Castles In The Sand

Castles In The Sand

RON BRELAND

To order additional copies of this book, contact:
Xlibris Corporation
1-888-795-4274
www.Xlibris.com
Orders@Xlibris.com
30140

Contents

FOREWORD

I would like to dedicate this book to all of those fine men and women who stand on the wall of freedom every single day. They stand on that wall in the freezing cold, pouring rain, and desert heat. They serve in desolate lonely postings all over the world, oftentimes never knowing whether or not they will return home, eat a home cooked meal, or hear "I love you, daddy." one more time. You might call these occupational hazards. In our world, they are a way of life.

They stand in cramped guard shacks, lie in over watch positions pestered by sand fleas, and fly in the dark to places unknown delivering everything from ammunition to holiday cheer to those deployed to some of the worst places that you can imagine. Who would choose to live this way? Anyone can volunteer for this; but if it were easy then everyone would be doing it.

When you read these pages, know also that with each deployment, near death experience, and heartbreaking absence comes equal turmoil on the home front. It's been said that the hardest job in the Army is that of an Army Wife. I couldn't agree more.

If you ask most folks, they most likely either know, or are related to someone in the military. If you ask those same people what their nephew, niece, or friend does in the military, many will rarely have a grasp on the profession of their loved one. Even those with little or no knowledge of their friend or family members daily routine will tell you with a gleam in their eye, wistful with pride as they say, 'He's in the service.' Or 'She's in the Army.'

For many years I have seen many of these same people tell me about their former military service decades ago. These people are from a bygone era known as 'The Greatest Generation'.

They remind me of the day that I graduated from Airborne School down at Fort Benning, Georgia. I was older than most of my classmates and at the age of twenty-seven I reveled in the youth around me and it literally lifted me through the course. When my wings were pinned on my chest, I tried to stand at attention while looking at the frail older gentleman in front of me. He was wearing a trucker's hat with a pair of jump wings on it, with about a dozen or so pins tacked to it. He asked me how many jumps it took to graduate from Airborne School, and I told him that the requirement was five. He told me that he only had four during his service in World War II. If I were any younger at the time, I might have thought myself a bit cocky in already having more than this 'old warhorse' standing before me. I was indeed honored by this nameless gentleman, a hero of the Greatest Generation as he told me briefly of his four jumps at Sicily, Salerno, Normandy, and Holland. Being stationed at Fort Bragg at the time, I was very familiar with all the drop zones named for these famed operations. I was truly honored, and in awe of this living history. He was more than an old retiree; he was a national treasure.

Veterans love to tell stories, some more than others. Some are willing to share their experiences, and some are not. It's very common that a lot of veterans don't often talk about their service because many of the incidents are painful to rehash and are probably best left alone. We all have our own ghosts, and many memories left on battlefields all over the world. This may have been true in the past, and I don't fault anyone for that. I on the other hand, find it somewhat therapeutic and cleansing to share these times with others. I chose this format for this book because most people love a short story, and I am no different.

This is just a collection from my many privileged years in the United States Army. No two duty stations have been the same, and I have had a great many blessings both in combat and at home.

The United States military is a cross section of society. Soldiers, Sailors, Airmen and Marines come from every corner of this great land. They all have their own idiosyncrasies, accents, and particular ways about them; however, they all have one thing in common. They all love their country. Far away they are the servants of their people, but in their own right should be viewed as kings. Protected by walls of earth and sandbags, they create their castles in the sand. They bet their souls on what they believe, and their very lives on what they know.

This book is once again dedicated to the Greatest Generation, and this one, and every one in between who have laid many a sacrifice upon the alter of freedom so that we may live in the best country in all the world. God bless them all, and God bless the United States of America.

*Freedom is the sure possession of those
with the courage to fight for it.*

CHAPTER ONE

GROWING UP IN THE ARMY

THE GIFT OF LIFE

I entered the Army with the hopes of going to war in the Middle East. I came in on the eve of Desert Shield and Desert Storm and dreamed of doing good things for God and country. In basic training I was trained by men who were sincerely preparing us for war. And then later on in my technical training, at the U.S Air Force's Fire Academy I was trained extensively on how to protect and save lives. Up to now my career was a dichotomy. I know both how to preserve life and take it, and sincerely hoped that I would make a good soldier even though deep down I hoped the latter would never come to pass. I was now a third generation fireman, and was proud that I could be in the family business, but somehow still do it on my own through the Army.

It was mid December 1992 when I found myself in the position of being an expectant father for the first time. I was a young soldier stationed at Fort Campbell, Kentucky. I was proud to serve with the 101st Airborne Division; young, and full of vigor. What I never did expect was for something so small and fragile to absolutely drop me to my knees. And then he arrived.

At 1413 hrs. on December 23, 1992 my first child was born. Ronald Gary Breland II entered the world at 8 lbs., 5-½ oz. He was perfect in every way, and he had the reins on me without so much as the slightest effort. Not so unlike most new first time fathers, I was a little young and very confused. Could I raise this child? Would I be a good father? Could I handle the responsibility? While on duty at the fire station I was one of the 'go to' guys. In a crisis I was cool and collected, and my crew and I quickly formulated the answers to any variable that would arise in a bad situation. But somehow this little person had the fear of God hovering over me and I was swimming in a sea of doubt.

We had chosen to go through the Army's Midwife Program instead of a traditional doctor. I can't say enough about this program. The midwife that we were assigned to was a young Nurse Midwife named Captain Graham. She was a straight shooter, and very professional. She eased many of the 'first timer' tensions that I had about becoming a father, and the entire pregnancy and childbirth process. I attended every single class that I could and left no stone unturned. I figured that the fewer surprises the better. CPT Graham was a little surprised that I showed up to the breast-feeding class, and as you can imagine I was the only man there. She laughed, and the expectant mothers snickered as I posed questions about particular brands of breast pumps and what my role in this particular task was.

Like most first time fathers, I muddled through it. I attended Lamas classes and everything I could sign up for. By the time the big day arrived, I thought I was as ready as I could be. When the big moment came, CPT Graham was very calm but poignant in her guidance. As his tiny head crowned she placed my hands on it, with her hands cupping mine. We gently turned his head, and like every birth, once you get past the shoulders it's all downhill from there.

Everything went smoothly from there, and my 'number one son' as I've come to call him over the years has enriched my life as he's turned into a fine young man. The bravado that seemingly permeates the stereotypes of military men today isn't far from the truth in some areas. I am no different, especially when it comes to childbirth. I have worked with the nurse-midwives in various Army hospitals throughout my career when having my children. I am one of those fathers that don't believe in waiting rooms, unless it pertains to friends and in-laws. The fact that I have 'hand delivered' all of my children gives me no greater pride, and I wouldn't have it any other way. I have recommended it to my friends over the years, as there is no price on witnessing this miracle. Although I am through with having any more children, I still highly recommend it to anyone who may be thinking about starting or continuing a family.

Somalia 1993

In early June, I had heard something about the battalion needing drivers, due to a shortage, to go to Somalia. I figured that I'm an Army firefighter, and if I can drive a fire engine then I can surely drive a Humvee. It seemed simple enough to me, and I was hungry to get my feet wet, so to speak.

I called my Squad Leader at home, and he told me "Sure, why not. Go ahead and volunteer." It wasn't clear to me until a few days later that he wasn't taking me seriously, as he and I were driving over to the company to see the Company Commander about me calling my Battalion Sergeant Major at home and volunteering for the mission in Somalia. As we walked into the orderly room, three soldiers were standing in front of the Commander, being told that they were not going to Somalia for one reason or another. I thought, 'Oh damn, I'm really in trouble here', as they didn't have their squad leader with them. I figured that they too had made the mistake of bypassing their chain of command as I had somehow done.

The 1SG and Commander both had grins on their faces, and this made me just a little more apprehensive. This, as you know, is because a 1SG doesn't ever smile, if he can help it. The Commander spoke up, and he told me that the Battalion CSM liked firemen, and where I should report to the next morning. I did, and that is where I met the man who would become my squad leader and mentor for the next five months. He was going ahead of the main body of the unit as a member of the advanced party, and I eventually caught up with him at our base camp.

I suppose I hadn't realized how long the flight could be for us. First we landed in Gander, Newfoundland, then Shannon, Ireland. We were not permitted to get off the airplane in Shannon due to a recent terrorist threat. I longed to stretch my legs and get a breath of fresh air, but this would have to wait. The next leg of our journey took us to Cairo, Egypt. I of course had never visited any of these countries, however even at night Cairo seemed mystical. I can still see the Nile River lit up by green underwater lights and the laser lights show on the pyramids as we took off. It was truly a sight to see. The last leg of our commercial flights took us to a little country called Djibouti in northern Africa, and then finally Mogadishu Airport.

We had to switch to a military transport plane in Djibouti because the commercial airline we had been traveling on couldn't travel any closer to the combat zone with support from their insurance carrier. That really made me think about where we were heading to, although I suppose if I had thought about it sooner it would have made sense.

It was early afternoon when we landed at Mogadishu International. Little did I know at the time, but we would be on a convoy within the hour taking us to our new home. While offloading equipment, a huge metal case containing two M2 .50 cal. machine guns, I had a flight bag in my left hand and the handle from the weapons case in my right. I was already exhausted from traveling, and then hauling this stuff around, that I guess I just lost my head. I had a cigarette in my mouth, and, as I turned around, a man introduced himself to me. As he grabbed the lit cigarette out of my mouth he said, 'Welcome to Somalia, I'm General Montgomery. You know son, smoking is bad for your health.' As he said this tossed my smoke on the ground, and stomped it out. You can only imagine how fast I was imagining what was left of my career in the Army dissipate into nothing.

The convoy to our base camp, 'Swordbase' was uneventful; however the issue of a live magazine prior to boarding the trucks was a well-needed wake up call for many. As we started off at the airfield and traveled down 21 October Road, one of the guys in my truck hadn't seated the magazine in the magazine well of his weapon securely, and we watched as it dropped down to the ground. A few Somali kids wrestled around for it until the biggest kid finally won out. We thought he was in deep shit for losing his ammunition but it turned out okay for the most part. In a combat zone, ammo is lost and found like cigarette butts on the ground all the time; we just hadn't learned that yet.

ARRIVAL AT SWORDBASE

Upon our arrival at Swordbase, I was a little disoriented, but I did however gain a little confidence in the double-stacked mil-vans that made up our perimeter. I had been inside them before, and knew that they were steel. That heightened my confidence level of keeping things out of the camp that didn't need to be there.

We arrived, and in the late afternoon hours I was tired. I wanted to get settled, and try and get some sleep . . . none of which happened. I soon met up with my Squad Leader again, and it was good to see a familiar face. He showed us around, and gave us the low down on the area, and everything they'd seen thus far. They told us that there were mortar attacks every night since before their arrival, and I would learn all too soon what they were talking about.

The first night there, mortar explosions woke me up, and it scared the hell out of me. My 'room' was in an old war torn building that, even by ghetto standards was rough. We fit eight men into a very small space, and realized all too soon that living in close quarters can be rough. We made the best of it. The American soldier is very resourceful when he has to be, and in more ways than one.

I was shacked up with SPC Mims, a rather large (round) guy who was Jewish, and that he could only eat the tuna fish MRE's because the rest all had something to do with not being kosher. Like I said though, he was a large fellow, and certainly didn't look like he was missing any meals. The other guy in my tiny cubicle that was separated from the rest was SPC Brian Pilcher. He was a former Nightstalker, from the 160th Special Operations Aviation Regiment. He was a large guy in stature, but spoke softly. He would later become the 101st Airborne Division soldier of the year. Brian was a big guy, and I was certainly glad that he was on our side. He was a born killing machine, and he lived for a deployment. He was a natural. Although this was my first deployment, Brian was already a veteran, and he helped me a lot upon our arrival in getting used to my new way of life.

During the first night's mortar attack, we were told when we heard the first explosion; we should immediately 'get your shit on!' This meant to get your flack vest, kevlar helmet, and have your rifle at the ready. After three or four mortars, the attack was finally over, and the troops who had been there a while already seemed to go about their business as though nothing had happened at all. I was amazed. These mortar attacks would continue for weeks. Actually, we joked about it often. We would say, 'if the Somalis had a place they could actually zero their weapons, they'd almost be dangerous!' I think it was about the fourth or fifth night that I actually got more than an hour's sleep. I remember thinking 'this is gonna be a long tour if I don't ever get any sleep.'

THE ARMS ROOM

Upon our arrival in the Mog, I didn't know what exactly to expect. Life in the Army for me at this time had consisted of "the good life" as most would agree. You see, I'm an Army firefighter and, as such am exempt from most of the mundane tasks that are expected of soldier's in line units. I deployed from Fort Campbell, KY; an absolutely wonderful place. I truly loved the post, serving with the 101st and the surrounding area as well.

I was in one of six, 6-man teams Army-wide that were to deploy within 18 hours with our deployable fire engine, and set up anywhere to provide protection for our aviation assets. The aviation guys always loved us, and they were great to hang out with. Our duty was always the same: 24 on / 24 off, with a 3-day break, called a 'Kelly-day' every two weeks. We never pulled details, CQ, Staff Duty, KP, and did I mention . . . we never went to the field. Life was sweet, but all this would soon change for me.

After joining the Army because I wanted to go to Desert Storm, I believe that I just wanted to experience 'Army Life' as I thought it was, not the sweet lifestyle that I'd become accustomed to.

When I volunteered to go to Somalia, I tossed the idea around the fire station with a few of my buddies, and we all decided to volunteer. Well, you guessed it . . . no one else was willing to give up 'the good life', and I was the only one sent. I was more than just a fish out of water; I was about to get a rude awakening. However, my Squad Leader made my transition easier than it could have been.

I learned soon that I would soon become the unit armorer, the gopher, and whatever else was needed . . . like a lot of guard duty. I grew up in Somalia, so it seemed, and attended the University of Mogadishu as we later called it. Many of us had our first deployment and combat tour in Somalia, and, although we 'grew up' there as far as our careers were concerned, a piece of all of us still remains there.

I was introduced to a small conex container by my Squad Leader, and learned that this small 6 X 6 steel box was to be my new arms room. I was not armorer qualified, but in Somalia, that didn't matter. I quickly learned about many weapons, the M60, the M2 .50 cal., MK-19, and stored more ammo and flares than you can shake a stick at. After about a week or so, I got moved into a huge 40 foot MILVAN. The 'sweat-box' as I called it would be the place where I spent most of my time for the rest of the tour. I issued and received ammo, learned about the weapons, and the Army. I also pulled more guard duty than I ever thought possible. I was no longer in Kansas . . . Toto.

Every day at guard mount, our squad leader would inspect the troops, check their equipment, and put out necessary info. He was a rock, and that solid professionalism is what got me through a lot of tough days.

I remember thinking . . . 'damn, if a mortar hits this damned arms room while I'm in it, at least I won't feel anything. There was more ammo, grenades, claymores, M203 ammo, endless belts of crew-served weapons ammo than I thought we would ever need. SFC Morang, our First Sergeant, didn't see it that way though, and I just kept the ammo coming.

Myself, and the other guards would occasionally receive harassment fire from a small tent village just off of our corner of Swordbase, and then we would return fire. We had no target, but it would keep the harassment fire down for a time, and let them know that we were paying attention. Being a tent village, who knows what the actual body count was. They said we probably killed or wounded from ten to twenty people every time we had a minor engagement like that. War is hell, and there is always a price to pay.

At the end of every guard shift, my guys would come to me, and get anywhere from 5 to 20 rounds to replenish their basic load of ammunition. It became somewhat of a joke after a while, and we would take bets among the Soldiers who would shoot the most rounds. But they would always come back and get their stuff from me, and we would talk a while. It almost became normal. It's truly amazing what you can get used to.

The 4 Horsemen. We were inseparable, and as our first combat tour was coming to an end, decided to get a few pictures. The blue berets were issued by the United Nations to denote U.N. forces.

THE FOUR HORSEMEN – THE BEGINNING . . .

In our first weeks on Swordbase, everyone adjusted rather well, and being a resourceful bunch, set up our hooch as best we could. After a couple of weeks of being shacked up with three other guys, I decided it was time for a change. Living in close quarters can be tedious and aggravating at times. I started asking around for some wood, and that's when I met Will, Harv, and Veno. We would eventually become the Four Horsemen.

They all volunteered to help me out, and we set out to find some wood. Well, we were told we could have some 2 X 4's, and a single sheet of plywood. That wasn't going to be enough for the job, so we decided it would be better to ask for forgiveness than permission. We ended up liberating some more wood from a unit we thought didn't need it as badly as we did. I've said it many times before; but the resourcefulness of a deployed soldier is unmatched.

Will and Harv were particularly good at carpentry, and Veno was strong as an ox, so it worked out well. Those three guys dove into the task head first, and I found myself being more of a spectator. Before I knew it, I had a 10 X 10 foot frame made out of 4 X 4's, with a small frame extending up to waist level on the outside lip. This was my balcony. We couldn't change the shape of the building, so we built up instead. With a double-sheeted plywood floor, and a solid wall on one side, I now had a second story penthouse. It was great. There was a small ledge that separated my hooch and Veno's place. It was soon separated with a plywood wall, and a small hole cut out for commo purposes. At the end of the day, we were all exhausted, and we sat over in Will, Harv, and Veno's hooch for a bottle of water and an MRE. Now that we all had suitable accommodations, it was time to block any light that may creep through the battle-scarred walls of our building. After all, we didn't want to give the Somali's any free targets. We acquired a light set, and we all had actual working light bulbs. Up to now it had all been chemlights and flashlights.

We were all sitting there, after the construction site was cleaned up, and Will pulled a bullet out of his magazine, and whipped out a Gerber tool. He would use the pliers, and wiggle the bullet out of the actual casing, and then twist a small piece of wire with a loop on the end of it. He would use his lighter, and heat up the bullet and as the lead in the center melted, he would insert the twisted end of the wire, and hold it there until it set again. He then had a little "charm" to hang on his dog tags. We all did this, and thus became the Four Horsemen. There would be many adventures to come that we probably shouldn't have done, but that will be later.

THE POLISH RIFLE

There's a guy in every unit who's a jokester, pulls pranks, or is constantly making someone laugh, and ours was no different. He was one of those guys who was quiet for the most part around the hooch, but when he did pipe up and say something; he usually got you really good. He could be just absolutely hilarious.

He was an extremely hard worker, and he was always moving, doing something. Well, being in our unit, he was kind of a 'go-to' guy. If you needed something done, he would do it. He may have been less than conventional about it, but he always got it done.

One day, he was moving some equipment with a forklift, and everyone was working as usual. Someone runs into my hooch, and says, "You gotta get down here man, you gotta see this". Nothing in Somalia was normal, so even if this was something new, I doubted it would surprise me.

I walk out my hooch, and there stands our little comedian holding his M-16 rifle, and the barrel is completely bent at a 90-degree angle. It looked like something in a cartoon, or a polish joke. He just stood there laughing, and saying, 'Can you fix it?" This was another one of those times when I thought, 'What the hell am I doing here, I'm a fireman'. We got his rifle fixed up, and drove on. I'll never forget how funny he looked standing there with his 'polish rifle'.

SQUAD PT WITH PSYOPS

One gloriously hot and crappy morning, my squad leader called us all out to an open area to do some PT. We dreaded the morning hours, because, if you didn't get up early enough, and the sun broke over the horizon, then you were definitely in for it. The heat was pretty much unbearable, but somehow we managed.

Our Squad Leader started PT, and we tried to keep it together and at least try to be professional. We were terrible about joking around in formation. We were always picking on each other and stuff, but we kept it clean for the most part. I recall fondly the thousands of extra pushups I had to do for being a smartass.

Well, there we were, standing at attention. Everyone heard the Blackhawk's overhead, but it was so common that one rarely paid attention. Our Squad Leader was just about to bark out some exercise and these little 3 X 5 pieces of paper started raining down on us. They had some message written in Somali on one side, and silhouettes of soldiers and tanks on the other. The Blackhawk's we heard overhead were apparently dropping 'propaganda' or messages of good will down to be distributed among the locals. It's a tool that the folks over at Psychological Operations use to distribute messages to the masses on occasion. Apparently the pilot misjudged the wind, and literally hundreds of these papers were dropped right on top of our camp, namely our training site.

These messages were intended for the Somali people, however, the wind apparently shifted and spread hundreds, probably thousands of these little psyop pamphlets all over Swordbase. Our Squad Leader released us to snatch up on a token piece of memorabilia from the tour, and continued on with PT.

THE MAN WHO COULD GET AWAY WITH ANYTHING

Have you ever known anyone who seemingly gets away with anything and everything? They don't really hurt anyone, but it just kind of gnaws at your soul just knowing that if you tried something like that, someone would probably tell you to either go pound sand, or they'd beat the tar out of you.

Well, this guy definitely fits the bill. I'm sure that the mass majority of vets from the Mog know who he really is; they just don't realize it.

The man I'm referring to is (drum roll, please) . . . Ty Kendrick.

Ty was an AFN radio disk jockey, that ran the afternoon show, and he was absolutely hilarious. Many of us likened him to the Vietnam era's Adrian Cronauer of 'Good Morning Vietnam' fame. Ty was always uplifting, had a joke, and had an 'on the air' love affair with a young lieutenant named "Missy. (*Missy, we know who you are, but still don't know where you live)

Like any new soldier in country, Ty broke the ice easily, and then gradually flew off the handle. He cut loose with no fear of repercussion whatsoever. Many commanders disliked his on the air style of wit and humor, but the Soldiers loved it. They could never pin anything on him though because General's Garrison and Montgomery loved his show. (Raise a beer for the little guy!) Even on a convoy, we would find ourselves taking a radio along so as not to miss Ty's afternoon shows while at another camp.

When he got the show off and running, he 'patented' his opening lines. The morning guy would introduce him, as they do in the civilian sector. Next, there would be this drum roll, and then . . . "From Mogadishu to Mombasa, from the empire state to the golden gate, with more crap than a Christmas goose, I'm SPC Ty Kendrick, and I love you Missy!"

Everyday would vary slightly from the one before, depending on the action during the night prior, the morale around holidays, etc. His show was very close to the heart for most of us.

And oh boy was he just absolutely infatuated with Missy. He'd make comments about how much he loved her butt right on the air. Even as outspoken as I am, I felt a sense of shock every now and then while listening in. I dedicated a song to the Four Horsemen one day. It was Gary Wright's "Dreamweaver". Ty said, no problem, he'd get it right on the air. But when he got on the air, he gave my name, the song I requested, and then followed it up with, "I don't know what they're smoking over there at Swordbase . . . . think they're going through some sort of Jimmy Hendrix Phase or something". It was so funny. I have three cassette tapes of Ty's show, including the dedication. They're about worn out now, but I cherish them to this day, and my stomach hurts from laughing so hard.

TY BLOWS GATOR'S COVER . . . ON THE AIR!

Logically speaking, the modern military is merely a cross-section of society . . . . as it were. And, like society, is not without its problems and concerns. One such problem throughout both entities is infidelity, and the military is no different.

Many of us have no doubt heard the phrase "What goes TDY stays TDY", and that phrase never held so true as it did for a man named 'Gator', in the Mog.

Gator, as he was affectionately known by many of us in the Mog, was a Marine officer, a lieutenant as I recall, and an interrogator. He was a very popular guy; always hosting a barbecue, volleyball game, or some other social event in his spare time.

Many of us didn't know this at the time, but Gator was a married man. And none of us would have probably ever known except he was messing around with some enlisted female for quite some time. This was common knowledge among those close to him at the time, however; hell hath no fury like a woman's scorn.

Apparently this young lady with whom he was having intimate relations found out that he was married, and decided to exact her revenge . . . publicly.

She called Ty Kendrick while he was on the air. This was the perfect time to call because the whole country always tuned in to Ty's show. After all, he was practically a celebrity. So, she gets on the radio, and has a conversation with Ty for a minute or two, and then proceeds to tell the whole world that she found out that Gator was married, and what a lowlife she thought he was.

For reasons unknown, Gator decreased in popularity in the following days, as all of Kendrick's listening audience saw him for what he really was. I'm not sure how it works in the Marine Corps, but I'm sure that the Army Military Intelligence community wouldn't put up with such embarrassment.

Oh well, tough luck Gator. Better luck next time.

TURKISH WHISKEY AND ROSANNE

It was just after Thanksgiving '93, and Will's wife, Melissa had just delivered their first son. Will couldn't get home because of the hot situation we were in, and it really began to wear him thin. His wife even called the AFN station and dedicated a song for him on AFN Somalia. If there are any country music fans out there like me, the song "Wish I could have been there" can be a real tearjerker but was absolutely appropriate under the circumstances.

Harv decided to spice things up a bit by somehow 'securing' a bottle of Turkish whiskey. It was horrible stuff by our standards; it was pretty much toilet water.

Well, when in the field, once again, a soldier can always be resourceful in a pinch. We raided the Class I freezer and acquired (steal is such an ugly word) a bunch of dry ice. We also had a ton of odds and ends from MRE's that were never eaten (hot cocoa, kool aid, sugar, salt) stashed in our hooch for future use.

So, we cut some water bottles in half with the lid still screwed on, placed the lid end inside the bottom half of the bottle, and used 100 mph tape to secure the two together. We then made a cup of Kool-Aid, doused with a shot of the Turkish whiskey, and plopped a chunk of dry ice inside. The bubbling effect of the dry ice was a nice touch as the drink rolled over 'boiling' like lava.

Well, I have to say that it lightened our spirits a bit; at least it did for me since I'm such a lightweight drinker. Harv had this giant boom box with a little 5-inch T.V. inside it, and the only channel we could get in over there was Armed Forces T.V., or AFN. The only show we could manage to tune in was 'Rosanne'. I'm glad we didn't have anything worthwhile to eat, because I think I would have surely lost it over seeing Rosanne. But the whiskey was good, and that night I think we all got just a little closer.

A VISIT FROM DAD

Please allow me to digress a little here. Although there are many stories in this collection, some funny, some just damned hilarious, and some horrifically serious, lest us not forget not just the soldiers, but also the families that were involved.

Upon being notified that I was onboard with the mission, I told my son, and then immediately called my father in Louisiana. This was on a Friday morning. I hung up with him about 9 a.m., and surprisingly by 7 p.m., he pulled into Ft Campbell to visit for my final weekend before leaving. I remember being at my now ex-father-in-law's house, laying out my gear, and packing my ruck and duffle bag in the living room.

We ran out to Wal-Mart for a few incidentals; all of us. My dad, step mom, mother-in-law, father-in-law, wife, and son. We went out to dinner that night, and barbecued at his house the next night. My son sat on the floor, about 6 months old at the time wearing my boonie hat and a pair of sunglasses. He was so cute. After the BBQ, the men retired to his back deck for cigars and a couple of beers. This was the first time I ever heard my dad and father-in-law speak of their time in Vietnam. I was truly in awe, because not only was I sitting there with family, I was also in the presence of the recipients of (between the two of them) 2 purple hearts, a bronze star, and almost 2 1/2 years of collective combat time.

I listened intently to every word, never missing a point, or a change of the beer bottle. I couldn't sleep that last night, as I finally laid down at about 2 a.m. My dad still made it a point to get up with me. That morning was the first time I ever saw the old man cry . . . ever, as I pulled out of the driveway. I got up about 3 a.m., still not being able to sleep, and picked up my son out of his crib. I sat in my chair and held him for about 2 hours, weeping as the pain of leaving him had come to a head. He was so precious, lying in my arms; so ever trusting, cheeks bulging and long eyelashes closed and dreaming. Thank God he would never have to see and experience the things we had to. He was my inspiration to make it home in one piece. He might still be daddy's boy, but I would always be his daddy too.

My ex-father-in-law drove me to the unit, and then to the airfield, after a coffee run at a quick stop. His words inspired and mentored me more than I could ever express. Between our talks on the deck, my dad crying, and that drive to the airfield, I knew that this was going to be the real deal.

I am still thankful to this day for my Squad Leader, the Four Horsemen, and all my compadres that made it possible for us all being able to get back home.

MY DAD AND THE REAR DETACHMENT 1SG

Upon seeing one of the D-boys being drug through the streets on CNN, my family, like so much of America was in dismay, and a state of extreme anger.

I was on my way back to my hooch one evening, and a guy runs up to me and says, 'Hey, the 1SG needs to see you right now.' I met SFC Morang at the entrance to our TOC tent, and he was smiling. Now, I'm concerned. He puts his hand on my shoulder and explains to me that since the footage was shown on CNN, my father had tried calling our rear detachment. Well, the Rear Detachment First Sergeant back at Fort Campbell was a Puerto Rican guy who had a very strong accent. And when a concerned parent calls wanting to know about his boy, their patience runs a little thin when they can't interpret the accent on the other end.

Apparently my dad was talking to this guy, who obviously and unfortunately had no answers for him. You see, when the body was being dragged through the streets, the whole world saw it, and no American parent knew whether it was their child or not. I can certainly understand my father's frustrations. I can also empathize with that poor old First Sergeant. While the main body of a unit is deployed, the Rear Detachment is responsible for taking care of family members and dealing with the results of unfortunate events like that poor warrior who lost his life.

My dad calls over and over, and not understanding this guy very well, proceeds to tell him that if the Army is going to have someone there to answer phone calls, then they had "better be able to speak freakin' English."

I got all of this second hand, of course, however, it made me feel good that without even talking to him, my old man could still reach out and show his concern half a world away. I called him that night, and through yet another mortar attack, got cut off the phone. That probably didn't do much for his nerves, but at least he knew I was alive.

Thanks Dad.

OUR LAST NIGHT IN THE MOG

Our last night in the Mog was a beautiful thing. I recall throwing bags up on trucks and taking pictures with the Four Horsemen, and the somewhat sense of disbelief that we were actually going home. Any soldier who's deployed can tell you that when it comes time to re-deploy, the rumor mill gets out of control. We're going home tomorrow, then it's next week, then it's on hold, then it's back to the original date. And after it's all over, the thrill and hopes of finally going home are what create the stress, especially in younger soldiers like me at the time.

I remember getting to this huge hangar area with about a thousand cots spread out all over the place. My Squad Leader said, "Grab a rack, and get comfy, it's gonna be a while." I didn't care if we were there for another six months by then; I just knew that we weren't at Swordbase anymore.

We finally got word that we would be leaving sometime the following morning, and although we could actually relax, we were all very anxious. Most of us stayed up all night, and watched AFN T.V., smoked about a thousand cigarettes, and tried very hard to relax. Not a chance. This was impossible. I hadn't seen my son in five months, and the following day was his first birthday.

I calculated the time difference, the travel time, and if all went perfect, I would meet my number one son at Hangar 1 at Campbell Army Airfield at 23:45 with 15 minutes to spare on his birthday. No such luck, but that's another story.

As for the Four Horsemen, I was going home to my wife and son. Will was going home to his new son, now a month old that he'd never seen. Harv was going home to a cheating wife and her boyfriend, who would eventually meet him at the airfield (the both of them), and Veno . . . what can I say about my boy Veno? Veno was going home as single as he was when he left. He would later marry and have two beautiful children. Visiting in-laws at Fort Campbell a few years later, I would catch up with Jim, and catch up on lost time.

As we boarded the plane, the engines revved up, and just as the wheels left the ground, I don't think there was a soul on board that didn't flinch just a tad from the fear of a mortar or rocket propelled grenade maybe hitting the plane at the last second. Thankfully, this was not the case, and we were off . . .

GANDER AIRPORT

After flying half the night, we ended up stopping at the airport in Gander, Newfoundland. It was December; there was a huge snowstorm. Of course being from Ft Campbell, we all couldn't help but think of our comrades in arms who died here just a few years before.

A planeload of soldiers from the 101st was sabotaged, as the History channel has it, and all died. There is now a memorial in a field behind the Fort Campbell Burger

King where a tree has been planted for every soldier that died that day. The memorial is well kept and is in full bloom every year. It really makes you wonder about those lives lost, as I look at those towering trees when I visit there from time to time.

Anyhow, we were laid over there for almost a full 24 hours until the weather broke enough for us to take off again. I remember the kindness shown to us by the people of Gander, as we were seemingly lost in time. All we really wanted to do was to get home again, however, I reflect fondly nowadays on the kindnesses of the people there during a special time for all of us. I ate a burger in the airport terminal, and remember thinking that there were many times that I might not ever taste a greasy airport burger again. It never tasted so good.

ARRIVAL AT CAMPBELL FIELD – CHRISTMAS 1993

Our arrival back to Fort Campbell was seemingly uneventful. I spent many nights awake at Fire Station #3 on Campbell Field in the past, and when we landed, things looked as quiet as ever. We landed in a huge civilian jet, and at 0400 hrs. on Christmas Day there isn't much traffic. So I thought. As we taxied off the runway and down the parallel toward the main Hangar adjacent to the fire station, I didn't notice anything at first. And then a light shone so bright through my little airplane window. There were people, lots of people that seemingly came out of nowhere. As I stepped off the plane, Major General Jack Keane, the Division Commander shook my hand. With a slap on the back, we were guided towards the hangar and our families. Simultaneously, the fire station bay doors opened up as my fellow firefighters pulled the trucks out with lights flashing and air horns blaring. It was a sight to behold. The Division band was playing music; there was food everywhere, and my son never looked so handsome as I walked up to his tiny silhouette.

I spotted him about halfway across the tarmac to the hangar, and don't even think I could see or hear anything else. 'I love you daddy', he said. It was the first time I'd ever heard him speak and those few little words absorbed me wholeheartedly. He was no longer the little baby that I cradled in my arms just five months before. I was torn between the happiness of being home and the bullet that drove itself straight through my heart over suddenly realizing all that I'd missed. But it was Christmas, and my blessings were many. There is truly nothing in this world like coming home.

CHAPTER TWO

SPREADING MY WINGS

U pon arriving at Fort Bragg, North Carolina I was more than overjoyed. I reveled with the seemingly endless opportunities that lay before me. Up to this point, I had requested a slot at Airborne school down at Fort Benning at least four times during my career. Most of the time I was at a post where jump slots were not readily available or in a jump unit where such a thing would be practical. However every request came with it a similar comment, which was usually something like, 'You're a fireman, why do *you* want to go to jump school?' Each dismissal was a little more disheartening than the last but I didn't give up.

At Fort Bragg, the Airborne mentality, lingo, and lifestyle emanated from everywhere. For those who are not familiar with this, it must be a lot to take in at first. You can't go a hundred yards on Bragg without seeing a formation of paratroopers in Class A uniform, with perfect maroon berets and jump boots so shiny that you could read a newspaper in them.

I longed to be a part of this elite fraternity and I would soon join them. After six years of denied requests I finally received the approval I desired. A mere thirty days after my arrival at my new unit I would head south on I-95 towards Fort Benning and the age of twenty-seven endure the same as my classmates just out of high school. Every drop of sweat and crackle of my knees would be worth it. My knees still crackle to this day, only a little more often than then. I still think it was worth it.

After graduating Airborne school I drove away from Columbus with a sense of a destiny fulfilled. Our graduation came in the wake of a scandal involving a hazing ritual by the Marines which their superiors drove their wings into their chests leaving a bloody mess. Twisted as it may be, I still wanted it. My classmates and I approached our instructors and requested our 'blood wings'. With a wink of an eye, and a nod towards the cadre offices he simply uttered under his breath, 'backs off the wings, and backs against the wall'. It was exhilarating and suspenseful all at the same time. I felt the pins on the back of my wings pierce my chest. By the stickiness of my t-shirt I could tell I was bleeding, but I really didn't care. I drove all the way back to North Carolina with those wings embedded in my chest, and woke my son up to pull them out. It was truly a great day for me.

A BIRTHDAY TO REMEMBER

On April 27, 1997 I turned twenty-seven years old. As far as birthdays go, it wasn't a particularly notable one. It wasn't my 18th, 21st, or 40th birthday, and other than turning another year older it was really just another day of the week. I was determined, however, to make it notable in some way or another. I had just graduated jump school two weeks earlier, and after my five jumps at Airborne school, I'd received my foreign jump wings on an Australian joint Airborne operation just days after my return to Fort Bragg. Many paratroopers wait years for the opportunity for a foreign jump, so I counted my blessings. Anyway, after only two weeks on jump status, I found myself having a birthday, and wanting to do something unique.

I decided that I would reenlist for another six years. We had an Airborne operation scheduled for that day, so I requested through my chain of command that I be able to reenlist at the Iron Mike memorial en route to the jump. For anyone who's ever been to Fort Bragg, you know that the traffic circle where the Iron Mike memorial stands leaves a lot to be desired when it comes to parking. My unit lined up cattle truck after cattle truck full of paratroopers around the edge of the memorial, and there were a couple of hundred paratroopers in attendance. I wouldn't have had it any other way. After the reenlistment ceremony, we all loaded back up on the cattle trucks and headed out to Pope Air Force Base to chute up for the jump.

It was late evening, and as my feet hit the ground the sunset was perfect. I was with my paratrooper brethren, I'd just reenlisted, and as far as birthday's go I don't think that I could have squeezed anything else into the day. It truly was a birthday to remember.

THE STORY OF US

My Darling Helen

Shortly after I received notification of my divorce being finalized, I was feeling liberated and without need of another. My ex wife lived across town as did my three boys. I saw them every other weekend, and continued jumping out of planes, running into burning buildings, and started bull riding. I suppose that my liberation made me feel a little bit invincible, and perhaps it really did. Then again, sometimes it's more fun to be lucky than smart. I would soon see the wisdom in this. It's not so much that I was a thrill seeker, but I was doing everything that I had always wanted to. Looking back, I never minded being a family man . . . just not with her. We both married young, and did not possess the wisdom necessary to succeed at a place like Bragg. Fort Bragg is just one of those places that will make a good marriage stronger and destroy a weak one. It's a real challenge either way, as I found out.

To unwind during the week from all my adrenaline pumping activities I would go out to a dance club called 'The Palomino'. The club played country music and had a dance for everyone. I loved dancing, and enjoyed being single once again. I had many loyal dance partners, and never got involved with any of them beyond the dance floor. It was a mutual respect that I did not expect to find out in 'single man's land'. It was a welcome comfort, and I enjoyed going out every Wednesday night immensely. I'd iron my jeans and a shirt so stiff you could serve breakfast on it. I enjoyed looking nice, and my dance partners didn't seem to mind either.

One particular Wednesday night, I walked up to a girl whom I'd only watched from afar. There were lots of pretty women on the dance floor, and flaunted it in this mass 'meat market; but I enjoyed the relative safety of my regular dance partners. To this day I'm not still sure what made me approach this beautiful blonde, but I'm ever grateful that I did.

So I walked up to this girl and introduced myself. I held my hand out as if to lead her to the dance floor and she replied with, 'Hi, I'm Helen and I'm married.' This was simple and abrupt. With all due respect to her, I didn't see a husband around, and she seemed to enjoy dancing as much as I did. I had no idea. Nonetheless I left it alone and went back to my group of friends and just continued dancing.

It was about four months later that it was confirmed to me that this same girl was going through a separation. I felt relatively safe talking to her, and at the very least, watching her dance, which I enjoyed immensely. To this day I still can't recall what was making me feel so bold that night, but I walked up to her with arms spread wide open. In a loud voice I said, 'Helen, how are you?' and hugged her close. She patted my back, and I can only imagine her surprise in thinking to herself, 'Who is this?' By some miracle I broke the ice once again, and apparently I didn't make a bad impression.

Later on in the evening she apparently decided to take a chance herself. I was having a beer with my buddies, and someone grabbed my free hand. I honestly thought it was one of my buddies messing with me. As I turned to see which one of these rogue cowboys was messing with me, I saw Helen standing there, leading me to the dance floor. It was a slow song, and we talked about seemingly everything in those few minutes. For those of you who have slow danced before, you know that at the end of the dance there is a point where you finish and separate your bodies. This didn't happen to me. The disc jockey spun up another slow song and Helen and I held our embrace. We continued dancing and talked some more. I found it very difficult to keep my eyes on hers and not stare at her well-formed curves. After all, I am a man. Somehow I stayed fixed on her eyes and we finished yet another dance and I thought that I was doing really well.

The following excerpt from a personal journal that I've maintained during our entire relationship is a short story that I wrote describing the night we met. It was actually the second time that we met, however she doesn't remember to this day blowing me off just four months prior. Here it is.

It all happened one Wednesday night, in a place far, far away . . . . in a land called North Carolina. I went out to go dancing at a sultry country joint called "The Palomino". Wednesday nights is generally a meat market at this place, but this was no normal Wednesday night. On this Wednesday night, I would meet the woman who would become the sweetest, sexiest, most caring and wonderful woman I had ever met. And her name . . . was Helen.

When I first ever saw Helen, it was a few months prior, and we exchanged names, but nothing more. I watched carefully, for months, taking note of her every dance step, and wishing they were all with me. Her long, flowing blonde hair twirled with every line dance. She was a delightful eyeful, and always a pleasure, (as she is to this day) to watch. Not even speaking in the meanwhile, I watched, wisely from afar, for several months, only longing to be nearer to her. And on the Wednesday night in question, I made my move. Anyway, I was out with a few buddies on the magical night, and I spied Helen from afar. She was the most breathtaking vision of beauty that I'd ever seen. Her long, flowing, curled blonde locks flowing with each dance step . . . . my heart just stopped. Her glasses, which her pretty face framed perfectly, were only adding to her potency at this point. Dressed in solid black, from her boots, to her jeans, and on up to her denim vest, which only enhanced her natural features just so . . . what can I say . . . I'm only a man.

I slowly walked up to her and gave her a hug like I knew her, and I watched as she somewhat struggled . . . not quite remembering my name. I knew this was the case, and eased my name into conversation. It was brief, but we soon parted, and went back to our own groups of friends. What would seem like an eternity to me now, but what were actually only moments that night, I was standing near the entrance to the dance floor. As I was speaking to one of my buddies, I had a beer in my left hand, and I felt the softest, most caressing touch graze my hand, take it, and keep going. I turned around quickly, and once I saw who it was, desperately handed my beer off to my buddy while still in motion, as Helen, my angel Helen, was leading me to the dance floor for a slow dance. My buddy laughed at this, but then again, he was the one standing there holding a beer, while I was holding Helen. No contest.

Holding her on the dance floor, and moving as one together, we would have put Fred Astaire and Ginger Rogers to shame. It was the most delightful dance that I'd ever had, and holding this angel was sending my heart into a frenzy.

There comes a time towards the end of a dance, that you know the song is about to be over, so you somewhat separate from the other person, and thank them for the dance. Helen only held me close as the second slow song begun, and we danced another. This was a dream come true, as I thought I died and went to heaven. With the soft, slow music, and holding her close to me, I could not have asked for more. She was absolutely the most beautiful woman that Id ever seen (and she smelled really good too).

Towards the end of the night, I learned that Helen had to go because she was out with a friend going through some trying times (Yet another sign of Helen's angelic nature). As she was leaving, I walked her to the door, and was praying to God for a hug. I never prayed so hard and so fast in my life, by the way. I had not yet asked her for any information at this point. I was awaiting my chance to strike at the opportunity, when out of the blue Helen comes out with, "So, do you want my number?" She had beaten me to the punch; however, the result was the same. After walking her and her friend to her car, I was flying on cloud nine, and the rest of the night was a blur, actually, but I did have a smile on my face, as I still do now.

Well, there you have it, the story of us. It may seem a little cheesy, but Helen loves it and that's all that matters to me.

CHAPTER THREE

KOSOVO

The Magnificent 7 – With a small band of firefighters and one fire engine, we evolved fire protection on a mountain camp into an effective machine. During our six month tour we had over fifty responses, and fortunately never lost a single life due to fire.

THE RUSSIANS ARE COMING . . . OR IS IT US?

There are many people throughout the Army that will tell you that it isn't a very important thing to be a Paratrooper. The people that say these types of things are never paratroopers. You will never hear those words cross my lips, nor from anyone that is close to me. Being Airborne is much more to me than it is a lot of folks. To me, a paratrooper is a much better soldier than most of the others. A man who is willing to exit an aircraft with nothing but a chute strapped to his back with his buddies is a revered man indeed. These men are willing to risk it all on a day to day basis while in training, not just when the balloon goes up to deploy to some hot spot somewhere around the globe. Although when the call does come in, Airborne units have eighteen hours to be packed, board a plane and go 'wheels up' where they will forward deploy to parts unknown for as long as six months to a year.

I have always had the utmost respect for paratroopers. Throughout my career I would attend air shows just to see the airfield seizure demonstrations. The mass exodus of billowing parachutes all lined up in a row as they exited a C-130 was a sight to behold. I'm not sure exactly when it happened, but I can't recall a time when I didn't want to jump out of planes and be one of the elite.

While deployed to Operation Joint Guardian in Macedonia and Kosovo, I met up with a guy who was heading up a team to go outside the wire frequently and inspect the many outposts where other soldiers had taken up residence for the remainder of their tour. Oftentimes these outposts would be nothing more than an old bombed out building with some triple strand concertina wire around it.

They were living rough, but our team would see to it that they had everything they needed and some of what they wanted. Our group was a Quality of Life Assessment Team, or QLAT. It is exactly what it says.

The leader of our team was a young Captain out of Fort Bragg, like me. He and I immediately clicked, and being a fellow paratrooper he immediately placed more responsibility on my shoulders than the others. I was also the junior ranking individual on the whole team, but it really didn't matter. The young Captain was the Force Protection Officer for Task Force Falcon. He reported to the Commanding General on all Force Protection matters, and aside from being the Task Force Fire Chief, I reported to him. It was probably one of the best duties that I'd ever pulled during my career. Our efforts made a direct impact on the soldiers' lives, and it was very gratifying.

I would check their area for fire safety hazards, while another NCO would inquire about their needs for more frequent mail runs, weight sets, and any other amenities that we could provide. Another member was the Task Force Environmental representative while yet another served out of the camp hospital from the preventive medicine office. During one mission, we would attempt to make a daylong trip to one particular outpost to check on some troops. Their camp was right along the edge of the Russian sector. The entire country of Kosovo was split up into different regions. Each group from the Multi-National Brigade East was assigned a different area to even up the workload. It was a good idea, as our sector was busy enough.

We had a grid coordinate, a town, and a unit to find and it all seemed to be in place. The drive that day was actually a pleasant one through the country. The greenery of the countryside was beautiful as we wound through the side roads and byways. This area of the Balkan region offers a wide array of terrain. In a single day one could experience everything from mountains to forested areas to rural villages quaint in their surroundings.

It was in one such small village that we reached our objective, or so we thought. We pulled into the small town and fully expected to soon see some soldiers. We had only our team with us, and an interpreter was not available for this particular mission. We had gone out many times without an interpreter, however most soldiers that I know are highly creative and know how to 'wing it' as we had done before. The outskirts of our base camp was primarily an agricultural area. Most of the time I had to find commonly sounding words or use hand gestures with goat herders and farmers, however this day would prove to be different.

As we got out of our vehicles, we realized that we were possibly in the wrong area, but the presence of school-aged children playing outside seemed natural enough. My most recent tour to Iraq has changed this and I have become a little callous in such situations whether children are involved are not.

I saw a few soldiers near what looked like the village schoolhouse, but they certainly weren't ours. The Captain and I walked towards them as the rest of the team remained near the vehicles. We all had weapons, with the exception of one civilian contractor among us. At first, we realized that perhaps we were just a little off course and not in any kind of real trouble. This would soon change as my boss and I were staring at well-aimed AK-47's. The confrontation was a tense one, but only for a minute or two.

Maybe these soviet soldiers were just having a bad day, but the tension soon broke. One of the soviets noticed the wings on our uniforms, and the Airborne tabs on our shoulders. About the same time, we noticed their patches, which were well camouflaged by their European camouflage pattern. They were paratroopers as well. You could virtually see the light bulbs come on over everyone's head. They offered us a hand and we stood up. Prior to that we were on our knees with our weapons slung on our backs and our fingers interlaced behind our heads. It wasn't a completely hostile situation; however I wouldn't care to be in it again any time soon.

My Captain buddy looked at me with a sigh of relief as things were turning out okay. I felt a little primitive after that because we were reduced to a few airborne words in broken English. All hope was not lost though. I didn't speak Albanian, Serbo-Croatian, or Russian but I did speak 'Airborn-ese'.

Before we left we took a few pictures and I wound up cutting off my combat patch and jump wings in trade for one of their airborne patches. We all shook hands at the conclusion of our visit, and everyone was satisfied with their trinkets from the visit. My paratrooper buddy and I were sweating it out there for a while, and were glad to walk away with a lot more than a souvenir patch.

Mount Sera – This mountain was the backdrop of our camp, and was a beautiful sight to wake up to every day.

'I SAY AGAIN . . . YOUR MEN ARE LOST!'

About two months into our tour a National Guard unit showed up and we went from working every single day with seven firefighters to working every other day with twenty-nine. It was much a needed and well-deserved relief for my men and me. We had developed standard operating procedures for fire safety and inspections for the whole base camp. We were wired into emergency phone networks with the airfield, MP's, and the command group. We'd established ourselves as a tight unit known to work hard and fast to get it done.

Just after the National Guard got there our next higher unit changed from one battalion to another. I met with the command and was pleased to see that even though they were from Germany, their Command Sergeant Major was a paratrooper. He was very personable, and we gave him his first ever ride in a fire engine. I'd given literally hundreds of 'first rides' throughout my career. I could never get over however old, or how much rank any of them had; they all turned into little kids inside my fire engine. It was always good to see what a thrill it was for them.

Our schedule had now changed to 24 on / 24 off and it was a chance to breathe. My guys were motivated though. I think that we were all used to the high operational tempo, and we weren't sleeping very well. On a deployment you're never really 'off', but we had a great schedule worked out. The only was that we would work was if it involved a security issue on the base camp, a huge fire off camp that the General wanted us to assist the locals with, or if an incident got way out of control on the camp. Thank God for us that the Army is hugely safety conscious.

The Battalion Sergeant Major approached me one day and asked what we were up to. He said that he had a dilemma. As I mentioned before, the OPTEMPO was high and resources were short in supply. He asked me for a vehicle, a Humvee, of which I only had one. It was my command vehicle, which I used as Fire Chief during our shifts. He also asked me for two of my men to take along with him on the same mission. I needed my men and my vehicle for the next morning at 0700 sharp, but I told him I had no problem with it as long as everyone was back in time and my truck was in one piece. I was reassured that my guys would be back by midnight and there wouldn't be any problems. Murphy's Law is always in effect.

About 1:30 in the morning I walked down to the TOC to see what was going on. There were more people than usual in there, especially at that hour. My imagination was going wild. I ran into the night Battle Captain, whom I had worked with before with a few emergencies. He saw me coming and said, 'Houston, we have a problem.' I immediately thought the worst, and feared the worst for the men I had sent out. We were being deactivated upon returning home from this tour, and I talked to the men about expanding our experiences. One of the men I had sent out that night was a real redneck and told me plainly, "Sergeant, I think we should get our hands into ev'ry cookie jar we can while we're here". We were going out with a bang, and gaining experiences that most guys in our field would never see. I questioned my leadership decision at this point and asked myself what the price of experience should be. At that point I wanted nothing more than to just get them back safe and sound.

This was definitely a leadership lesson learned, as I probably shouldn't have panicked too early in the game. Apparently, the Sergeant Major had got caught in a winter storm and got my truck stuck. A Humvee is made for just about any type of terrain, so to get one stuck is pretty rare. Then they all had to walk to the nearest shelter they could find, which happened to be an old Albanian brick and stone house with the fireplace burning. From all accounts, it must have looked inviting because they looked no further. When an aged man opened the door, our Sergeant Major told me he immediately noticed a belt buckle prominently displayed on the fireplace mantle. It was simply three letters . . . KLA. This man was either a former or current member of the Kosovo Liberation Army, a rebellious group of bad guys whom we tried to disarm during our tenure there.

The man must have noticed our guys eyeballing the belt buckle, because he immediately motioned to them as if to say that it was a long time ago. My guys and the Sergeant Major stayed up all night pulling guard and making sure everything was as quiet as it was as when they got there. The night went without incident, and when they returned my men fell out of exhaustion. We delayed training that day and most of my other guys made sure that everyone around us was quiet so as to let them get some good rest.

We never let the Sergeant Major live that one down though. I felt like a father telling the son that he couldn't borrow the car again, and that my guys couldn't come out to play anymore either.

Years later at Fort Leonard Wood, Missouri I would run into the Sergeant Major again where he attended my graduation from a service school. You guessed it; we told that story again.

THE BABY

Since our deployment to Kosovo, I had seen literally hundreds of children in my travels. Like most children abroad, they all had this inherent knowledge that American soldiers like to be good natured and generous whenever possible. I must have been in a rut or something somewhere along the tour, because I was a little bitter at not seeing my own children for so long. I had my oldest and infant twins back at Fort Bragg. I longed to see them, and it was easy to put children in general in the back of my mind.

That all changed one day when we heard the news that a newborn baby had been found in a farmer's field just a couple of hours old. It was winter, and the Balkan winter's can be particularly harsh. By the grace of God alone this child had survived. An American patrol had passed the field when a farmer notified them that the child was still alive.

The child was brought to the hospital where she was treated and loved with the utmost care. For about a week or so, you couldn't go an hour without hearing someone mention 'the baby'. I won't mention the base camp where we were at but the rumor was that the hospital personnel were going to name her Bonnie Steel. They ended up settling on Rose Steel instead, thank God.

One of the National Guard guys that worked with us was an enlisted man. In the National Guard, some of the guys are quite a bit older than those of equal rank on the active duty side. Most of my junior enlisted guys were single, and this guy was certainly not. He was a grandfather. I knew he was a lot older than my guys, but I don't think I would have ever guessed that he had kids old enough to have kids themselves. He was more mature than the others, as life had made him.

He approached me one day and asked if it would be okay if we could go down to the hospital and see the baby. I told him that the chain of command had already put out that several soldiers had already tried to adopt little baby Rose, and the flood of visits had pretty much killed the staff's motivation to allow visitors. I'd also been in the Army long enough to know that there's a way around everything provided you're properly motivated.

We decided to go to the PX and purchase a small gift for baby Rose, which proved to be more of a challenge than it would have been back home. Inside a forward deployed PX, the selection is generally limited with no consideration to infants. They had more combat knives and CD's than anything else, but nothing for a baby. So we settled on a red, white, and blue angel pin from the cashier and a belated birthday card. We stashed the stuff in our cargo pockets, as we couldn't be openly trying to visit the baby.

We walked into the hospital and found ourselves face to face with a guard, a private. Getting past this guy shouldn't be too hard, but he was still an obstacle. I introduced myself to this young warrior and told him that we were from the Fire Department and here for an inspection. Technically, you can do a fire inspection anytime and right now seemed like as good a time as any.

It was almost too easy, so my partner and I decided to give the hospital a thorough once over to ease our conscience. When we came to the inpatient section where baby Rose was resting, we knew right away that we were in the right place. We went in and although I recognized one of the medics, I didn't really know anyone there to well. Human nature tells us to keep close to what is familiar to us, so I approached the medic and asked to see the baby.

My buddy and I both got to hold her and it was a nice touch of reality in a sometimes-surreal place. I had not held a baby for a few months when I left my infant twins behind to deploy. My callousness was washed away in an instant, and for the first time in months I felt my fatherly instincts return as I held that tiny baby.

A Serb church in the town of Klokot. U.S. forces had to guard the church due to the gold inlays on the walls. The detail and beauty of this church would rival that of St. Pauls Cathedral.

AN UNFORGETTABLE FIRESIDE CHAT

On the way back from one of our many missions out into the countryside, I remember pulling off to the side of the road so that we could take a break from the long road trip. I remember standing there talking with my buddies. It was absolutely freezing outside, but the call to stretch our legs, and for a nicotine fix was a driving force. We decided to make a public relations call to a nearby farmhouse just to assure the locals that we were indeed there in good faith with our overall mission. It was really a dual purpose mission in that while we were mingling with the locals we could also conduct a presence patrol and perhaps give them a sense of comfort knowing that KFOR troops, Americans in particular were taking a vested interest in their safety and perhaps ward away any KLA (Kosovo Liberation Army) members intent on any wrongdoing.

As we neared the house, we approached what appeared to be the backside of the dwelling. It looked to be a sturdy house made of stone and mortar, and complete with a large chimney that topped out at about forty feet or so. The smell of the smoke billowing out of that chimney gave me warmer thoughts than I'd had in months.

The area of Kosovo where the American sector resided was primarily an agricultural area. The simple people of this region were merely trying to survive the genocidal dictatorship that was predominant in the region, and our enemies were always trying to intimidate them.

As we came upon the house, we admired the obviously tedious work put into this home that was undoubtedly built by hand. As we rounded the corner of the house, the smell of the fire was more noticeable and just the thought of it was enough to warm up my mind a few degrees. What we saw next would leave me somewhat speechless.

From the path that we used to approach this old farmhouse I never would have suspected that the chimney that warmed our thoughts was supported by the only remaining standing wall. As we turned the corner, we found a family of four sitting on a small bench in front of the hearth. At this point, I believe that we were equally startled in seeing each other. In my Americanized mind, I suppose that I never dreamed that I would see such a sight. Each member of this family was scantily clad in tattered clothing, and I observed that the fuel for the fire in the fireplace consisted of books, sticks, and rags as well. The older boy stayed with his parents; however the little girl was more curious than any of the others. She was a dirty-faced cutie with bright blue eyes and was absolutely adorable. Wearing an ensemble that would make you cry, she was a little trooper as her culture and environment had forced her to become.

I had lowered my weapon by now, and offered a large gloved hand to her small, dirty, bare hand. She accepted, and as I saw my own children flash through my mind I couldn't help but smile. Her pureness of heart and smile were enough for this warrior to smile back and recognize this unexpected optimism in the form of a small child. I removed my ballistic helmet and slipped off the black wool watch cap underneath.

As I motioned to place it on her head, she just smiled and stood there, semi-paralyzed. I don't think that she was expecting more than a handshake from this tall, armed stranger.

The Fire Chief from the town of Gnjilane and I posing for a quick shot. We forged a mutual aid agreement and I frequently visited his firehouse. We helped them out with resources, and he was genuinely appreciative.

Her father immediately got up and headed my way. As a soldier I didn't feel threatened by this man, however thought that I may have committed a faux pas as a parent to another's child. His smile reeled me back in, and the hurried gait that I mistook for anger just a second before was clearly now an excited appreciation. He outreached his hand to me far before he reached me, and hugged me tightly when he did. I didn't understand his words, but as a father I could read his heart. To this day I can still see that little smile. As a father of a daughter myself now; had the roles been reversed I could most assuredly say that I don't think that I'd have been any different from the man I met that day.

CHAPTER FOUR

ALASKA

9-11

I t was one of the most turbulent moments in our nation's history, and I have yet to meet a single one of my countrymen who can't recall where they were or what they were doing when, for a moment time actually stopped. It was one of the worst days that most of us can imagine. Indeed a tragedy, however, our country showed its might in a single nationwide effort to unite. The fall of the Twin Towers in New York City will undoubtedly be a highlighted moments in our history. I only pray that no one ever forgets that with being the most powerful country in the world presents opportunities to those who would do us harm and see us as a target.

Although no amount of memorials, flowers, good deeds or well wishing will bring back the over five thousand Americans that lost their lives that fateful day, our homage to them and to the future generations, as I see it should be to attack terrorism where it sleeps. I don't think that this places us on par with our enemies, but protects our own future generations from such atrocities.

Here is my little piece of September 11, 2001.

I was on duty at the fire station at Fort Wainwright, Alaska when the bunkroom lights came on almost an hour early for some reason. One of the guys on the early morning radio watch was watching the news, and realizing that we were on an Army installation that this would soon affect us all. All of the firefighters made our way hastily to the common room where we were glued to the television. With every second of horror that ensued we were in sheer awe. I likened it to folks back during World War II hearing of Pearl Harbor over the radio for the first time. I simply couldn't believe it. I called my wife, Helen, and woke her up to see the news. She was pregnant with our daughter, Abigail, at the time and I remember being hesitant to wake her up. But then again, I was probably going to be really late getting home, and this was bigger than all of us.

Fort Wainwright used to be an open post. By this I mean that there were no closed gates, not even a guard on the main post gate unless the MP's were checking for drunk drivers on a weekend. I recall my arrival in June of 2001. As I drove through the main gate about ten o'clock at night, the sun was high, and I remember thinking how nice it was to be on an open post. The threat of anything remotely dangerous was obviously minimal. It just felt safe.

Almost immediately after the planes hit the towers, Fort Wainwright went from a THREATCON (Threat Condition) 'A' to a THREATCON 'D'. There were guards on the gates, civilian contractors were positioning concrete barriers up to create serpentine entryways, and all gates but the main one were shut down completely. This of course presented some problems locally that no one had thought much about even as much as an hour before the tragedy.

With only the main gate open, both military and civilian workers were stuck in traffic all the way to North Pole. The town of North Pole, Alaska is 19 miles down the Richardson Highway, so delays were inevitable.

Usually getting off work around 0800, I didn't see home until around 1030 that morning. We had a huge dry erase board in the common room, and by the time I had left the fire station we had written over a hundred names on it; all fallen firefighters who gave the ultimate sacrifice. By my next shift the following morning, the final tally would be 343.

When I walked through my front door, I really didn't know what to expect. Helen was sitting in her big comfy chair, sobbing uncontrollably with a box of Kleenex in hand. As I walked through the door, here eyes met mine in a reddened watery gaze. I hated seeing her like that, but I also knew that we were by no means the only ones touched by the day's events. It was the horrible sensation of being a small part of something so wrong. It was our country joining a fraternity of those already struck by terrorism. It was felt in my home and in our hearts. It was a singly catastrophic moment that was the beginning of a series of events in our lives.

2002 ALASKAN GOLDRUSH – OUR WEDDING

I wasn't around for the original Alaskan Gold Rush of the late 19th Century, but Helen and I were getting married in Alaska at the Northern Lights Chapel. This may sound like a cheesy, Las Vegas style wedding, but it's actually a beautifully modern looking chapel on Fort Wainwright. We decided to relive some of the history of the area and have a themed wedding. We would have our own Gold Rush. It was exciting, and we tediously prepared everything down to the last detail.

We had tied shovels and picks with bows to the ends of the bench style seating, the pens were seated inside an original gold pan filled with little gold spray painted rocks and the attire was something to see. Denim and flannel were the order of the day. Helen and I had purchased matching shirts for us and another matching set in another pattern for the best man and maid of honor. I don't think I ever saw so much flannel in one place before, except on an episode of 'Home Improvement'.

We arrived at the chapel early that day, as did about a dozen dedicated and wonderful friends to help us set up our reception. In the Army family, everyone helps out with everything. There were kids everywhere, the kitchen was buzzing with activity, and being a Platoon Sergeant at the time, I assumed the role of overseeing virtually everything so Helen wouldn't have to.

Things seemed to be going well enough. That was, until we realized that we left Helen's shirt at home in the dryer. My best man and I jumped in my truck and broke virtually every land speed record known to man to get home and back in time. The planets must have been aligned because the wind was at our back and we hastened to the chapel with time to spare.

Our son, Kevin, was the ring bearer. A very self-conscious child, Kevin did a great job presenting the rings inside an old fashioned gold pan. His excitement over being a part of the ceremony was undoubtedly one of the highlights of his young life. Our daughter Abby was only two months old, and was beautiful as a girlfriend of Helen's carried her down the aisle as our flower girl. She was draped in a century old baptismal gown that was hand made and absolutely gorgeous. We wouldn't have had it any other way.

The Chaplain who performed the ceremony was an old paratrooper buddy of mine. Back at Fort Bragg, just a few years before he was my battalion chaplain. He was a good man, and due to the fact he knew us when we were dating permitted the wedding to go on as planned without the standard marriage counseling classes. So there we are, waiting to get married. The guests are seated, Helen's ready, and I am for some strange reason a bit nervous. I wasn't nervous about the wedding, the commitment, or Helen. What was unnerving me at the last minute was that we were about five minutes from 'show time' and the Chaplain hadn't showed up yet. I was of course concerned, so my buddy who set up the whole thing for us, and a Chaplain's Assistant called to see if the Chaplain was on the way.

Apparently, he completely forgot about the wedding. In twenty minutes flat he was walking through the front door of the chapel, wearing a suit, with bells on. I told him that Helen and I would get him a watch with a fresh battery the following Christmas. It was only a minor glitch, and actually took some of the tension off of our big day.

The Chaplain finally kicked off the ceremony with an apology to all the attendees along with a witty anecdote about how, like this ceremony, in life things don't always go as planned. It was absolutely perfect. As I peered out into the pews it was as though my future was flashing before me. I had looked forward to this day for so long; it was hardly believable. Rarely in lives do our dreams come to fruition, so when it does it is truly savored. I had a buddy queue the music as she proceeded down the aisle; and she was absolutely beautiful. She had flowers in her hair and looked as though she was walking on air.

The reception hall inside the chapel overlooked the lake in the center of the post. We danced together, and then one with Abby and I and Helen and Kevin as well. It was so nice to be connected with my best friend in this way, and it really was a dream come true.

CHAPEL MORNINGS WITH DARRIN

About a year following 9-11, I had turned the reigns over to a buddy who took over my platoon as the Platoon Sergeant. I was leaving Alaska in just a couple of months and really didn't have a job. I talked it over with my First Sergeant, and there was a chapel that needed a Noncommissioned Officer because there were a couple of troops down there with little to no supervision. It wasn't much of a job, but it served a purpose in the interim. The best part was that I got to work directly alongside my buddy, Darrin. Darrin was a fellow paratrooper and a good man. He had come to us from Alaska from Fort Campbell where he had served with the 160th Special Operations Aviation Regiment. He was a first class warrior, and I liked him immediately.

You see, Alaska is a garrison environment. At least it was before the Global War on Terrorism. No one ever really deployed from there, so you knew you were going to get some good fishing and hunting in over the three year tour. Again, that was all before the war. Our unit was a Headquarters element, and every section in our unit had something to do with running the post directly. We had the post fire department, air traffic controllers, range control personnel, and it also included the post command group. Our function was to run the post on a day-to-day basis, and then push out any units that were called to deploy. However, though it all, we stayed. For most of us it was a good break from the breakneck pace of the line units that we were used to.

My first day at the chapel was a Thursday, which was our training day. Every Thursday all the Chaplain's Assistants would assemble at the chapel for some training on tasks from hand to hand combat to the technical tasks associated with serving a Chaplain. Prior to training though, Darrin and I would cook up dozens of pancakes, eggs and sausages, and plenty of coffee for all those attending. This was by no means standard, but it really was a nice touch and a great way to start the day.

During the week, we'd have to report to work by nine o'clock in the morning. After physical training, we'd shower up and get to the chapel early. At this time in our careers, I had already completed two combat tours and Darrin had three. We were warriors in probably the most un-warlike posting in the whole Army. It was disheartening at times because the war was raging on and we were merely spectators. I suppose it just gets in your blood after a while. With as much experience as we both had at the time, we longed to be leading a squad of men, charging towards Baghdad. However this wasn't happening any time soon.

We'd show up early and put some coffee on, watching CNN. As we heard the reports of our fellow soldiers charging into the cities, it truly pained us to be on the sidelines. In retrospect I am now appreciative for the break in the pace that I had for my twenty-two month tour in Alaska, however, I always liked to keep my edge. We were two 'lifers', sitting this one out. But every morning you could just about set your watch to the time when Darrin's truck would pull up.

Most of the time I'd already be in the chapel. I'd hear the creaking of the old chapel door as it opened and just smile. It was very comforting to have such a good friend who had 'been there, done that' and understood exactly where I was coming from.

It's often been said that fellow combatants have a bond that can never be matched; a closeness that only they know. Many moons ago I had only heard about it, however, after living it a few times I can wholeheartedly agree that this fraternal bond is eternal. Although Darrin and I had never served together prior to now, it was clear to me that we were on the same page in many areas.

He's just one of those guys that; if you ever needed him in a pinch would be there for you. I now live in Kansas, stationed at Fort Riley with the 1st Infantry Division. There's not a doubt in my mind that if I needed Darrin here with me that all it would take is a phone call, and vice versa.

Just seven months later I would find myself in a whirlwind caused by the war. Three weeks to the day after signing into my unit at Fort Riley, I would once again be wearing desert camouflage and boarding a plane for Iraq.

My second tour in Alaska was a quick one, however after being a platoon sergeant, getting married, having Abigail, 9-11, and driving out of there to Missouri to retrain and change my job after thirteen years I can say it was a good tour overall. Darrin was a big part of that time in my life, and made a lot of things more bearable than they could have been.

Even since I left Alaska our friendship has continued on. Aside from my wife and children, he's only one of a handful of people I ever called during those precious few phone calls I was allowed to make from Iraq. I hold his friendship as one of my true blessings, as true friends don't come around very often.

THE PRINCESS

After Helen and I started dating, we realized that we had four children between us already. I had three boys from my first marriage, and she had one son from hers. We compared notes, and after a while, I didn't think that I could actually learn anything else about kids, generally speaking. Children can surprise you, and they will every chance they get.

With my oldest, I could not have been more proud. He quite obviously looked like me, and deep inside the ego of a young father, the miracle of birth of a son that's your spitting image is just the icing on the cake. He was perfect in every way, and was my world. I can recall a fishing trip we took one day when he was about six years old. I was off from the fire station, and his mother was at work. It was in North Carolina down at a small pond. After buying a bucket of crickets for bait, about fifty; I though that we might catch a few sunfish, and it would be a good day for he and I.

What I didn't know at the time, however, was that the fish were waiting for us and were they ever hungry. After his first fish, I considered it luck and proceeded to bait his hook once again. As I cast my own line out into the water, he started whooping and hollering again as we both watched the bend in his rod signify the tell tale sign of yet another fish on the line.

What I didn't know then was that this would continue for about the next two hours and when it was all said and done we had about forty white perch in our bucket; only about ten of which that I caught. It was a great day, and in this surreal moment I recall thinking that it just doesn't ever get much better than this.

I had seen the bumps and bruises that little boys get just by being little boys. After all, I had done all this myself once upon a time; and in retrospect they were all good bonding moments between my sons and me. I had twin boys, a challenge to say the very least. I learned early on that whether you're serving food, getting them dressed, buying toys, or anything of that sort, what you do for one must be done for the other. The logic behind this of course is because by the very nature of being twins you have two very distinct personalities to take into consideration. It's a delicate balance, but it can be done.

It's clear that up to now I had experienced the whole gamut of emotions and experiences with my boys. When I met Helen, Kevin was about six at the time, so this wasn't unfamiliar territory for me. He was the child of a single mother, loved video games and Pokemon. I was in somewhat of a comfort zone as I'd been through this before, so to speak, and once again I really felt comfortable.

Four years later, Helen and I would find ourselves in Alaska and one morning I was lying in bed when Helen called out to me from the bathroom. As I approached the door, she was sitting on the edge of the bathtub with a pregnancy test in her hand. By the miniature hieroglyphics in the tiny window and the directions on the box there was no doubt that she was in fact pregnant. We decided that we would go to the hospital the next morning to get a blood test and make sure. Of course the results were positive, and I was absolutely ecstatic. I suppose back then that I'd never even though about the possibility of having a girl. Helen and I had all boys up to now, and it didn't even seem a remote possibility that a girl would ever be on our horizon.

Being that we never had a child together before, I explained to Helen about my experiences with the Army's Nurse Midwife program, and that if she was comfortable with that, I'd really like to work through those folks. This was due to the fact that as long as there were no complications then I could deliver our baby myself. I was really excited about the possibilities.

During one appointment, we were given a tour of the maternity ward of the hospital, and met several of the staff. To my surprise, we were introduced to the woman who would become our nurse midwife, Major Bristow, as well as the department head, who was by now a well-experienced nurse named Lt. Col. Graham. It was another surreal moment that just felt like destiny in the works. I explained to Helen that the good Colonel was that same young captain many years before that assisted me with the birth of my oldest. She remembered me, and we joked that delivering babies together was becoming a habit. She asked if I had any others, and I told her since our first experience together I had delivered my twins at Fort Bragg, and was really looking forward to working with her and her people once again.

Life is funny sometimes. I often wonder what the odds were that the same nurse who delivered my oldest with me would be in the same duty station when we were entering our last collective pregnancy.

The months went by and Helen fell ill with a terrible case of morning sickness that lasted a very long time. My chain of command at the time was very supportive, and due to our needs at the time I was moved from the fire station over to the unit to work for the First Sergeant. With my new work schedule I could be home every night and this proved to be very beneficial for all.

One of our very good friends at the time came back from a three-month school in Alabama the night that Helen went into labor. It was Alaska in June, and when he returned from his trip he thanked us for 'waiting' for him to come home to have the baby. This was of course a huge coincidence, as he also thanked us in advance for not calling him that night so he and his wife could have a little 'mom and dad' time. With the tedious and busy shuffle that was our life at the time, I suppose the writing was on the wall. But nobody saw it.

After my friends' homecoming, Helen and I returned home and went to bed. Just a couple of hours later, Helen informed me that it was time to go to the hospital. We were both very tired, and I scoffed as I thought she was joking. Nope. Sure enough, her water had broken, and we were on the way to the hospital. When we arrived, Helen was made as comfortable as possible by the awesome staff in the maternity ward, and I hurriedly called everyone I could think of.

This mass 'all call' was a challenge. On Fort Wainwright, all of our friends lived within three blocks of each other, and we all lived within two minutes of the hospital so neither time nor distance was a problem. The issue was that a month before I decided to test everyone during a hospital visit where Helen was having false contractions. I made one phone call to a buddy who had never had children before. He and his wife had two children from her previous marriage and I knew I could throw a red herring his way without arousing suspicion. I called his cell phone and said, "Helen's seven centimeters . . . we're at the hospital . . . I gotta go." Our other friends had three children and she was a registered nurse, so they were definitely not an option for my practical joke.

By the time they all made it to the hospital, there were four parents and seven kids waiting for the latest news in contractions, centimeters, and labor. When they came down the hallway, I stood there staring at my watch. They all had that look on their face as if to say, "Well, what's going on?" Tapping on my watch I said, "This is a test, this has only been a test! How come it took you all twenty-eight minutes to get here?" Apparently the mothers had changed their children's clothes, taken a shower, and prepared for the long haul. I suddenly realized how much trouble I was about to be in. They walked past me and into the observation room where Helen was resting. I heard her tell them that it was a joke from the beginning, and she of course had no way of calling them as I had our phone.

What I had not realized up to then was that when they showed up, the husbands were left with the children in the waiting room, and the buddy whom I called felt horribly out of place. I felt bad afterwards as I found out he was in tears after the emotional roller coaster that I put him on. Later on we all had a good laugh about it, and he has forever since been known as Mr. Sensitive. I still think it was a good practical joke.

When the big day came, and it was time to call everyone (again), the other wives told me that Helen herself would have to be the one to call because they wouldn't believe me. That was fair enough considering what I'd already put them through. Once again, they all made it and we hunkered down for our long journey.

Our nurse-midwife, Major Bristow was clearing post by now, heading off to her next assignment. We surely hated to lose her as she was possibly the most informative, comforting, and genuinely concerned nurse we'd both ever experienced. She had actually signed out of Fort Wainwright by a few hours at that time, but told us to call her anyway if 'anything' should happen. During our numerous appointments she told us that she loved taking care of expectant mothers but had never actually experienced a live birth herself, other than her own of course. I suppose there's somewhat of a sense of closure to it all seeing that newborn enter the world and cry for the first time.

Helen and I talked about it and decided that it would be a shame if we didn't invite her to Abby's birth, at the very least. All of the key positions were filled except one. Helen was in labor, Lt. Col. Graham and I were delivering, and one of Helens girlfriend's was cutting the cord while another girlfriend manned the camcorder. We openly invited Major Bristow to be a participant, and she did a great job coaching Helen and comforting her when necessary.

Helen did a fantastic job as a laboring mother. We did our best to keep the ice chips flowing and the pillows fluffed. Her efforts were absolutely phenomenal and I couldn't have been more proud of her. Our baby girl was the culmination of the best of both of us. She was our miracle. I had hoped that she would be just like her mother.

I would have different bonding moments with her than I had with my sons; different but special in their own right.

When Abby came out, it was an absolute shock to me. I'd never delivered a girl before and this one was my daughter. She was absolutely beautiful. I felt this wave come over me that to this day I still can't explain. My heart was filled with pure love, and my knees were weak in such a way that there aren't even words to describe it.

Abby is now two and a half years old. She knows she's my princess because she tells me so. She also tells me that she'll never leave me. Helen's always saying that Abby is lucky to have such a sensible mother, and she's right. I see Helen in her eyes, and her mannerisms and character are both her mother's as well. I just think I'll believe my daughter's promises a little bit longer.

CHAPTER FIVE

OPERATION IRAQI FREEDOM

When we all left Alaska, I was heading off to Missouri to attend training at The U.S Army's Chemical School. After thirteen years as a firefighter, I was changing my career to better my chances of promotion and retirement. I also knew that with the change to such a career field that it was only a matter of time before I would be of to the desert again.

After signing in at Fort Riley, we moved into our home assigned to us by the housing division. It was a nice four bedroom with a garage and a fenced in back yard. By any standards it was a nice home and we were glad to have it.

My mother was living in Florida at the time, and had some rough times coming her way. We decided while we were still in guest housing that we could move her, my grandmother and my teenage brother in with us for a while until they got on their feet. I called my brother, Gary, and he and I meticulously planned their trip to Kansas down to each pit stop for gas and food. It worked like a charm. The day we signed for our keys to housing, I was at work at my new unit. I was getting signed in, and being placed where they needed me as I was going to be a part of the rear detachment until we al got our desert training in order to ship out to Iraq. This would only prove to be a short few weeks.

When I got home from work that day, I found an old pickup truck in my driveway with a ton of furniture in its bed. My wife met me at the door, and I queried as to what this furniture was doing here. Our household goods wouldn't be here for a couple of weeks, but we had a house full of furniture on the way. Since my family was arriving in a few hours, Helen wanted to make sure that at the very least my grandmother and mother had a bed to sleep on, and dressers to put their things up. Having never met her in laws, I just couldn't help but be impressed with how poised she was. She never ceases to amaze me.

I had attempted to see my boys, however my ex-wife was not willing to come to Kansas and my training schedule left virtually every minute accounted for until our departure. It was a huge disappointment; however, I just prayed that I'd live through the tour to see them again.

Just a few short weeks later we were all standing in front of the gym, getting our last shots and getting briefings before boarding a bus bound for Atlanta, Georgia where we'd get on possibly the longest flight of our lives.

The following is a journal that I kept for a year while in Iraq. Prior to leaving, Helen and I had no idea what kind of communication capabilities were available in the desert and agreed to keep journals to keep up on things both at home and abroad. After the tour, we would read each other's journals at our leisure, gradually catching up with lost time. It was a good idea, and with Helen's support would later become the motivation for this book. I never dreamed that I could write so much, but when you're not sure whether you'll live long enough to see your family again you'd rather write than sleep. After all, it just might be the last chance you get to say something to the ones you love. It started out for me as a venue to write to her when I had no time for anything else, and inevitably grew into writing to her just about every day. It's really interesting how it developed. I've edited the following version, as some events and places should still not be mentioned due to operational security. However, my Helen has the original, as she should. After all it's hers; she just chose to share most of it with you.

20 OCT 03 – D-DAY (DEPARTURE FROM FT RILEY)

After leaving post, our journey takes us across the country via a charter bus. The hours go by, and the lines in the road just melt into each other. This is but the first night of many away from my darling Helen, and I will soon start to see our children grow up in pictures over the next year. I have done this with Gary and the twins for a long time now, but with Kevin and Abigail as well, I think it will be more than I can bear. Most of the guys are asleep now, and after dinner at Golden Corral in Columbia, Missouri, there's not much else to do but sleep from now on. I am fighting the urge to stay up. Stay up for what? I know I need to get all the rest I can right now, and stockpile up on sleep while I still have the time. God only knows what the next year will bring. I wonder if everyone on this bus will make it home. I wonder if any of them will remember this somewhat carefree night, relaxing on this bus. I surely hope so.

21 OCT 03 – D + 23 hours

The driver pulls over at a rest area to get some coffee, and after I wipe the sleep out of my eyes I believe that I recognize this place. After the pain of leaving Helen and the kid's at the gym on Fort Riley just less than a day ago, I find myself hanging in suspended animation. This rest stop is between exits 1 and 4 just over the Tennessee border. I've driven over this same stretch of highway many times in my life, as I was stationed here for three years. I am in Clarksville, and after all the heartburn of not seeing the boy's due to my ex wife; this is just the icing on the cake. I am only about two miles from the boy's house right now. I am a cross between anger, frustration, hurt, and at the same time trying to shake all this off because I know where I am going. I need to have my head on straight, and I will.

Tonight, we also stopped at Baltimore, MD where we took flight to the Azores, off the coast of Portugal, and then a short layover in Frankfurt, Germany. I was able to speak with Helen, the kids, and Grandma in the Azores, however, we were short on time in Frankfurt, and I have to get used to being in long phone lines again.

22 OCT 03 – D + 46 hours

We will reach Kuwait tonight, and I will try to call again, just to let Helen know we arrived in one piece. Everyone has been either sitting down or asleep for nearly two days now, and the anxiety really hasn't started to show yet. In Kuwait, after a few briefings, I'm sure at least one or two will show some. I don't expect too many issues though. We have all been together up until now, however many of us will go our separate ways, over to different companies, and perhaps different base camps. Matt, Brian, Dusty, and I have been there since the beginning, but they are going to at least two different units after we reach Iraq.

25 OCT 03 – D+5

Arrived in Baghdad, Iraq the day before yesterday, and was greeted by a buddy at the airport. The plane was delayed in taking off from Kuwait because Baghdad International was closed due to receiving mortar fire. Lovely. When we finally got there and checked in, the reception LNO said there would be no chow before lunch, but my friend hooked us up. He and I took Matt, Brian, and Dusty to the chow hall and got 30 plates to go. When I asked the civilian if it was possible, he said 'no', but then my buddy spoke up, and, being a Major, they of course said yes.

Yesterday, we milled around Camp All-American a lot. We occupied a tent with the 11 people we came with, and established a water point, and scored some ice. Later in the evening, we acquired some more ice, a valuable commodity here, and bedded down for the night pretty early. There have been a few explosions around here, and not much can be done about it. Sometimes it's EOD blowing up a weapons cache, and sometimes it's not. We saw a few Apache helicopters flying around in the area today, this offered little comfort against the random explosions, and none against the heat of the day.

Today was actually somewhat of an interesting day. We tried to get out to the main Baghdad PX, but were then bumped by some other people on the random bus that travels through the American complex in Baghdad. Try again tomorrow. I need to get some pads of paper, and envelopes, and get the letter writing moving. It's good for morale, but also helps to pass the time. I hope that things at home are going better for Helen. I know that it must be a strain on everything with the kids, the family, and now me being gone. She is the purest form of love that I've ever seen. I miss her so very much, and long to be with her. I know that this will all be over one day, and that this God-awful place will be behind me, and the rest of us.

We were told that helicopters only fly during certain days of the week, so we'll have to try and get out to our unit later in the week. The unit is in no big hurry to get us up there, and we are truly on our own for right now. We are, however, making the best of things. The troops are holding up well. Most spend their time waiting for a phone somewhere. The phone company here is charging an arm and a leg for the phone usage. Phone cards are sold like hotcakes, and spent even faster. It's really a crime that they are making a killing off of us like they are. Dusty and I went down to the Internet Café tonight after supper, and got charged $3 per hour to use the web. I only shot out two emails, one to my lovely Helen, of course, and one to Uncle Steve. He and a veterans group of his want to use me as a case study for vets and such. I told him I'd oblige, and signed off the Internet, which was terribly slow. Tomorrow, my buddy said he'd like to show us around a bit, and said he'd take about four of us around town. He's got access to a Toyota 4WD vehicle, and his offer was most generously accepted. He really has been a Godsend to us. He's helped us get meds for the troops, chow when we needed it, and lent a hand at everything he possibly could. I'm really grateful for his help.

26 OCT 03 – D + 6 1920 hrs.

Today was interesting enough, I suppose. It really goes to show you how quickly you can get accustomed to some things. Today it was nearly 100 degrees, and the sun is always high in Baghdad. The troops all got up around 0600 to get ready for chow. The interesting part is, I was already up by 0530, and I laid my head down last night around 0300. I stayed up late sending out emails, and attempting to call Helen. After nearly 14 years I have always said, 'Joe will always be Joe'. Myself included, to be sure. I see my soldiers running around calling their families and girlfriend's back home, and it seems to be their central preoccupation during this time of calm before the storm. During my first two combat tours, I did the very same thing, only late at night so as not to let the troops see me rattled. It's that primal desperation that all of us go through at one time or another; a thing that we all quietly share, yet devotedly try to keep to ourselves. Any vet who's straightforward will admit that. So, as it turns out, I found myself dialing an endless series of numbers from one type of phone line, and one country to the next, only finally able to reach my wife by pleading with the post operator to dial a calling card number and reaching my wife on her cell phone. This escapade started at around 2150 hrs., and came to a close around 0250. Sometimes, even surrounded with your buddies, armor everywhere in the sky and on ground, all you need for everything to be okay is to hear that one angelic voice of the one that loves you truly.

2035 hrs.

As I sit here writing, a mortar has been so graciously donated to our camp on the south side. Lights then go out, and power is restored eventually, when the threat is believed to be gone. Again, it's truly amazing what you can get used to. I gave a refresher class this afternoon on 9-Line Medevac requests. We invited a neighboring Infantry unit to join, and they did. It seemed to go well, and the troops seemed to be thriving for information. They are hungry, thriving only to do their job, and serve. I see a lot of myself in these kids. I see myself 10 years ago in a little town called Mogadishu, Somalia as we naively attempted to rescue a nation from itself, and save the people who could not, and did not want to be saved. This sounds familiar.

As we sit here in Baghdad, an ancient city of beauty and full of lore, it's hard to imagine anything like that now. This city, this country, has consumed itself over years of neglect through the greed of a sadistic dictator with an unquenchable thirst for God only knows what. Only the minority, such as our mortar donors, seem to not mind the uncertainly of their lives, their futures, and their country.

The guys and I did happen to see Saddam's main palace and Uday's palace as well. Saddam's palace belongs to the 1st Armored Division, and Uday's place belongs to an Engineer Brigade. It feels so good to just write that. Saddam's boys were not the nicest kids on the block. Qusay was a particularly rough kid. He loved animals, so much so that he kept a private zoo. Except he loved torturing his people more that he loved animals, and his zoo mates benefited from this. He would simply torture his people, and feed them to the more ferocious of the critters in the zoo, the tigers in particular. I'm glad to see the property being used for a better purpose nowadays.

27 OCT 03 D+7

Today the men seemed a bit uplifted. If I had to guess why, I'd say it's because of the tension, and nervous excitement in the air. This morning set the tone for the entire day, as it often does. Unable to get a hold of my friend, I decided to leave a message at the hospital inviting him to have supper with me tonight about 1800 in seeing as we leave tomorrow. Around lunchtime, I headed down to the hajji shop to get some smokes, and see what wares he was peddling today. After that, we went over to the 82nd ABN DIV dayroom to catch a movie. 'Tombstone' was the flick of the day. I love the movie, but it would approve an ill choice later in this day. During the movie, we heard an explosion, and decided that no bells and whistles were going off at the time, and it must be EOD. Those guys are often setting off charges to blow weapons caches, mass amounts of ordinance, and explosives.

I had a long talk with Brian, or "Mo", as he is affectionately known as around here. We spoke of Helen, and his girlfriend, our children, life in general, and how important for these young Soldiers to know that, over here, it's all about the man standing next to you. Over here, nothing else matters, moment to moment. We may fight for our country, loved ones, but make no mistake; none of that is here right now and each other is all we really have. We agreed that the troops would be fine, and he mentioned one in particular that he inprocessed with back at Ft. Riley that he hoped to keep with him. Mo has become really good at putting up walls in his life. He makes sure his Soldiers are always taken care of first, but still sees it as weak if he himself tried to call home. He's a deep individual. Once the time is taken to actually talk, moreover listen to folks like this, you can gain an incredible insight into their souls.

Just before supper tonight, about 1740 or so, I was finishing up with Hajji's internet café. Since we leave tomorrow, I wanted to send Helen one last email since we don't know how technologically sound it is out west. I also sent Uncle Steve a SITREP, and a quick note to Darrin Numbers, a good friend of mine who used to run with the Nightstalkers. He's a true warrior in every sense of the word, and I wanted to at least shoot him a note as well before we left. You know why. I recall the days following 9-11 that Darrin and I would watch CNN religiously following the inception of the war on terrorism. Darrin had come to Alaska from the Nightstalkers, and was the 75th man on the ground in Afghanistan. We were both angry and wanted justice. We were impressed with the precision of the surgical style bombings from the Air Force, and the deadly accuracy of American SPECOPS guys being reported almost daily. We actually wished we could go.

Tonight we mourn to loss of this morning's explosion. It was not in fact, EOD, but a car bomb that killed 39 soldiers, and destroyed the Red Cross, and later in the morning a series of smaller explosions, which killed another 15 people. The NCO's are upset because here we sit at Camp All-American, not 100 meters from the main road, with no ammunition for nearly a week now. Not a comfy feeling. While the cherries are bemoaning the loss of our fellow freedom fighters, many Reservists go on, laughing at the DFAC, talking about going on leave, etc. Rough day today. We'll pause for a moment, while we have the chance, and then move on. I hate to sound so callous, but I know that this will definitely get worse before it gets better.

29 OCT 03 D+9

After arriving at Camp Junction City last night, we immediately were taken to the Battalion CSM to be assigned to our units. I of course went to Decon, but there were a few surprises. Mo went over to Bravo Company Bulldogs, while Dusty, who was fresh off Recruiter detail as a Corporal, went to Charlie Company. Dusty was a hilarious guy, but I know he was nervous about going to the line and getting Team Leader time. After being a staff puke for so long, he now had to soldier. He went into recruiting as a Corporal, so he had no leadership time. Getting a Team Leader slot was somewhat of a 'baptism by fire'. Matt on the other hand, who was a young warrior in the truest sense, was not sent to the line but to the S-3 shop. He was immediately irate about this, and made no secret of it. Within the next two hours Matt talked to everyone from the Battalion CSM and Commander on down. To no avail, he was stuck being a staff weenie. To him, this was weak and no place for a soldier. He came up to the hooch and vented regularly that day, and I did my best to console his realization that he would not see too many convoys outside the gate.

In our in briefing with the Battalion CSM, we were told that a soldier was killed within the last 24 hours. It was CSM Falanika's son. Command Sergeant Major Falanika was, and still is a legend within the Airborne community known for his hard ass attitude, and his admiration by his troops. Matt Papke and I had inprocessed Ft Riley with this kid, and joked with him within recent weeks about how he wasn't Airborne. I remember Matt saying, 'You're Falanika's kid, and *you're* not Airborne? The kid told us that that was exactly why he didn't go to jump school . . . because he *was* Falanika's kid. I guess it's hard being the son of such a hugely respected and well-known man, and then coming in as a Private.

What a hell of a first day.

30 OCT 03 D+10 2110 hrs.

Tonight's movie was briefly interrupted by inbound and outbound artillery fire. The inbound was most likely mortars from Hajji, and the outbound was 155mm rounds from Paladins. The engagement lasted about five minutes, but was pretty intense. It sounded like we gave better than we got, but in reality we'll probably never know.

I spoke with the LT tonight, and apparently he leaves us in January. He is young and slightly bitter about his own situation. The Decon Platoon in this battalion is comprised of one LT, one SFC, two SSG's, about 12 Soldiers, and myself. We are a Brigade asset, and as such delved out to those in need of Decon type missions. Makes sense. However, we are also subject to all company and Battalion missions and are pretty much at their mercy at all times. I know that this sucks, and sometimes you just have to bite the bullet, but I think this whole scenario has proven to be too much for the LT. He's a bright young guy with a solid future that he will make for himself.

6 NOV 03 D+17

After an uneventful Halloween in Iraq, it has been a few days. I have been busy with Gate Guard/Escort Duty, maintenance on vehicles, and keeping up with the latest intel reports on what's been going on. The other day, we missed an RPG attack on the gate by just under an hour. I had just taken the men home for the evening, and as soon as sunset occurred there was a shot from 450 meters away. Ironically, the gunman fired the RPG from just a few yards from the Iraqi Police station. I spoke with Matt about this, and we both agreed that the soldiers and I were just plain lucky.

It has been presumed that the gunman, taking full advantage of the Ramadan holiday, waited in his perch until the exact moment that the sun went down, and then fired his RPG. During Ramadan, the hajji's can't eat during the day, and with the heat, and working too, they know exactly when the sun will go down, and they can get something to eat and take an afternoon nap as they often like to do. The gunman had his shit together; his only flaw that his aim sucked. Good for us though.

I have been keeping my precious free moments filled with writing letters to Helen. I have written several letters thus far, and one to the boys in Tennessee, and one for Kevin as well. I also sent Kevin and Jon some of the new Iraqi money. I thought they might like it. I so desperately miss Helen that sometimes I feel like a lovesick puppy or a giddy child from school days. I am so in love with her, and with each passing day I realize that I never even want to risk the chance of parting with her for this length of time again. Three combat tours. And with each one comes a price, in one form or another. With this one, I am parted from my true love, and I am missing the children terribly as well. Kevin grows so quickly, and his intelligence and sense of humor grow with equal speed. I hate to say it, but the pain of not seeing, and missing the boys is an old companion that I am unfortunately all too familiar with. And Abigail, my sweet Abigail. I miss her sweet voice calling Dada, and the sweet way she sleeps ever so close to Helen, and the darling way that she almost whispers Mama first thing in the morning. She, not so unlike all the boys, has been a victim of a deployment at a young age. Unknowingly she is robbed of time that hopefully she can forget without too much effort as she grows. For me though, it's time that will take an eternity to forget as I hear about the events during my absence. All the firsts that I will once again not be a part of. I really don't intend to sound so pessimistic, but today is one of those days that I had enough slack time to think too much. I want to process it in little parts now, while I am gone though, because I don't want it to come crashing down when I get home. The command is considering something called decompression time; a few days in Germany or somewhere for soldiers to relax and get used to not being in this environment prior to returning home. I already do not want this time. I don't want another day longer away from my Helen than is absolutely necessary. I do so hate the thought of decompressing at home, but I have confidence in my awesome marriage, and my dearly devoted family that I'm sure by then that they won't mind either. I don't want to be in a place where helos getting shot down, sand in everything, and IED's on the side of the road are normal. I'm not losing my faith in the Army. It's just that I think I am starting to realize that maybe I really have done enough for my country. Maybe now it's time to do something for my family and me. I believe it just might be time for something different.

7 NOV 03 D + 18

Today I have such a deeper understanding of my wife than perhaps I ever have. I have been very foolish, thinking that she shouldn't somehow love me as much as she does. It's almost like I've had this double standard; and it's only because I never expected to receive the love that I am willing to give. I think this martyr's attitude comes from never receiving it in the past, and I really should have known better in Helen. She loves me deeply, as I do her, and it literally pains me to not be with her. She is truly a gift from God, and I am indeed fortunate to have her. I miss her so. I think we got our work done too quickly today, because I wrote Helen two letters today, and I allowed myself to think about family more than I should. Is that possible? I don't think so, but I am missing them all so very much. I am really drawn to my wife today. I hope that maybe she will look at the moon tonight, and somehow see me staring back at it too. I know this is a pipedream, but I wish so desperately that she could know at this moment how much I love and miss her.

I learned today that there are Marines and Navy coming here to Camp Junction City. There are two possibilities: one, they take command, and we continue with our mission here under them, or, two, they completely take over, and we move to Northern Iraq and start over again. Northern Iraq is not nearly as developed as it is here, and it will be very stressful. The artillery boys are at it again, returning fire into the night somewhere, and this time it rattled the window above my cot. Hajji is getting a lot more accurate with his mortar fire.

9 NOV 03 D+20

After yet another exciting day on Ogden Gate Escort Duty yesterday, I was looking forward to my first Sunday off, and taking the time to try and call Helen and the kids. I have been unable for some time to get through now, and it is very frustrating. I shot out an email to her this morning, and tried to reassure her that although things are indeed rough now, it would certainly get better. There is a possibility that this will not be a yearlong tour, but only six months. I dearly hope so, as that will surely help.

She is not getting much help at home from my brother, and that is disappointing. I'm told that he's sleeping all day and staying up all night. This makes me very angry. Helen said he hasn't even cut the grass once since I left. I suppose it's too late in the season now to do that, but his lack of help is not very comforting at all. Never send a boy to do a man's job. Anyway, I was looking forward to the day off, but when I came home last night, I found that there was a mission to Habbaniyah, Camp Manhattan today. SSG Johnson was asked to go based on his familiarity with the area, and I was to take his shift as Escort 6 today. This was highly disappointing. The only good news is that one of our guys returned safely from Qatar last night. After the CH-47 crash last week, I am grateful for his safe return.

I am placing a sign at the gate today, marking the Escort Element as DECON territory. It just helps make it a little homier than just a shot up war torn building. I already have built sandbag walls around the front entrances and windows to shield us from mortars, RPG's, or grenades. It's not bomb proof, but will shield us from the majority of the blast and fragmentation. I learned these things from past deployments, and only pray that they come in handy now. I just want to make an indelible impression on these young soldiers. Well, I must get my gear ready for the day. The PX opened up yesterday, so I bought some post cards to send out to folks. There's not always time for a letter. Due to the poor phone and internet situation, I feel that if I take a lot of time to write other folks letters, even family, then I am taking time from writing to Helen. That simply isn't going to happen. I have to get geared up for my shift. It takes some mental preparation being on the tip of the spear. Today might be difficult. Someone hijacked one of our contractor's trash trucks at gunpoint yesterday, so we are now expecting a vehicle-borne IED. I can't even imagine a bomb the size of a trash truck. The size of that is proportional to the planes used on 9/11. We'll see.

11 NOV 03 D+22

Yesterday afternoon's convoy to TQ Air Base started ominously enough. The day was overcast, with a low fog hanging like a motionless oil painting over the camp. We had only 5 hours notice, and it was to be an overnight mission. The LT looked a little nervous, as he was the convoy Commander. He only found out about 10 minutes before I did, so we were both jumping through hoops to make it happen. In one hour I had the vehicles at the SP area, and the time hax on the board. The Soldiers were cleaning their weapons, NVG's, and packing a ruck for overnight. We ended up being done with everything about an hour early, and made it to the Battalion SP without a hitch.

That's where I found out I would be doing this same mission every Tuesday, and, I was in an armored Humvee, so I was a chase vehicle . . . a hunter. The rules of engagement haven't so much changed here, as they've been slightly altered since our mission started. If we receive indirect fire, such as inbound artillery, mortars, etc., we simply haul ass and push the convoy through. If we receive direct fire, such as an IED with a visible triggerman, or small arms fire of any kind, then myself and two other vehicles chase down and kill those responsible. In an instant it seemed like I was back on the QRF in Somalia. My whole job was to hunt down anyone firing at us and take them out. My soldiers had a similar reaction, right about the same time as I did, and they all looked at me at the same time. I simply told them that we had our marching orders, and as long as we all got to TQ in one piece, whether we had to hunt anyone down or not, then we were in the green. We only had one small incident on the way there. Along the MSR (Military Supply Route) out in the middle of nowhere, there's this guy and a kid and old man digging a hole on the side of the road. This looked awfully suspicious, so I told my driver to whip around and then radioed ahead that we were going back to check it out. I saw the LT's face as we passed him going back, and I think he was concerned. No one ever likes to think what it would be like to lose a troop, and although young and inexperienced, even the LT was feeling that. I was as well. We were going to confront the enemy on his own turf, one on one. In our Humvee we have a ring mount that my saw-gunner was perched in. I told my driver to creep up on this guy and about one hundred meters out to slow down to a complete stop. I would then hoof it in alone, and confront this individual. I told my saw-gunner that if this guy so much as flinched, he was to cut him in half. If something happened to the gunner, the medic in the seat behind me would treat him, and the driver would hop on the SAW. It was a good plan, and we were all straight. When we got to where the guy was parked, he had stopped digging, and was now on the road driving in the same direction as our convoy. We whipped around behind him, and I decided to follow him. If he did anything shady, I was going to shoot his tires out, and detain all three of them until we could get an interpreter out there. At this point, I was really wishing that we brought Salah with us. He's a no-bullshit kind of guy, and he really knows how to get the point across. The Iraqi driver made no such moves. I was looking for any shred of hostile intent to take this guy down. We followed close behind him for almost two miles, and then decided to pass him up and rejoin the convoy. We started around him, and as soon as we sped up he swerves out in the middle of the road as if to stop us. Now, a few things started swimming around my head. This guy was digging out in the middle of nowhere on a known military route. He also saw how long the convoy was, and know that we were part of it. He also knew that we were checking him out, and now he's trying to stop us from rejoining our convoy. Why would he do that? It would be so foolish.

We made it into TQ all right, and as soon as the troops were fed and bedded down for the night, I made my way around the camp looking for Eric Russell. Eric is a big burly guy, and he and I were Squad Leaders together back at Bragg. I found him near his hooch and he gave me a huge bear hug in front of everyone. We talked for a bit, and sat down over a cold bottle of water. When we jumped together back at Bragg, especially on late night jumps, we would always go to KFC afterwards and we would each get a 20-piece pack of honey BBQ wings. We'd be all dirty, and have camouflage all over our faces. Those were some great days. We both lived out in the country, and we would carpool to work on the days we had jumps and have our chicken ritual after, celebrating that we lived through another one. It was nice seeing Eric, but I also realized that I was surrounded by a whole camp full of paratroopers. God, I miss that. Eric and I got our foreign wings together as well, and we talked a lot about our kids. Both of our oldest boys played together a lot. When I showed him pictures of Helen and the kids, he looks up at me, and says, 'you gotta be shittin' me! How did you trick a beautiful girl like that into marrying an old man like you?' We laughed until late, and I made my way back to our vehicle, which the four of us ended up sleeping in. It was an armored Humvee, so I popped the hatchback, and crawled in the back to sleep on a bed of rucksacks. I tied off the hatch-strap to the antenna, and put my fleece on. I popped a chemlight, and, lying there under the stars, could only wonder what Helen was doing then. She was probably curled up in our canopy bed at home. I thought about our close call that day, and wished so desperately that I could call Helen. I so miss the sound of her voice. It's so comforting to me. Wishing I were next to her in our bed, I drifted off to sleep under my poncho liner, and tried to stay warm. I woke periodically through the night and looked in on the troops.

After our return this afternoon, we downloaded gear, and I was back briefed on what had gone on in the last 24 hrs. I brought a plate of chicken back from the Hajji restaurant on TQ. Eric took me around the camp in a Gator vehicle that morning early, and showed me the nearly 20-mile perimeter of that huge place. There were units from 82nd Airborne, 3rd Armored Cavalry, and a host of support units. They had the Hajji restaurant right there on camp, and they were comfy, no doubt about it. There was more wire than I'd ever seen on a camp before.

We were sitting in the hooch eating our takeout when the artillery boys starting lighting up someone. They must have fired about 15 or so rounds from those howitzers. We came to find out that a scout patrol was just outside hurricane base down Highway 10 from us. They had been taking incoming mortar fire for a while, and the patrol was calling for fire. The noise was so loud, that it got everyone up. We turned out the porch lights and watched the fireworks from outside in the dark. It really was impressive. I thought of Helen, and how we laid in bed all day one day back in North Carolina, listening to the rain hitting the windowpane. Or the night we stayed up in Missouri watching the lightning storm from that dinky little apartment we had. I wouldn't wish for her to be in a place like this in a million years, but in a really dysfunctional way sort of reminded me of that. I hate having any kind of experience without her, except those here of course.

13 NOV 03 D + 24

Last night we spent the night at Camp Manhattan, near TQ Air Base. The purpose of our mission was for the Battalion Commander to investigate an incident that occurred the same day I got back from the TQ mission. Apparently, three soldiers were pulling duty near the old ASP in Habbaniyah, and the SPC decided to pick up some UXO. An NCO out there told me that it must have been complacency, because the soldiers out there are used to seeing these things. The soldier picked up the UXO, and it detonated, blowing off both of his arms. He also had shrapnel to his face, and two other soldiers had minor injuries as well. It's a shame, because every soldier, from Basic Training forward is taught that you never pick up any kind of UXO.

This time, we took Highway 10, which is the most dangerous road in the world right now. I was the trail vehicle, which was unsettling to those in my vehicle. Typically, with IED attacks, the first and second vehicles are targeted, as well as the trail vehicle. It makes sense that the first couple are targeted due to the amount of antennas on those vehicles. An antenna marks the vehicle as a command vehicle of some sort, thus painting them as targets. To take the long way there is about 2 ½ hours through TQ and then another couple miles. We took the shorter route yesterday, and made it in 26 minutes. We were absolutely hauling ass, but made it to Habbaniyah without incident.

We spent the night in an empty building. I had supper with Mo, my buddy from Riley. They are always busy over there. They receive mortar fire every night, and return with equal force. Last night was no different. They started in on us about an hour after dark, and went on into the night. After a while, we drifted off to sleep, the booming sounds now distant.

This morning we woke up early, and got mounted up. Yesterday was Thursday, which is ceremony day for the Hajji's. On ceremony day, they hold weddings, funerals, and everyone with an AK-47 is authorized to display celebratory gunfire on Thursday. Friday, (today) is like Hajji's Sunday. It's the last day of his weekend, and is typically a recovery day from ceremony day. These days are supposedly even more special now because of Ramadan. Today was not the case. Just short of the halfway point between Habbaniyah and Ar Ramadi, our convoy was hit with an IED. The third vehicle was lightly peppered with shrapnel and my vehicles driver's side windshield was shattered by a large piece of shrapnel. My driver, PV2 Simmons, received a few small cuts directly in his eye. When we got hit, we immediately hauled ass out of the kill zone, about a half-mile down Highway 10. We all got out and pulled security near the median, and Simmons, still hurting, pulled security with us. SSG Lebov was the senior medic in the battalion, and had volunteered for the mission because she didn't want to send her soldiers down Highway 10. Under fire, she irrigated Simmons' eye with an IV bag of saline and still managed to shoulder her rifle in a defensive posture. She's a warrior of the highest caliber. I held rear security and kept my eyes peeled for anything moving. When we saw the Quick Reaction Force pulling up to our rear, and two OH-58 helos circling the attack site, we decided to press on. I put Simmons on the truck as the SAW gunner and SPC Dorelus in as the driver. All the soldiers performed very well, and I was thankful that they were there. Hajji was on the money with his detonation time, and we were all very fortunate to survive the attack. We didn't ever see the triggerman, but our soldiers were ready nonetheless. Every person in that convoy wanted a piece of Hajji, but none more than me. They hurt one of my Soldiers . . . one of my guys, and I wanted some payback. We made it back to Camp Junction City still in only 38 minutes, counting the attack and the security stop. This was still good time. We immediately took Simmons to the Battalion Aid Station, flushed his eye out some more, and patched him up. He'll be out of the flow for a few days, but his eye should heal up in no time. Of course mention was made of his Purple Heart almost immediately, and he sure does deserve it. And for no other reason than he's one of my soldiers would I trade places with him in a heartbeat. Simmons is pretty tough about the whole thing, but that doesn't change the way I feel about it.

I also found out after the debriefing that we are to do another escort convoy to Champion Main this afternoon. Champion is right around the corner, about a 10-minute ride, but if any of us took anything for granted before this morning, they surely won't ever again. It shouldn't be an overnight trip, so I already feel a little better. I think in this case, for us here in DECON, that it's good to hop up on the horse so soon after a major incident. Most folks probably wouldn't agree, but they're not in my shoes either.

I remember taking a knee, pulling security in the middle of Highway 10, and thinking that someone just tried to kill us. Screw that shit. I didn't miss a single detail, and I was looking hard for ANY sign of the triggerman. I was just a trigger squeeze away from some kind of justice. At least in my head anyhow.

My Darling Helen, I'm going to try and lay down for a little bit now before the next mission. I love you so, my darling. Kiss you later.

Well, the mission to Champion Main went well. We took trooper gate out across the Euphrates River to the camp. The bridge made me a little nervous, however, we were lucky, and everyone got there and back just fine. The LT and I are learning each other, and working very, very well as a convoy leader team. He is in the lead vehicle, and I am in the rear. We both have just as much at risk, with the antennas on our vehicles, and we are reading each other on the road really well. Our communication on the radio is second nature, and we rarely have to speak a full sentence to know what the other is trying to say. It will be sad when he leaves here, and the Army in January. I will have to learn another LT, but I won't take it easy on that one either . . . he he. The soldiers are gaining confidence in their leadership, slowly but surely. It seems rather dysfunctional, but they grow very fast here. In garrison, it would take at least six months to a year to foster the team spirit and esprit-de-corps that we already have here in the last three to four weeks. The downside is that it takes extreme circumstances to enable that.

My love, I know that this journal seems to ramble on in ambiguous thought all the time, but I wanted you to get a realistic snapshot of what I'm thinking, feeling, and what goes on in detail on a daily basis. Some things are very hard to convey in words, even here. And some events will simply have to wait until I get home to work them out. I'll be honest; today was a particularly rough day, as you have read here. But no amount of the right words can truly express how I feel today. I look at Simmons, sleeping across from me, and I am deeply saddened by today's events. Here, I look on my Soldiers as my children, and just as when I'm home, I feel a parental hurt when they suffer in the least way. The LT came back from his meeting tonight with the Command Staff, and my soldier will get his Purple Heart. It really is the least that they could do. He really does deserve it. One of the soldiers outside the platoon made a joke about being a status symbol of sorts. This is true to a degree, but he is lucky to not receive it posthumously, as we all were. I also kindly reminded the platoon that if you asked him, Simmons would probably rather not have it than have it. We were very lucky indeed today.

16 NOV 03 D + 27 0630 hrs.

My Darling Helen, it is now 0615, and although I was looking forward to my first Sunday to sleep in almost a month, I couldn't stay in bed. I received your package yesterday, and I was so excited when I stopped by the hooch from the gate. I built a small hutch for my area yesterday, and we cleaned up the bay last night. I just wanted everything to be perfect. We all cleaned the bay, spaced ourselves out since Haines and Eason finally showed up, and our hooch looks very nice now. I went and took a shower. I think I was a little nervous about opening the box. I made my bunk, up nice, went to take a shower, and folded my laundry which I hand-washed the day before. I finally sat down on my stool, kicked my feet up on my cot, and opened it. I immediately saw your letter and Kevin's as well. I also appreciate the notes from Joseph and Austin as well. I dearly love your letter honey. I had to just sit there and read it three times. I know my ears were turning red, because I just couldn't stop smiling. I appreciate everything in the box. I immediately passed out a piece of candy to everyone in the platoon. It's almost expected, but not really mentioned around here. The platoon is tight, and everyone shares everything with everyone else. It's nice to see how tight people can be. It's like the 4 Horsemen on a different scale. Also, any type of food like that must be eaten somewhat quickly because of critters around here. It's between 35 and 40 degrees at night, and the rats always come in and are looking to get warm, and for food. Anyhow, I must have been up until midnight last night reading your letters and just being happy. I can't even tell you what a morale booster that was for me honey. It really showed me how far down I've slipped in the few short weeks since I arrived here. Everyone is starting to talk about the upcoming holidays, and I can only imagine now how busy the PX and Wal-Mart must be at home. Even the PX here is already selling Christmas cards and stuff. I wrote out your Christmas card last night, and it took a lot for me to do that, sitting here, in the surroundings that I am in. However, I still have to lead by example, and show the troops that we need to do things as normal as possible with regard to things at home. I love you my darling. I am going to go and fill out some post cards for the children now, and get them off to the mailbox while I can. The mail only leaves here on Tuesday's and Thursday's, but I don't like to put it off. Plus, if I send it out like that, there will be some days that you will get more than one letter in a day. That's why I sent so many so far.

We've had six convoys in the last 4 days, and the men are tired. Somehow, they are still dedicated, and although the battle rhythm decides our pace, we are adjusting well. Simmons is feeling much better. He no longer has his eye patched up, and is feeling much better. He should be ready to go on missions again in the next couple of days.

17 NOV 03 D + 28

Hello my love. Today I am on the gate, but we have almost 30 people and 6 vehicles. The changes I suggested are starting to take place, and things are getting smoother by the day as far as the escort business goes. I actually have a few minutes today to write during the day. I sent another letter off this morning, and I'll probably start another this afternoon sometime. Due to all the people I have today, I am building some more furniture for our folks. SSG Johnson only has a small shelf, and I am going to build him one like mine. It's very nice. You know I love to putter around with tools whenever I get the chance, but here it's a real luxury to have any kind of furniture at all. Our quality of living here solely depends upon us. We will beg, borrow, and "acquire" just about anything that we can to make life easier . . . and we do. Busy day today.

18 NOV 03 D + 29

Hello my love. When I read your emails today, I didn't mind the comments. I absolutely understand how much you must be going through right now. It did concern me about Mom and Jon watching Abby, and then no one being anywhere in sight when you had to wake up and get her anyway. That really pissed me off. I'm not so much bothered by the fact that it happened, but that I know that they're not giving you the same respect as if I was there. If I was home, I know that that wouldn't have happened.

Today was a rough day. It was very depressing. I listened to some tunes this afternoon, and before I knew it I realized that I was listening to everything that reminds me of you, and I was lost for a little while there. I took the squad out for some PT, and then went and ate supper with Matt. I feel somewhat better now, but I actually got a chance to rest up a little today, and I want to make sure I can get some sleep tonight for the gate tomorrow. I have found that free time; in any small amount is as much an enemy to me as Hajji is. It invites depression, and gives me too much time to think. It may sound foolish, but it's absolutely true. We're going to watch a movie tonight in the hooch, and relax a little. The platoon is pretty tight, and it always feels better when the whole team is here at night.

24 NOV 03 D + 35

My Darling Helen, it seems like forever since I've touched this journal, however, I got to email you twice today, and although it's taking me a few days to write a letter,

I keep the letters ongoing by writing the date and time whenever I pick it up again as I'm sure you've seen by now. It seems surreal sometimes, but it has become my reality here. I catch a few hours of sleep, and the cycle starts over again. Last night was our second all night excursion in a row out in Ar Ramadi on mission for the locals. I pulled security as part of the Battalion QRF, and the nights were long. We were placing concrete barriers around Iraqi police stations to protect them from car bomb attacks. The first night, (22 NOV 03) we left about 2030 hrs. and returned about 0845 hrs. the next morning. Then last night, we left earlier than normal, about 1830. I didn't like that too much; it was just a tad too bright for me, and the streets in the downtown market were way too crowded. We handled the crowds, and the only constant bother were the local kids begging for a 'torch'. The local children love chemlights, so I snapped a couple, and sent them on their way. Everyone is very poor here, and, I suppose even after our IED attack that injured my soldier and tore up my Hummer, I still have an inkling of compassion left in me, although I'm not sure how. The kids here have the same look on their faces as mine do when I give them a chemlight. I'm sure this place could have a future if they really wanted to work at it, but honestly I don't think they want it. There was a lot of shooting last night. We must have heard tens of thousands of rounds. The tracers lit up the night sky like the Fourth of July. We were in the center of the Ar Ramadi slum neighborhoods when the shooting started. Some of the shooting was closer than I'd liked, but then again so is all of it. I looked around, and there were tracer rounds everywhere buzzing buildings, and skimming rooftops, but mostly soaring into the night air. The worst part of the night was the ride back through Ar Ramadi. There's a bridge that crosses the Euphrates River, and it make my ass pucker every time we cross it. You can see the holes in the steel from prior explosions and it's very unnerving. Before we made it to the bridge though, we were on Highway 10, and three little kids were aiming toy guns at our convoy. I drew my weapon up on the one kid, whose weapon didn't have an orange plastic piece on the end of the barrel signifying it as a toy. I came so close to smoking that kid. We've been back for almost three hours now, and I'm still pretty pumped up. I know that when I eventually lay down and crash pretty hard.

Last night before we left, I was talking to the S2 about the area we were heading out to, and we saw something on CNN. They were showing an expose on the R & R site that the Army runs in Qatar. It also had a brief note about a single IED attack that had happened before one of the soldiers went on R & R. The LT and I just stared at each other in shock. He recalled talking to his wife and her asking about if it was really as bad as CNN portrayed it on the news. He told her the truth, and told her that it was worse because the news couldn't possibly have enough time to cover all the attacks. We laughed as we remembered the one day nearly two weeks ago that passed without an IED attack.

Hajji is getting smarter. Last week he set two separate IED's. The first one was a small one, and also a decoy. The unit followed their SOP, and got out of the kill zone, then pulled security and observed. What they didn't know until it was too late was that where they stopped was the kill zone as well, and a much larger IED was set. This one kid from our Brigade got out and was only four feet away when it detonated. I heard they couldn't even find all the pieces of that kid. I hope and pray that he didn't feel it. I'm sure there will be more memorial services back at Riley, and I hope that Helen and the kids don't go. We were supportive when I was still home, but I'm sure it's different now. I don't want them to have any grim reality checks when the kids don't attend anymore right now, especially since they have so much to deal with right now. It really is an emotional roller coaster being separated under these conditions, and that would probably be too much to bear.

I found out a little while ago that there is another mission tonight, but I am not going. I have Escort duty tomorrow, and Nick Johnson is going instead. The last two nights have been exhausting, and he really does want to share the burden. Last night I took one of his SAW gunners with me, giving my guy a break. The gunner has to perch himself through a ring mount, half his body exposed all night long. With exception to the obvious dangers of that, it also gets really cold at night, especially in the wee hours around 0200 or so. We have three SAW gunners, so I'm sending my guy out with him tonight. When I took his guy with me last night, I know Nick wanted to go really bad, but I wanted to show him that I could take care of his guy under fire. I absolutely have the same trust for him, as it should be.

I only got to talk to you for a few minutes today before I got cut off. I called 101st FSB at Riley, and they connected me. It was very nice of them to help out with a morale call, but it really was a tease, unbeknownst to them. I need so desperately to hear your voice my love. I don't have many needs here, but our occasional phone call is something that I cannot seem to get used to not having. I know that having our cell phones spoiled me, but the phone lines here are ridiculous.

THANKSGIVING DAY D + 38

Well honey, this certainly wasn't the Thanksgiving I had in mind this year, not even for here as it turns out. I was on the gate, of course, but I did let over half the troops go just before they served the holiday meal at the DFAC. I think it was actually better for me to work today. Most of DECON sat around the hooch and watched movies, and bummed around. I made my guys go to the DFAC and we all ate together. PV2 Haines asked who was going to say the Thanksgiving prayer, and I told him I would lead our squad at the table just as I would in battle. The meal was actually a bit nicer than I anticipated, but not even close to home. I was looking so forward to our first holidays in our new home this year.

On a dimmer note, just before I held the guard mount this morning, a shot rang out, and I thought it was odd to be so close within the compound. My first thought was that it was an accidental misfire. Sometimes that happens when soldiers forget to clear their weapon properly, and a round is accidentally fired. I remember thinking, 'damn, someone's gonna get the ass chewing of a lifetime for that'. Unfortunately, it was a soldier committing suicide instead. For some reason, the poor soul saw no other alternative, and used his weapon against himself in front of a bunch of people. The soldier, by the name of Sweet, was one of my escorts just a couple of weeks ago, and as I recall, nothing was really out of the ordinary. Another one of my escorts for today apparently witnessed this, and he was really disturbed by it. First of all, I can't believe that the unit actually sent him out for escort duty after that, but then the kid started getting jittery and chain smoking and stuff. I never met this kid before today, but I could sense something was wrong. I asked him off handedly if he was okay, and his words just started pouring out like a deluge. He kept asking me why anyone would kill himself, much less on a day like today. I walked him over to my Hummer, and drove him over to talk to his chain of command and his chaplain. He would be okay after all, but not right away.

His chaplain, by the way, happens to be very good friends with Chaplain Davis. Apparently, they grew up together, and went to seminary together as well. I asked him to write our names down, and give Chaplain Davis and his family our best.

After all that this morning, it seemed like that's all everyone could talk about. While on Escort duty, I made all the soldiers write at least two letters home to family, and study for the soldier of the month board to take their minds off of things. It seemed to work okay, but you could still hear chatter here and there about it all day. It is very sad though, in many ways. First thing is that his parents will never have another Thanksgiving without being reminded of this, and the thing that sucks for everyone else is that because of his selfish act, the phones and internet were immediately cut off until the next of kin is notified. The last time a guy died in action here, the phones and internet were off for two and a half days. I hate to sound selfish, but I really wanted to talk to you today honey. I really wanted to talk to you on Thanksgiving Day, and for you to hear my voice and tell you how very thankful that I am for you. You are a gift from God to me, and I don't want to ever let you forget that. Well, I only wish you could understand how much I really am there in spirit, and I love and miss you very much. If we just can get through the time then we'll be just fine. Good night my love.

28 NOV 03 D + 39

Today was perhaps the most uneventful day since we've been here. We did some mission planning for tomorrow's operation at an old Iraqi Special Forces compound on a chemical/radiological survey. This is actually an NBC mission, one of the first since we've been in country. But we've got an early start tomorrow, so this will be short tonight. Plus it's our night to use the phone and computer, so I'm getting up in about three hours.

29 NOV 03 D + 40 0500 hrs

It is now 0500 hrs., and I just got back from using the phone and the internet. I just talked to you a little, honey. I can only imagine how much is going on back there. I sure wish I were there to help with everything. I'm actually glad that you vented to me. I really do understand how frustrating it must be to hear that I called Gary when I couldn't get through to you. I only hope and pray that you know how much I love you. After we got cut off from the 1st Engineer Battalion Rear-D Staff Duty NCO, I'm glad we got to play email tag for a few minutes. I actually felt a lot better about things after that. I hope it did for you too my love. These times are very hard for all of us, and God will help us through it all. You and I above all should have an easier time than most because of us. We're Ron & Helen, and although that may not mean much to anyone else, it means everything to me, and I don't care what anyone else thinks or feels about it, not even family if they don't understand it or have a problem with it. I'm really glad you spoke your mind to Mom and Grandma the other day. I'm sure it must have felt at least a little bit liberating to tell them how you felt. I also know that things can get tense in a household at times like this. I wonder if you've received any more of my letters. I dearly hope so.

I'm so glad; at the very least, that we had an opportunity to play email tag for a while. I was on the computer way longer than I was supposed to, but after our phone call, I decided that I would stay on until someone kicked me off of it, which eventually happened. Oh well, I will try again on Sunday to call you. Early this morning is our phone time for Decon; however they made Sunday a free for all day for the whole battalion. It's a little rougher on Sunday, but I will try to get on sometime then. I hope to at least be able to talk to you for a little longer then, since I have the phone cards that Steve sent. I copied all the numbers down after you forwarded them to me, and I'll keep them with me in case I get the chance to use the phone during an odd time.

I love you my soul mate, and I sincerely hope to talk to you again soon. Your voice is very healing to me, and just hearing it takes a lot off of me from the everyday stuff here. I am on the gate today, and I will write again very soon. As I got off the computer tonight, you said Angel was doing something with your hair. I hope you are getting a chance to relax and do girly things every now and then. I miss you more than words can say my love. I will sign off for now and pray for you and the children. Kiss you later.

10 DEC 03 D + 52

I missed you particularly much today my love. The days all seem to melt into one another, and occasionally, when we look up, we see that another week or two, another month have passed. One thing is for sure though, and that is that it all counts towards our year, and it's always one day closer to coming home. You know, especially with a one-year tour ahead of us when we left, I suppose even then I knew that this day would come. I have started to lose touch with a lot of things. I don't miss things like Wal-Mart or fishing anymore. I just want to get home to you my love, and hold you forever. It's almost like being in prison, where hope of leaving any time soon is a far cry from reality, and you just kind of deal with everything as it comes, no matter how much it is, or how long you have to stay up.

Tonight Nick Johnson and I got caught short. A couple of the soldiers were found to have a little rust on their weapons, and Nick and I had to clean the entire platoon's weapons. We did it in about 3 hours, and, although it really sucked to have to do it, at least it's done. We have a lot of young soldiers, and it's been a long time since I've had soldiers this inexperienced. We just have to baby-sit more often now. It's not really like we have anything else to do. Outside of mission, which is a constant, everything is NCO led, but due to the fact that there are only two of us, it's very difficult, but we still manage somehow.

Good night my love. I'll start another letter tomorrow, and try not to bitch too much about stuff. I love you my darling. Kiss you later.

11 DEC 03 D + 53 2330 hrs.

Today was a horrible day. Our guard shift at the gate was going well, and then the explosion. It was just north of us, just inside the wall at Champion Main, the camp immediately adjacent to Junction City. Apparently, a hajji came into the camp, and was searched by their search team. He made it through the search area, and when his escort got into the vehicle, he drove about 100 meters into the camp when the car bomb was detonated. The two hajjis inside the truck and the escort were killed immediately, in an instant. Four other soldiers were injured from the blast as well.

Our search area was only about 400 meters away from the blast, and could feel the blast wave over my face like a rough wind. About 10 seconds after the blast, I asked an EOD guy coming through the gate what they had going on over there. He told me that he was the only EOD in the area, and that he had no idea what it was. My heart sank. I suddenly realized that something was horribly wrong. I immediately stopped the flow of traffic coming into my gate, and repositioned my people to make that happen. We called for reinforcements, and placed them as they arrived. I even stopped incoming military vehicles, and used the vehicles themselves to block access points in my area, and pulled the soldiers from the vehicles to use as guards. Amidst the chaos, somehow, it all pulled together rather quickly. The Brigade Commander and Command Sergeant Major showed up within minutes, and asked what was going on. There were two lieutenants out there, both green in their careers, and they maintained the radios on site. I briefed Devil 6 and Devil 7 that I had stopped traffic, repositioned personnel, beefed up my positions with reinforcements, and was awaiting more soldiers to arrive.

The whole thing started about 45 minutes into our shift, and took up most of the afternoon. We came back and went for a short run, even though I must have run about a mile or so with all my gear during the afternoon. After our shift was relieved, I back briefed my troops about what had happened, and what a great job they did. It was a somber time, and I told them to keep quiet about any details they knew, and to route any questions through me.

Later in the evening, I was down at the Mayor Cell, working on the Escort SOP for the Commander, and a call came out over the radio that Devil 6 & 7 were looking for me. My First Sergeant and Battalion Command Sergeant Major walked me down to Brigade Headquarters. When we walked through the door, The Brigade Command Sergeant Major (Devil 7), yells, 'There's the guy!" My heart was pounding, and I really wasn't sure what was going on. Devil 6 walks up and shakes my hand, and palms a new OIF Brigade Coin in my hand. Devil 7 said that what I did today was what being an NCO was all about, and that I was an example. They asked me what I thought about what happened, and I told them that I was only doing my job, and that as far as I was concerned, the only thing that happened today was that a soldier lost his life, and four others were injured. I said, "That's the only thing that happened today, sir." He nodded his head, and shook my hand again, as did the Command Sergeant Major, and bid me a good night. It was a solemn moment, and then we left. As I walked through the door back into the Mayor Cell, my Battalion Commander was putting it out over the radio net that I had just received a Brigade coin for doing such a good job. I was truly humbled. But I also felt awkward as well. The only reason that I had to do any of if was because another soldier died. If I had my way, none of it would have ever happened. War certainly is hell; there's just no other way to say it. We truly are at the tip of the spear.

A guy that worked in S-3, which I have been on all my convoys with thus far, came in late tonight. I asked him where he'd been, and he told me that he was tasked with going over to take care of the investigation of this morning's events. He told me that he had to do a bomb crater analysis from the explosion, and that he'd never seen anything in his life like that. They use the crater as the point of origin, of course, and then fan out to look for debris. The distance from the blast to the last piece of debris is the bomb blast area. He said that there was nothing left of that poor kid but his head and a few of his ribs. He looked pretty burned out by the time we ended the conversation, and I told him I'd be there if he needed anything.

12 DEC 03 D + 54 2130 hrs.

Hello my love. Today was certainly a lot different than usual. Today on the gate, we changed our procedures, and normally we allow around 500 to 600 hajjis and vehicles on post every day. Today, we only allowed about 20 all day. After yesterday, we are searching everything twice, and doing physical searches about 200 meters away from the vehicles as well. We are also confiscating anything that could be used as a remote detonating device, including cell phones and calculators too. Being on that gate makes me absolutely paranoid, but the training value is excellent, and it allows us to keep our edge out here. I look at my guys every day, and try and tell them what a good job they're doing as often as I can, because you just never know. I really have taken them all under my wing; so to speak, because they all deserve the very best of whatever I can give them while we are here together.

This morning, a guy in 1-16 INF died from being struck in his Hummer by an IED. We were told that the explosion was so severe; that pieces of shrapnel went clean through his vest and plates like it wasn't even there. They are the enemy's most frequently used weapon. That's two soldiers in two days, all within 500 meters of the camp. Hajji sure is getting bold. The command believes that if we stop using Highway 10, and just stay inside the walls, then we just hand the Iraqi extremists another victory.

I'm going to try to call you tonight my love. The phones have been down due to the families needing to be notified. I will never despair over that my love. It is somewhat disappointing that I can't always call you, but I also think about the families that are about to find out that their loved one is never coming home again, and only two weeks before Christmas. I can't even imagine what that would do to you and the children. I really do try my very best to not think about it, but it's almost unavoidable here because it happens just about every day.

I'll sign off for now. I love you and the children so very much. I can't even tell you how much. I miss you all every day, especially you my darling Helen. I pray for you and the children every day and also that I might return home to you sooner than later. Kiss you later.

13 DEC 03 D + 55 1838 hrs.

Hello my love. Well, it was a relatively uneventful shift today, and at least nothing blew up today. Well, at least at our gate. There were a few small explosions outside the gate, but only that we could hear. We couldn't even see a plume of smoke or anything. Just a normal day I guess.

14 DEC 03 D + 56 2047 hrs.

I was walking back from guard mount this morning, and about 20 rounds from an AK-47 off in the distance. I remember thinking, 'just another day in Iraq', and didn't really give it much thought after that. The day wore on as usual, and then came my guard shift. The afternoon was relatively slow, and with less traffic than usual, the troops were in good spirits, as they felt more comfortable with our newer search techniques. Today is Sunday, and although it is somewhat of a down day for most troops, it's a regular workday for Hajji. Usually, on Thursday's, there is a lot of celebratory fire due to it being ceremony day. Today, however, was not that day. About halfway through our shift, we got a lot of gunfire from the village due south of us. My SAW gunner was on the rooftop, and the LT was up there with him. The gunfire was going steady for about 5 to 7 minutes when one of the regular hajji contractors came through my gate and told me that it was on the radio that Saddam Hussein had just been captured. He was upset that we might start engaging the village due to all the gunfire, but that it was his village and his people were so very happy that this day had come.

I have to agree with that guy. He shook my hand, and in that instant, I felt it light a jolt of lightning running through me. Once again, I felt the hope of a nation in the palm of my hand. At the same time, I also felt that in some strange way, us being here was suddenly worth it. This guy has been on the world's most wanted list for years, and I felt just a little prouder because my wife and children can sleep just a little better tonight. This is what it's all about. I could not be prouder to be your husband my love, or the father of all of our wonderful children. No, I didn't have direct contact with the bad guy this time around, but I actually don't mind sitting this one out. I'm just glad that he's been found. If I could have, I'd have done a little celebratory gunfire of my own today. We are far from being out of the woods on this deal honey, but from your end, I hope that you can breathe a small sigh of relief. I'm going to try and call you in a few hours my love. Kiss you later baby.

15 DEC D + 57 2015 hrs.

After the week and a half of no power or heat whatsoever, the platoon pulled together the other day and bought a generator for our personal use. A day after we got it, our Commander told us to get rid of it. She said it wasn't brought with us from the States, so we can't have it. I even got one of the hajji contractors to deliver free fuel to us for the entire tour. I even bargained him down from $370, down to $200. and the generator was brand new in the box. You would have been proud honey. These hajjis's have no respect for anyone that takes their first offer. It's actually part of their culture to argue like that. It's kind of like trying to get our families to do something for anyone but themselves, except here, no one takes it personal. Oh well, we'll just take it one day at a time.

16 DEC 03 D + 58 1100 hrs.

Today came with more rain and a lot more mud. I swear, my love, that I'd do anything to see our yard again. I haven't seen grass in forever and a day. After last night's fiasco with the generator, I think it sent a message to the chain of command. All of a sudden, out of nowhere, we get another power transformer (2000 watts), a 220 coffee pot, and satellite cable is ordered for us. What the hell? I think the unit just realized that DECON has been put on the back burner for longer than anyone else. Plus, we take on all the missions that no one wants to take, like Escort and the Gate Security. The Army is so funny sometimes, how it operates. People will make or break any unit. I've always said that, but I wonder how this will all work out when you build good soldiers within a unit that's already broke. We'll see.

2206 hrs.

Apparently, DECON is in the hot seat again. We sent a soldier on leave, and did not retrieve all of his sensitive items. It's a pair of PVS-7 Bravo's (Night Vision Goggles), and it appears that the guy took them with him on his two week leave to Mexico with him. He's a PFC, and one of Nick Johnson's soldiers, and he's worried sick over the whole ordeal. I am worried for him, over what the chain of command will do. If a sensitive item is lost in the rear, then it really is a nightmare. There are lockdowns, double-arm interval searches, long-term mass punishments, etc., but under combat conditions, I have seen this chain of command be unforgiving for so much lesser offenses. Line unit Engineer outfits are rough like that. Typically, they eat their young, developing soldiers out of nothing but brute force, and unwavering loyalty and discipline, even if it is not 100% real. All that matters is the bottom line, and that is results, even if it means burning your best man, and doing someone dirty just because it can be done, and for no other reason at all. It has its moments; however, this is the reality of the situation.

17 DEC 03 D + 59 1800 hrs.

Good evening my love. Well, we got off the gate at 1600, had a short platoon meeting until 1645, and then went to the Battalion Christmas Tree Lighting Ceremony at 1700. Busy day. Then Rafael took all the Soldiers to supper with him, and Johnson went to eat by himself. I'm sitting here in the hooch by myself, and decided to catch up on some writing. Wish you were here right now . . . he he. Anyhow, at 1900, we have a class on the M2 .50 Cal Machine gun, and then at 2100, we apparently have another platoon meeting. Rafael is an idiot. It was a pretty slow day on the gate. There's an older guy here in town, an elder Ba'ath Party leader that is going around saying that Saddam isn't really captured, and the locals are eating it up. Here in western Iraq, it's primarily agricultural country, and the population in general is easily manipulated by the local extremists, as well as us.

Also, we've been extended, so that we have the gate thru 29 DEC 03, instead of it ending on the 19th. All the Soldiers will be off on Christmas Day, so Nick Johnson and I will have to train a whole new crew to do our soldiers jobs for just one day. What a pain in the ass. Also, after last night's episode with Nick's soldier taking his NVG's home on leave, Nick is getting an Article 15. I can't believe it. At this point, they're not sure whether it'll be a Company Grade or Field Grade Article 15. He admits that he should have handled things a lot differently, and maybe I'm being partial here, but Nick is an excellent NCO, and I'd just hate to see anything happen to him that's too bad. We'll see.

I'm going to go and try to check my email later on my love. I'm hoping that maybe we can purchase some phone time, and that will make our communication a lot easier than it has been. I miss you so much my love. I'm more tired than I have been in a while. I forgot how exhausted I get. I asked my soldier on the night shift last night to wake me up at 0230 so I could go and call you, but he said I actually sat up and started to put my boots on, and then just collapsed on my cot. He said he wasn't sure what to do, but didn't have the heart to wake me up again since I was obviously so tired. I appreciated the extra two hours of sleep, but only in the morning. And with it came the sinking feeling that I didn't get to talk to you my love. It's a lose/lose situation. I'm sure that this awful tour will end sometime; unfortunately too long from now. And no tax exemption, no promotion, and not even these great soldiers that I have now, will be enough to make me want to stay here not one minute longer than I have to. I'm sending another soldier home this week. He's a single soldier, and he'll end up being home for Christmas. Although it's the right thing to do by the Army, the soldier, and as a leader, I can't help but be envious of his good fortune. I suppose everything happens for a reason, and I can only hope to find out what that might be.

21 DEC 03 D+ 63 1900 hrs.

Hello once again my love. Today was, unfortunately, a painstakingly slow day. At least I got to talk to you again, and for a good while at that. It was 0630 when I called you, and I loved hearing your voice just waking up. You didn't have to tell me that Abby was asleep next to you, because I could hear her breathing. And then I asked you to hold the phone to her ear while she slept so I could talk in her ear. I don't tell you this on the phone, but I really do notice everything. I notice yours and the kids tone of voice, if you're having a good day or not, depression . . . . I notice all of it. It's just part of being deployed, but it makes me still feel connected to you all, even though that's a small part of everything. It's okay though. I know this sounds weird, like I'm just babbling about bits and pieces of everything, but that's me tonight. I feel so disassociated with everything right now, and all I can really do is hope and pray that you and the children love me the same as when I left. I know that before I left was a very stressful time for all of us with moving to Ft Riley, moving family in with us, getting Kevin ready for school, getting ready to deploy, etc. I wish only that I could have let you know then just how much I love you. I wish only that I could have loved on the children more, spent more time with all of you. I admire your strength, and your desire to always do the right thing, my love. You are my greatest strength, and my greatest weakness. I would do anything for you my love. I know that I say that, but I think I failed you in that I didn't do everything I could have as far as not trying to come here. I am proud to serve, to be sure, however, it takes me away from you. I try to be as reasonable as I can be, and tell myself that a 6-month rotation is not at all bad, but it still pains me so. My darling, as a soldier, I normally wouldn't think that a short rotation is a bad thing, because it is eventually expected, but a 12-month tour is without a doubt the worst thing that has ever happened to me. Every day pains me more than the one before, without you my love. I could tell you, but you already know the unbearable nature of this time apart from each other. This is the worst possible thing that the Army could put us through, a combat tour. Again, a 6-month tour is a lot to ask of anyone, but this is more than I ever could have imagined.

22 DEC 03 D + 64 2026 hrs.

Hello, my love. I found myself not just thinking about you, but also daydreaming about you all day today. Even one of the guys thought I was a little out of it on the gate today, but I assured them all that I was fine and everything was okay. It was so surreal, like I was asleep, but still working the gate and functioning at the same time. In fact, I thought I was particularly good on the gate today. I remember thinking that everything is better with you. I just wished at that very moment that I could have told you that. Every day here makes me realize more and more how lucky I am to have you in my life. Out of all of the things that God has to do for all of eternity, and he still thought to bring you into my life. I have to be the luckiest man in the world. I do love you so, my darling. I need you like the air that I breathe. Without you I am nothing, my love. You truly are the best part of me, and when we're not near one another, and then I feel so empty.

After our guard shift at the main gate to our camp, we paused for a group shot. Pictured here are elements of our platoon from the 1st Brigade Combat Team, 1st Infantry Division out of Fort Riley, Kansas.

CHRISTMAS DAY D + 67 0530 hrs.

Merry Christmas my love. I got up at 0345 this morning, got my weapons report in extra early, and headed down to the MWR to call you. I feel blessed that I actually got through so early, but it was only about 1900 on Christmas Eve at home. It was so great to hear your voice, my love. It was a great way to start off my Christmas day here. All the NCO's are working the gate today, but there's no inbound, or outbound traffic today. We're expecting a lot of resistance from the so-called freedom fighters and Ba'ath party loyalists. All intelligence reports from the last month have indicated that there will be some type of attack on American bases today. We are just shy of two hours from Baghdad; and out here in the western part of Iraq, out in the country, we are somewhat exposed. There are a lot of troops out this way, but we are spread a little thin out here. I just hope that things go well today. During my last combat tour, I almost got killed on Christmas Eve, and early into Christmas morning, so I'm hoping this Christmas will be a little different. I don't think I'm asking for much. It's weird having mixed emotions that are really extreme about the greatest holiday of all. I'm just glad I got to talk to you this morning, my darling.

I just don't want to die on Christmas day. I'm sure everything will be just fine. I love you Helen, more than anything in the entire world. You are my world. I'll try to write more later on today.

28 DEC 03 D + 70 2230 hrs.

Hello once again my darling Helen. I got to talk to you earlier, but we got cut off. I tried and tried to get the line back, but no luck. I hope so badly that you're not worrying, but I know different. I really wanted to but didn't get a chance to tell you that we have only another week on the gate. Our last day is 2 JAN 04. We turn it over to another company within our battalion; however they are getting it as a punishment. Like most people in our shoes, I don't think they'll do as good a job at it as we did, but I'm just really proud of my guys for dealing with such an intolerable amount of stress for as long as they have. I really couldn't have asked for better guys. I know I say that every tour. But seriously, if God hadn't armed me with these people right here, right now, then we may have not done so well.

I miss you so much my love. I was reading your email earlier, before I called, and you mentioned something about wishing you could just peek in on my day sometimes. I feel the same way my love. I wouldn't even care if it were during a really stressful day or something, just to catch a glimpse of your day-to-day goings on. I miss everything about you my love. I even miss it when I do something stupid, and your eyes turn green. It really is sexy, although at the time I'd never tell you that. It's funny now, but when it's happening, I wouldn't dream of giggling about it.

I organized some music on my laptop here, and made a file called Helen, with all the songs that remind me of you. I listen to it when I write in this journal. I think it really helps me to connect with you while I'm writing. Otherwise, I might just drift off into an endless sea of blah blah blah about God only knows what. Speaking of, if I write much later than this, then I'll probably fall asleep typing. I love you my darling, more than anything.

30 DEC 03 D + 72 0630 hrs.

Good morning sweetheart. I pray that you are well today, even though it is 2130 hrs. at home. It pains me to think that I missed you when I called yesterday. I did however, talk to Jon for a while. He assured me that he was working a lot of hours and paying you the 15% that we all agreed on. He mentioned that he had a lead on something to do with his schooling, and that it was free. He also mentioned that mom just up and left to go to Colorado. Then she sent me an email about how she wanted to spend some time with her boys one on one, and how she'd like to do that after I get home, after I spend some quality time with you and the kids. At least she's recognizing that she realizes that you and the kids are my main priority, and nothing else. That actually does my heart good.

1 JAN 04 D + 74 2230 hrs.

Today was a day filled with both relief and sadness at the same time. It was our last day on the gate, and the whole platoon is both relieved and overjoyed about that. After the first guard shift, all the troops returned from the gate, received mail, ate some lunch; pretty much the normal stuff. We also had a formation for some promotions, and I think that that actually helped with morale a little. About a half hour, if that, after that formation, someone came into our hooch saying that the Commander wanted everyone back for another formation. Everyone was making jokes about how the command is already starting the New Year out right, with multiple formations and extra bullshit already. On the way down, we heard some people talking about an accident of some kind. Our battalion had a convoy leave for Baghdad this morning to take a bunch of soldiers out to go on leave, and to retrieve those returning from leave. Among those returning was PV2 Simmons, my soldier who was driving my vehicle when the IED went off. We had been able to get him home for Christmas, and I was glad, because he surely did deserve a break.

My heart just sank. At formation, the commander told us that a vehicle had been traveling along in a convoy, and that it had somehow overturned. The driver was uninjured; however, the TC was killed instantly. It was a 5-Ton cargo truck, and it had 15 soldiers in the back as well. Most of the soldiers in the back were from a National Guard Engineer Unit that's attached to us for the deployment. One soldier was pinned under the vehicle, a young female, and they had to get a crane to get the truck off of her. Apparently she was not breathing, and had to have CPR administered to revive her. Another soldier had a broken ankle. Overall, with exception of the TC, all of them were lucky. It could have been so much worse.

SGT Murphy, a buddy of mine who works at the TOC, was wandering around aimlessly after the formation. I approached him and said, 'Hey Murph, what's up?' His face was beet red, and his eyes even redder. The guy who was killed was a good buddy of his, a fellow combat engineer, and Murph was not taking this very well, as expected. We stood there, and talked in the middle of the street for about a half hour, miraculously with no traffic for the entire time, until I had to go to our next guard shift.

I went down to his hooch to check on him just a few minutes ago, and Murph was out cold. It had been a long, emotionally exhausting afternoon for him, and he was simply whooped.

Well, my love, we took our first casualty in the battalion today, a hell of a way to start the New Year. We'll pray for those lost and hurt, and hope for a better day tomorrow.

2 JAN 04 D + 75

Well, today was supposed to be our first day off as a platoon since we got here. Just before lunch, we got a call that the senior leadership wanted to see me in the TOC immediately. I was scared to death. I thought something happened to you or the children. When I got there, I was informed that an Army fuel truck was traveling on Highway 10, and struck an IED, then, was simultaneously hit on the opposite side with an RPG. The truck was carrying 5,000 gallons of fuel at the time, and the two-man crew of the truck was being shipped out on a MEDEVAC bird momentarily. The driver has third degree burns on over 70% of his body, and the other soldier was minimally injured.

We mounted up on the DECON 5-ton trucks with all the water and hoses, and got to go play 'fire department'. It was an exciting couple of hours, and we finished fighting the blaze with some local Iraqi firemen. It was interesting to see them operate, and for a moment, we were all just a bunch of firemen. It was a welcome lighter moment; lighter than we're used to over here.

So much for our day off.

As a decontamination unit, we were the nearest resources for mass water application. With no notice, we adapted our vehicles and turned our men into firemen. Shown here is our joint U.S. and Iraqi firefighting crew in the aftermath of a destroyed fuel tanker from an Rocket Propelled Grenade and an Improvised Explosive Device.

9 JAN 04 D + 82

Hello my love. I just got back from the internet café where I got to talk to you on the internet for a bit. I tried so hard to call you all day during any spare time I could find, but to no avail. I know at this moment you are probably still waiting for my call, but there are about three hours worth of people in line, and I have to get up at 0430 again tomorrow. I will try again to call you instead of going to breakfast. No big deal, breakfast isn't anything to write home about. The DFAC is actually a subcontractor of Brown & Root, because the mission and country are not stable, and they have to be ready to pull out at any given moment.

Life here in the Sunni triangle is never stable, and every day is a coin toss as to who will live and who will die. I have to deal with hajjis all day again, but if it brings me one day closer to being with you again, then I will do it every day if that is what it takes. I already have a reputation with the locals, and I wouldn't be surprised if there was a price on my head out in Ar Ramadi. With all that you and I have to endure on both ends with this tour, it actually comforts me a little to know that hajji has something to be concerned with when he comes on my post. I know you probably think this is some kind of weird game I'm playing with the locals, but my theory is why should they just be able to come on post and live life normally when you and I have to go without every day. I suppose it may be some sort of personal vendetta from me to them, but not really. Fear is often enough a good motivator, and if that's what it takes to keep them in line, then so be it. We all have our little part in this crazy war, including you and the kids. They even have the balls to bitch about being away from home in Baghdad for a few days at a time, so they can come here and get paid, I mean rally get paid. I searched a guy the other day, and he had $10,000 cash in his jacket. When I asked him what it was for, he told me that he had to pay his workers. The day laborers only make $2 per day. Someone's getting really paid.

Well, we got our mattresses today from the locals to go with our bunk beds. There's something about sleeping on a box spring with nothing but crossed-metal and a soft sleeping bag on top of it just isn't comfortable. I prefer the cot, but that's probably because I'm an old soldier, and set in my ways. I had bought a mattress a while ago, and had it with my cot, but I chose not to use it with the bunk bed until all my soldiers had mattresses as well. No big deal.

I will close for now my love. I have to get up very early, and I'll try and call you then. I love you my darling. I sent out two cards and a letter today for you as well as a postcard for Kevin. I sure hope he likes the mail I send. Okay, good night my love. I will dream of you tonight.

11 JAN 03 D + 84

Today was a generally good day. We had a few missions, and although the family doesn't agree with me, I generally tell Helen everything that happens, as long as it doesn't violate any operational security issues. We have an open and honest marriage, more than the majority, I believe, and that's what helps keep our marriage strong and healthy even across the miles. Helen asked me today in a phone call if I ever thought I would be *this* loved. I told her of course not, but I am ever grateful that I am. We had an escort mission where we were the PSD (Personal Security Detachment). I was not the convoy NCOIC; however, I lead the way because the LT was more comfortable with it that way.

Anyway, I called you today, my love, before we initially left on the mission, and again after we returned the first time. I also called again later on after we got back from picking up our package downtown. After it was all said and done, the team did rather well today, and I'm glad they're on point like they are. Simmons drove for me, and Dorelus was my gunner. My guys are really good at whatever they do. These are chemical soldiers, and they're performance under fire is amazing. We can do escorts, gate guard, chemical surveys, or PSD runs out in town, and they never let me down.

I will keep this short for now, because I have to continue to get up early, seemingly for the next year, so I will have to start getting to bed earlier so I can get up and call you as frequently as possible. I love you my darling. You are everything I ever dreamed about. Kiss you later.

13 JAN 03 D + 86

Today is Nick Johnson's birthday. He is 33, and jokes about how much older I am than him. Of course I will be 34 this April, God willing I make it to then. This is such a bad place; I can't even find the words. We are going outside the wire more often than ever now. It seems as though the unit can't find enough things for us to do. Thank God there is no DECON mission here, but everything else weighs so heavily on us. The burden of duty is starting to weigh more lately than ever. I got Nick a Dominican cigar from the PX for his birthday, and we are planning a small gathering tonight here at the hooch for him. I have an old airborne buddy here who's a cook. He's the liaison at the Brown & Root DFAC, and I arranged a cake to be made for Nick tonight. He's on escort duty today, but I'm going to go out this afternoon and take it over for him since it's his birthday.

We're going to the range today over at the new ICDC facility. ICDC is the Iraqi Civil Defense Corps. It's another facility that's run here on Camp J.C., and it's designed to help hand the country back over to the Iraqi's. The Civil Defense guys are kind of like the new Iraqi Army. They have a strict training plan, and it's run like Basic Training. Most of the Iraqi's that attend really do want to see a new Iraq, and have a genuine interest in being a part of the reconstruction. Anyway, the range we're going to today is an AK-47 range, so the troops are excited about it. Most of them have never fired an AK before, and they're just excited to see something new. We're still on a 30-minute string for QRF. I told Helen that we only had it the other day until yesterday morning, but of course mission changes happen, and now we have it for another week solid. Anyway, while I was on escort yesterday, Nick took the Platoon outside the wire and did a 'snap-checkpoint' out in town. A snap-checkpoint is a TCP (traffic control point) that is setup based on immediate intelligence that doing this may impede or slow down the enemy's movements or traffic. Snap – checkpoints are working really well out here, but the only thing is that they tend to make the enemy really jumpy, and, in turn, make snap-judgments, like taking cheap shots at the few soldiers performing the TCP.

I miss you so much today, my love. I can't tell you how bad the nightmares are getting. I know I hadn't mentioned this before, but I really don't want you to worry any more than you are. Last night it seemed like every time that I woke up, I'd lay down again, and go right back into the fighting. In one of them, there was an explosion, and when I woke up this morning, I actually had a hard time hearing out of my left ear. I still do, even now, and I've been up for two hours already.

15 JAN 04 D + 88

Hello my love. I'm so glad I got a chance to talk to you tonight. You were on my way to Sears with Angel and the kids, and I couldn't help but think how desperately I wanted to be there with you. I called you after we got back off mission from Champion Main. We were there yesterday, and I bought you something. I had this guy make me a dolphin pendant for you from some of Saddam's gold. I thought the least I could do is get something from the bastard that made me leave my family for a year. It's a small token, and I know it doesn't bring the time back for us, but I just find a little humor in the irony of where the gold came from. I'll take what I can get at this point.

I don't think I can express how proud of you I am for handling everything so well these past few months. I always knew that you were the one for me. You're the perfect wife, the best mother I know, and so much more to me. You're my partner, my best friend, my soul mate, and the one who I'll be with for all time. I always told you that you are a better mother than what I've had, and that's obviously true. After all, you've seen it first hand. I'm a bit embarrassed by it all, but I'm not sure why. You know that I wasn't raised like that. Matter of fact, I wasn't raised by them, or that way at all. I still feel awkward, because even though you and I are a team, and *we* are still handling everything together as much as possible, I guess I just have so much disappointment in my family right now. I guess I just thought that if they ever disappointed me in any way, surely it wouldn't involve my wife and children. However, again I was wrong, and I do apologize for all the trouble. I would've never done asked you to take this crap on if I'd known it would turn out like this. I love you my darling, and I would do anything for you. I love you so very much my wife, and I am so proud every day to be your husband. I will sign off for now, and get back to this soon enough. Kiss you later.

Myself and SPC Valencia pause for a moment after a weapons cache raid in downtown Ar Ramadi. Buried in the owner's front yard, and hidden within the walls of the house were everything seen here and more.

16 JAN 04 D + 89

Hello my darling. Today was an interesting day on the gate. I had everything from hajjis with attitudes, to tires shot out on a diesel tractor-trailer, to soldier problems. I just came back to the hooch, fixed myself a cup-o-noodles, and tried to relax. When I got back I was really tired and just wanted some time to myself. I told everyone this, and for some reason, it didn't seem to matter. There is no privacy here, and it gets old quick. Everyone feels the same way at times, but tonight in particular, I just wanted some time to myself. I told you I would try and call you on Sunday; however I'm not sure that I'll be able to. The two phones at Battalion are now gone, and often times they were the easiest to use. Oh well, I will try, and if not then seek other means.

I believe that I'm very depressed, and I really don't want it to affect our family life when I get home. I just want to be the man you always wanted me to be, and to be a great father to all of our children. I know you love me, and I you my love, however these are troubling days for me. Out at the Escort lot today I was talking to a buddy of mine, and we were talking about how hard it is to see so many of our fellow soldiers die and get wounded all the time. I think this tour is particularly difficult for our young leadership, and seeing how they've never deployed before.

18 JAN 04 D + 91 1830 hrs.

Hello my love. I feel like I just got off a roller coaster. We had three missions today. The night before last, we had an all nighter in Ar Ramadi doing a raid on a house. We captured two terrorist cell members, and their family, but one got away. We seized everything from rockets to RPG's, to mines, weapons, anti-aircraft weapon systems, and some video equipment. Included in this were about 20 videocassettes of attacks on coalition forces (us). The terrorists study our responses on the video to see how we react, and to improve their offensive attack techniques. Inside the house were two children, surrounded by all this stuff. It really was heart-breaking to see, but then you could also see the hatred in their eyes. Inside one room of the house, there were three generations of true, honest to goodness, American-hating people. It just is really something to see.

We took about five thousand pounds of ordinance and weapons out of there, but today we had to manually load the stuff up on trucks, one mortar round at a time. Then we had to go to Champion Main to pick up the EOD team. Then we came back to Camp J.C. and gathered up all our vehicles, and headed out into Ar Ramadi. We were headed towards the 'Five-Kilo' area of Tameen, a known IED hotspot. As if it matters, we live on one corner of the Sunni Triangle anyway. This whole area is just plain bad anyhow. Every day there is a constant sound of gunfire, mortars at least once a week or more, and the people in this area are Sunni Muslim, which are loyal to the Saddam regime. The Shiite Muslims are from the outskirts of the country as well as the border towns. They are not extremist Muslim. Actually, true Muslims are very peaceful people, and are very devout in their religion. Saddam and his people just took everything to extremes during the dictatorship.

Anyway, out in Ar Ramadi, we found a nice little out of the way area, which EOD regularly uses for their training, and we detonated all the munitions and ordinance that we found on the raid. We actually had an opportunity that few have here. We seized the weapons, and transported them back to post, and then we hauled them out into the desert and prepped them for EOD, which blew them up in a huge explosion. The explosion was impressive, even though it took almost every minute of our day off. It was a true sense o closure to know that at the very least, this batch of stuff would never be used against us again.

21 JAN 04 D + 94 2130 hrs.

Hello my love. Unfortunately, today wasn't very interesting at all, however we found out that tomorrow is my last day on Escort. That, of course, is good news for all of us. We are supposed to be getting four Hummers at the end of the month, but that can only be one thing; and that's that we are going to be on PSD (Personal Security Detachment) permanently. That means that we'll be outside the wire for the majority of the tour. I'm glad that I'll have more time as a team with the troops, but Ar Ramadi is a dangerous town, and not to be taken lightly.

The tour is getting very depressing for me here. I haven't spoken to you on the phone, or contacted you by internet in five days now. The communications have been up and down sporadically the entire time, but they're unreliable at best. I'm trying not to get depressed, or, at the very least, more than I already am now, but I miss you so very much my love. I don't really think we've been doing too badly here, but there are a lot of single Soldiers here, and we don't have the same priorities as each other obviously. I don't bitch about anything in front of them, but I feel as though they can see right through me when it comes to how I feel about you and the children. Everyone here misses someone, but it's no secret that I'm not doing near as well as I was when I was at home with my family.

With all the upcoming missions, especially living here right now, I can't help but think about my own mortality. It's an unfortunate reality here, especially with all that goes on here all the time. There's always another report of soldiers dying, getting injured, or something horrible happening somewhere off the camp, and you always wonder if it's someone you know. Running the Escort and Gate Guard for the last three months, you meet soldiers from all over the Brigade, and they get to know you pretty well, and that's good and bad. Like that one kid we had on Thanksgiving Day that shot himself in front of his friends; it was absolutely horrible. Just yesterday, one of the kids I picked up from Baghdad the other day, which was coming back here after two weeks of leave shot himself in the foot. He actually thought that losing the ability to walk normally, and risking a court martial was worth the effort and excruciating pain. He wasn't even back for 24 hours. I really hope that this doesn't become a situation that grows into something contagious. Things like this in a deployment are much like suicides, they are contagious, and I only pray that it doesn't become that way here.

Even though I would never do anything like that, and risk my family's future or anything like that; sometimes I get the feeling that my life will end here. I do get afraid sometimes, but it's not the bombs, the bullets, or being in a country that hates me not from where I'm from, or my politics, but for the God that I believe in. I just get the feeling sometimes that my life might end here. I certainly did not come here to die, but it is a grim reality that again; if anything like that could happen, then being here certainly adds to the probability of that. Sometimes I just think about things like, 'what if these are my last days? What will become of my family? Who will take care of them?' Then I remember that my depression shouldn't allow my faith to falter, and that God will always take good care of my darling Helen and our children, no matter what happens to me. And if I am blessed enough to make it home alive, then it's in God's plan for me to do so, and I should again consider myself blessed, and respond accordingly. I will never take my family for granted. I think I just need to accept the fact that I may in fact die here, and although I so desperately pray that that will not be the case, that it's also in God's plan, should it be his will. And if this is so, then I can only pray that my darling Helen not be bitter about this, if that's possible. I realize that that sounds ridiculous, but I know my Helen, and her faith is stronger than most people I know. I've known clergymen that don't have not so much the amount, but the type of faith she has. I am so blessed in having her in my life, as are our children for having them as their mother.

23 JAN 04 D + 96 0745 hrs.

This morning Rafael tells me that I'm taking one of my soldiers over to escort the 82nd Airborne Division Chorus to Hurricane. Hurricane is a camp located a few miles down the road from here, down Highway 10. I don't mind doing what needs to be done, especially going outside the wire, and especially with my soldiers, but damn, a little more than an hour's notice would be nice. Okay, enough ranting today. I have to go and get ready for the mission now. I'll write more later on. I have to get your letter in the mail today. It's already taken me about three days to write it, here and there. I've got another building project going on today, in anticipation of us taking over the PSD mission again. It should clear up some space here in the hooch, and give us all a little more well deserved room.

0820 hrs.

And with only ten minutes to mission time, while walking out the door, we get informed that the mission is not only cancelled, but that it wasn't even ours anyhow. I'm getting a little sick and tired of being so uninformed.

We went outside the wire today three times. We had to transport hajjis from the government complex in downtown Ar Ramadi over to the ICDC training camp just on the outer fringe of Camp J.C. It was a really unnerving day being outside the wire so much. I was with my troops though, and both Nick and the LT were there. The minute after we got there, and pulled into the government complex compound, some Iraqi Army soldiers started firing AK's inside the compound trying to keep the locals out. The locals were there to apply to join the new Iraqi Army (ICDC). It was worse than free government cheese day downtown. Then, we got to search about four hundred hajji's to prep them for transport. It really sucked.

Today really got me rattled.

25 JAN 04 D + 98 1818 hrs.

Today was interesting. Today was one of the two days a month, supposedly, that we will have Escort. We really thought we were done, but two days a month isn't bad at all. Anyhow, apparently there was another VBIED incident this morning at another American camp, and of course, everything shut down. A Captain from the Brigade Contractor's Office came out and started to instigate with me. He and I have never seen eye to eye on anything. He deals with all the contractor's, all of which are hajjis, and doesn't really concern himself with force protection like the rest of us. Anyhow, he shows up out there and tells me that he thinks that the way I deal with hajji is inappropriate, and although not illegal nor immoral, isn't the way that he'd have handled it. I kindly and respectfully reminded him that if he'd been working out here for 97 days straight, then he wouldn't take any crap from hajji either. I told him that I pull my weight around here, and I do my job. I also told him that hajji has no decent work ethic and tries to get over all the time, and because I do perform my job, that he doesn't like that. It seems that the good Captain took the hajji's complaints to heart, and reported something about me to the Company Commander. Apparently, she was told that I was on the verge of shooting someone and that I was on edge. Without even talking to me at all, she sends my LT out to the lot with Nick Johnson to replace me, and takes me off the Escort Lot in place. LT explains to me what has happened, and that the unit also wants me to go see the Combat Stress people on my own before they make it a command referral. I just couldn't believe it.

1940 hrs.

I just got back from taking a shower, my first in three days. I met my Platoon Sergeant on the way back, and he told me that he talked to the Commander, and that there was a mistake earlier in what was told to me about all this. I am in fact, command referred to go and talk to the Combat Stress folks tomorrow. So, I will follow the order, and comply. Hopefully, something good will come of all this. We'll see.

2210 hrs.

I just talked to you on the phone for about 20 minutes or so. I was glad to get through tonight, because today was such a hard day, with all the accusations flying around here. I know that I'm a hard person, and especially here because of the environment that we're in. But there are so many people that shy away from doing a lot of things, like going outside the gate, pulling any type of duty with the hajji's, etc. I just feel abandoned by the company command due to their lack of people skills and not dealing with things directly. I have certainly had better commanders, but never had one so inexperienced and lacking the people skills that you would think are a requirement. I will do my best to keep to myself, and do the best I can for my troops, and just do my job and come home.

26 JAN 04 D + 99 1245 hrs.

Well, I saw the Doc this morning. He was a reservist, and only in town for a few days, but he referred me to a Major who is an active duty guy who arrives tomorrow afternoon. The guy today was a Colonel, and after I told him why I was there, and a whole lot about my past, he told me without a doubt that I had unresolved PTSD issues from my other combat engagements. He also told me that I shouldn't feel weak in any way over this, but also that we are all our own worst critic. He also complemented me on being so honest in my own self-assessment, and said that it takes a lot of courage to not only be so honest, but to open up with it to a relative stranger. I told him that I really didn't see it that way, and that my main concern was that I spoke honestly with him, and that my wife's wishes for a true and honest assessment be met, and her other wishes be honored as well. He said that he really respected that, and assured me that, from what he could see thus far, he was sure I was doing a good job in keeping with that. I only hope that things go as well with MAJ Brown on Wednesday. I have to go back for another appointment in a couple days. The Colonel this morning said that he didn't think that I was completely broke, but certainly bent, and could most likely be straightened out in time with regular treatment. He said that there have been a few cases in Baghdad, of guys who were also in Somalia that had to be sent home due to the mortar attacks there that were prolonging their treatment. We'll see how things work out here.

1930 hrs.

We just got finished reconfiguring our manpower situation. PFC Lalicker leaves either tonight on a bird, or tomorrow morning on a convoy for his Environmental Leave. Haines was put on a MEDEVAC bird earlier. He was pulling some nails out of some wood the other day, and one jumped out fast, and landed squarely in his right eye. He's lost his vision from 12 o'clock to 3 o'clock in that eye so far, and now he's out of commission for about a month. He was sent to LSA Anaconda for eye surgery. Anaconda is in northern Iraq, and is in a much more stable area than here. At least he'll be able to relax for a while, albeit in a hospital, and with only half of his sight. We were out running as a Platoon, minus the Platoon Sergeant of course, when the LT flagged us down, and told us that Haines was leaving on a MEDEVAC. We all immediately grabbed up his things, and headed over to Charlie Med, where he was being taken care of. The doc there listed him as 'Urgent', so the MEDEVAC bird was there in only fifteen minutes from the time it was called. After we all got there, we made it just in enough time to see the twin Blackhawk birds fly away. We missed getting his gear to him, but the doc told us they couldn't wait because LSA Anaconda was a long way away, and they didn't want to risk flying in the dark over that distance.

After we all got back, most of the troops hit the showers, and one of my guys, Eason, saw our illustrious Platoon Sergeant in the shower. Eason said, 'too bad about Haines, huh?' to which he replied, 'what about Haines?' Apparently, he didn't have any idea that Haines was even gone, and he went frantic trying to get the information from someone, anyone. He really looked stupid, and the sad thing is that our lowest Private was the one to tell him. Eason talked to me later, and he commented that he thought it was really funny. I told him that I did as well, and I didn't want him spouting off to every other Private in the Platoon about this because it wasn't his place.

27 JAN 04 D + 100 0800 hrs.

I'm so glad that I got to talk with you this morning. I couldn't get on the phone, but we talked for a while on the internet as it was the next best thing. You told me about the new truck, how Mike is supposedly coming there in April, and about Abby on the toilet. It's interesting how much you can squeeze into a single conversation out here because we have to. Time is certainly not our friend, but I cherish every moment that we have together my love, even if it's nothing more than real time typed conversation on the computer. I will try to call you tonight though. I just hope the lines aren't too long.

I will be studying for the board today. I have the NCO of the Month Board in February. There are only three of us vying to win the board, and Jose Salazar is one of them. You'd remember Jose from the NCO barbeque we had at the house before I left. He's on gate guard for a month or so with his Platoon, and they're not doing so well, unfortunately. His guys let a cell phone and a Molotov cocktail get through the gate about a week or so ago. His soldiers just didn't catch it, but my guys did, so we confiscated the stuff, and ran it down to the gate to hand over to him. I think he was really embarrassed by the whole thing, but I told him not to worry, and that this would go no further, just tighten up the men, that's all. Sometimes going ballistic isn't the answer, especially with a buddy, and especially here.

1215 hrs.

We just found out that Haines never made it to LSA Anaconda, and that he was shipped to BIAP instead. We also learned that his eye injury is severe enough that he will be sent back home to the United States instead, and if his surgery and recovery are not as successful as we all hope for, he will probably be pushed through a Military Medical Review Board, and exit the military. Damn shame. I was actually starting to like the kid, with his smart-ass mentality.

My love, I finally got it. I just realized some things that you probably already knew. We've been watching a lot of military movies lately. And, as I watch those around me, some with many more years in than I, and even more with fewer, I can surmise the character of most men rather quickly. I can also see the depth of some men so clearly, as clearly as you tell me you can see mine. Being surrounded by the military 24/7 as I am now, I suppose I have become so hyper-alert that I am starting to see inside myself more clearly than ever before.

I have already told you, more than once no doubt, that I learned just a few years ago that I have loved the Army more than it will ever love me back. I still believe this to be true; however, not until recently have I realized that this will always be the case. Moreover, not only that, but it's actually supposed to be that way. The Army, as its own entity simply cannot reach each man individually. But collectively, each man can make a difference, serve his country, and love his Army for all he's worth. That collective effort can make a great Army, and preserve a great nation as it has done.

My successes in the Army have not been as personal as some men prefer, attaining rank early, achieving a greater pay rate, etc. My successes are in having a great partner, building a large, beautiful, and blessed family. The fact is that I have enjoyed my time serving my country. In recent times, here in Iraq, I must admit that they are harder than any I can recall, and, hopefully, the hardest that will come. I miss you so very much, my love, and although it pains me to not see you, be with you, touch you, and wake up next to you, I still have solace in that you and our children will be able to sleep a little easier due to the time here being, at least on a global scale, well spent. I suppose that I am having a better day today, than many in the recent past. I also believe that it's because I got to 'talk' to you this morning on the computer. I always have better days when I get to talk to you in some form or fashion. Hearing your voice, or even talking on the computer helps my hope and resolve to the very fiber of my being. I'd like to think that the same moon I look at night after night shines down on you and our children just a few hours later. This is but one commonality that we share, and a shred of what I make an effort to hold onto every day here. I realize, of course that we have many more things in common than this, but with all this time to think, it affords me the opportunity to pick out these little minute details of my day, that, hopefully are some of the same ones in yours. I realize that I'm probably rambling on by now, but I miss you so very much my love. I listen to your tape over and over again. I don't watch the DVD you sent much, because I only watch it when I'm alone. Even then, due to the lack of any time alone, I still have to be alert for anyone coming into the bay. I get within seconds of tears welling up in my eyes, and I really have to control myself, my physical nature, my posture, my emotions . . . everything.

1830 hrs.

We just got briefed that there was an IED attack on Highway 10 today. We actually heard about it earlier, but didn't get the details until tonight. Our battalion suffered more casualties today. On a convoy near Khalidiyah, a vehicle was hit with a very powerful IED. It took out a Hummer, and two buses full of hajjis. Among those killed were THE Commander and First Sergeant from Bravo Company, as well as two other NCO's. The entire senior chain of command was wiped out in an instant, and tomorrow the battalion is sending out another convoy to bring out a replacement for the commander. They're also taking Highway 10, which I don't understand at all. There's no rush whatsoever in getting the new Commander out there and there a safer, yet longer route to take. I just don't understand it at all. Why take such a huge and unnecessary risk. A lot of this command has never been deployed before, and I can take that into account for some things, but this is just ridiculous.

28 JAN 04 D + 101 0645 hrs.

Good morning my love. I would have tried to call you this morning, but due to the events of yesterday, the phones are still down, as is the internet. Last night, everyone was in bed relatively early, earlier than usual. The entire company is quiet this morning, and I just watched the convoy leave to take CPT Bavlinka to Habbiniyah to take command of Bravo Company. It's cold this morning, and very windy. The sky is overcast as well, an ominous overtone for the kind of day it is. I saw Mo the other day, on my way to take Haines' gear over to the helipad. He was staying the night here at Camp J.C., and then heading back. There was only one other reported injury on that convoy and that guy is in stable condition now. Mo's name was never mentioned, thank God. He's out on the road a lot, and I pray for his continued luck.

On a lighter note, I am going back to see the doc again today. This new guy got in last night, and I honestly can't wait to start. I talked a lot the other day, and I hope that I can be that open and honest with him. I really need to be, for all of our sakes.

I'm listening to the CD that you sent last week. It too is a mixture of happiness, sadness, and a whole lot of other stuff I can't put my finger on. I miss you so much, my love. I' told you this I'm sure more than once before, but, I usually don't do too well without you, and these days are no different. I love you so much, my darling. I'll write more later on honey. Kiss you later.

2022 hrs.

Tonight, we were issued a DVD that the company made of the tour so far. I provided the music for it, and it actually turned out pretty good. I can't wait to send it home to you, my love. I will wait though, until I have a videotape to send with it as well. I'll put together some pictures too, if I can get them printed out. It's not often these days that I get to do anything for you my darling. I so badly wish that I could. You are my everything, my love, and I long to be with you again.

I saw the doc again today, and we talked for almost an hour today as well. He told me that he'd like to see me again tomorrow. He told me that he thinks I need some time off, either in Ballad, which is up in northern Iraq, or a four-day pass to Qatar. He told me that he wants to talk about that tomorrow, and I'm not sure where this will go, but I'll pray for the best. I love you my darling. Kiss you later baby.

29 JAN 04 D + 102 0440 hrs.

Good morning my love. I just got back from trying to call you, but our phone was off for a couple of days. I tried to call Angel's number you emailed to me too, but that one was out too. So then I tried again to call the boys, and I did get through. I caught Gary just getting in from baseball practice, and he was glad to talk to me. Then Bailey came on, and he was telling me about some game that he has that Austin likes, but he doesn't like to play. And then finally, I got to talk to Austin, and he was so cute. The twins are talking so good now. Then Austin asked me if I was 'his daddy, or his other daddy'. If the roles were reversed, I would have grabbed the phone, and reassured Tracy that nothing really screwed up was going on, but of course that didn't happen. I'm not sure what's going on there. I think that Gary tried to get the phone back from him, but I heard Austin fighting to not give up the phone, and then he must have accidentally hung it up. I couldn't get back through after that. I was crushed; I can't even tell you.

I got a really short email from my brother, Gary also. He made mention that Mom had found a place, and that everything should be better soon. It was very short, and I think I got the impression that he might e a tad bit upset about all of this. I can't really afford to worry about that right now though.

We are supposed to take over as the PSD again starting in a few days, probably Saturday or Sunday. I'm not sure how long that will last, but it means a lot of time outside the wire, and living on a 30 minute string for an indefinite period of time. The time actually does pass pretty quickly when we're on PSD, but the inherent danger doesn't balance it out very well.

The days of late are so very hard for me. After the deaths the other day, and talking to the doc two, today will make three days in a row, and talking to the boys this morning . . . I just want to hear your voice more than anything in the whole world. I love you so much honey. The things that we have to do here, I just can't comprehend sometimes how you can love me so much. I feel like I could never show you how much I love you honey. You really are my whole world, my everything.

1400 hrs.

I just got back from a mission that wasn't. I was told this morning to get a crew and a gun truck and meet a convoy at our staging area. When I got there, I was informed by our Commander that our involvement was cancelled four hours earlier. I just love the decision makers around here. I took about an hour and a half to get the men and truck ready that could have been spent with all my guys. We have had a bit of down time in the last couple of days though.

We weren't supposed to take over the PSD again until Sunday morning, but of course, instead we'll be taking it over tonight. So, that's what we'll be doing for the next nine days or so. Living on a 30 minute string isn't so bad once we get used to it. It's just that we have to get to chow, use the phone, take a shower, or anything else we need to do in less than 30 minutes. After that, we can check in, and go about our business again . . . for another 30 minutes. We pick up our trucks tonight, and I already picked up our .50 cal machine guns, and everything else we might need for the next nine days. I'm extremely anal about packing everything we might need, especially while outside the wire.

2145 hrs.

Hello my love. We picked up PSD tonight, as expected, and the men are resting now. Eason always gets nervous the night before a mission, and he always hits me up for some small talk for a couple of hours. He's getting a little better, and I'm not so sure I was that different in Somalia. I must be getting old because he really does remind me of myself about ten years ago.

I talked to the Doc again today, and he wants to see me as long as possible before he goes back to Baghdad. The active duty guy hasn't made it in yet, so the Colonel is still talking with me. Today is the first time I actually broke down and cried since the tour began. I was talking about missing you and the kids and about how great our relationship and communication is, and how different we are from most couples we know. I told him how it really bothered me how I didn't get to talk to you in between visits, and he thought that was very interesting. At that point, I'm not sure why he was interested, and I told him that I was very needy for you. I also told him that I don't do too well without you. After all, it's not wrong to be needy for each other when it's your partner, life mate, soul mate, and best friend. After I explained that, he complimented me on my choice of my wife, and told me that I obviously had to know how lucky I am. Of course I do.

Tomorrow morning, I'm going to try and get up extra early and call you before we take off for the mission to Habbiniyah. We are escorting half the company down there for the memorial service for those of us we lost earlier this week. I hate that any of this happens, but I can't stand to hear that roll call and taps as many times as I have. I don't mean to sound selfish or cold, but it really does wear on you. I love you my darling, and I'll call you as early as I can. I love and miss you honey.

30 JAN 04 D + 103 2355 hrs.

Hello my love. I just got back from the phone tent, and got to talk to you for almost an hour (48 minutes to be exact). Kevin is just over 24-hour flu, and Abby sounds pitiful with her deep cough. You sounded really good though, up in spirits, and a little stressed about the windows getting installed, and Mom and the family moving out in a week or so. I have to tell you honey, it's a *big* relief to me that they're moving out. I know how things have been at home, and you have tolerated so much more than I would have. I love your strength, even when you may not. I can't believe how good you sounded on the phone tonight. I was really happy to hear it. That did more for me than most things could. You also had really good news that my truck would be delivered tomorrow . . . really good news there.

Well, we spent about 5 or 6 hours on the road today going to Habbaniyah for the memorial service for the four guys that were killed earlier this week. When we first got there, SGT Moreno, our supply sergeant got out to clear her weapon at a clearing area, and somehow squeezed off a round into the ground in front of her, about a foot in front my left boot. I was so instantly scared, pissed, and a whole lot of other things. That's how the day started, after a two-hour convoy through the open desert.

After we left the service, we headed across the bridge, (about a three minute drive) to TQ Air Base, where we ate lunch, and I got to see my airborne buddy, Eric Russell. He ordered some stuff for the unit for the deployment, and hooked me up with a few really cool knives. He got us some extension cords and some portable lights, and I was grateful. Eric always was the go-to guy for a good hookup. He's always been an upstanding guy, and family man, for which I always respected him. He's starting to prep to go home in six to eight weeks, and is looking forward to it immensely. He has two sons and a daughter, and his wife, Gabi, is very nice. I'm so glad that I found what he's had all along, and I think because of it; he and I are on a different (much better) level now. I certainly owe that to you my love. As I already know, you bring out the best in everybody.

It's just another thing that tells me that I was, am, and will always be the luckiest man in the world. You've brought out the best in me, as you always do, and a friendship I had before I even knew you is better since I met you. Back in those days, Eric knew how bitter I was. He and I served under the same 1SG that betrayed my trust. He was right there with me during all that, and we lived in the same neighborhood and shared a great many things.

You really do bring out the best in me, my love. In comparison to my last two tours, I have shared with you a great many differences with this one. Every cloud, even the dark ones have a lining, and this one is no different. Your love and warmth graces my heart, and gives me more hope and confidence than this place will sometimes allow, and I am grateful for it. I only pray for a safe return to you and our children, and also pray for a lifetime with you to how you my gratitude. It truly is a blessing to have you as my wife, and I love you more than I could ever say or show.

31 JAN 04 D + 104 0700 hrs.

Today is command maintenance day, so we will head off to the motor pool for a while, and check out our severely worn out vehicles, and then head back to the hooch to rest until a mission comes up. I reminded Rafael how tired we all get while on PSD, and after suggesting that we finish maintenance as fast as possible, so we could do that, we both agreed that it would be a good idea. Today we have a run to Champion Main, and it shouldn't be too hard. It's a five-minute run, but there's a bridge over the Euphrates River, and I just can't stand it. I'm just waiting for the day that hajji puts an IED there, or some type of bomb on one of the bridge supports as we're driving over it. I may be a little paranoid after all this time outside the wire, but I'd like to think that every leader would be compelled to think out, at the very least, every eventuality.

1130 hrs.

I just got back from doing maintenance down at the motor pool, and I am watching weapons while the Soldiers go and eat chow. I am watching your video that you sent just before Christmas. I've watched it about five or six times already, and I just can't seem to stop mashing the 'play' button. I have pictures of you and the kids above my bed, and there's not a night I lay down, no matter how short a time that may be, that I don't look up and pray for you all. I love you so much honey. If I play the video and write to you at the same time, it's almost as if you're closer with me, at least for the moment. I know that it's only 0230 at home right now, and hopefully you and the kids are sleeping soundly. I really do wish that I could say the same, but that will come for me when I get home. I am very tired today. We have to start mounting up for a mission this afternoon, about 1400, to Champion Main. It's a 'milk run', as we call it, because it's only over the bridge, about five minutes away. Champion is home to Headquarters, 82nd Airborne Division, and you know me; it always makes me feel better to be around jumpers. I think my guys are a little intimidated by all of it, but since we got here, I've had about four of them ask me to go to Airborne school. I realize nowadays that jumping is a young mans game, and I'm just trying to steer these youngn's in the right direction.

I'll write more later on, probably after the Champion mission. I'd like to try and call you again today, if both mission and time permit. I love you my darling kiss you later.

1630 hrs.

Hey honey. I'm so glad that I got to call you from Champion today. They have a lot more phones over there, but then again, it's Division HQ. I'm so tired from the day, I can't even tell you. We have to work so very hard just to keep our trucks up, because we put so many miles on them. The engines aren't used to this environment, and they're wearing out quickly. We'll see how it goes. Tomorrow is not a day off for the battalion, because they want to give us off on Monday instead because the Super Bowl comes on at 0230 hrs. here. I personally don't care about the game, but I could use the time to rest, and probably will. I love you honey, and I always will. I'm going to try and get some sleep now. I love you my darling.

1 FEB 04 D + 105 2300 hrs.

Hello my love. Well today has been a very exciting day for me. We got off to a really nice paced start this morning. Simmons got off the night shift around 0700, and then he and I went to eat breakfast, which rarely ever happens. Today was a light workday; because the Battalion CDR is giving the battalion tomorrow off so people can watch the Super Bowl tonight. It comes on at 0230 here. I souped up the gun trucks and had the Soldiers clean them out so we wouldn't have to do much else. Then, I went over to the PX, and then checked my email. I was absolutely delighted to get the pictures of the truck honey. I'm so proud of you my love. You did so well, I can't even tell you. I would have never trusted anyone else to do something like that, but you aced that one.

Then, I came back from the MWR tent, and found a package lying on my bed. It was of course your Valentine package, which I was so very excited to receive. Thanks so very much, my love. I went down to Support Platoon's bay to watch the video on their VCR. We don't have one, and they do, so I got about halfway through it, and couldn't watch it anymore for now. You're so beautiful honey, and the kids look great. It was so nice to see you and kids at our home, I can't even tell you.

After relishing in my good fortune, I decided to go over tonight after the crowd died down a little, and try to call you. I got through on the first try, and although we didn't get to talk for very long, we still talked longer than we normally are allowed. You were getting in the tub, and of course Abby was pounding on the door, and before you know it, she was in the tub too. I wished so bad that I could be there with you my love. I heard Kevin in the background, and he sounded pretty good too. I'm glad he's over that flu bug that he had. We've all had it at one time or another here and it really sucks. I wished we had more time to talk on the phone. I wanted Kevin to know how proud of him I was for his performance on the videotape. He was so cute singing up there with the rest of his class.

I am going to go now, my love. I took a nap earlier, and I am going to midnight chow with SPC Zhou, my second in charge of our squad. He's a little Chinese guy, and he's so funny. He and I both got naps earlier, so we're going to bring Simmons a plate since it's raining, and he doesn't like to get cold or wet. Matt Papke is also working graveyards still, so we'll grab some for him and his guys too. After that, we'll probably watch some of the pre-game show, but not the game. The battalion is off tomorrow, and I'm not giving up that time off just for some football game, not even the Super Bowl. Plus, the Saints didn't make it this year, so I don't really care who wins. I'm going to get going now my love. I'll try and call sometime tomorrow. I love you my darling.

2 FEB 04 D + 106 0100 hrs.

Zhou and I had an interesting late supper tonight. For some reason, he wanted to talk about his family. He's usually pretty quiet, but tonight, I think he just wanted a sounding board. He told me of his father and his admiration for him. He also spoke of his father's imprisonment in communist China in 1958, because of his convictions as a family man, and his thoughts on how the central government could make some changes to improve China as a country overall. The central government even asked him for his opinion, and when he gave it, he was detained and sent off to prison. In all that time, he only received one book to read, which was 'The Count of Monte Cristo'. I thought that was terribly ironic, and almost just plain cruel. He got out of prison in 1982, after Mao Tse Tung, the ruling dictator over China then, died. He mentioned how the prisoners were barely fed sometimes, and how they often ate grass right off the ground, and sometimes some added soil for flavor. My God, I can't even imagine. After being released as a political prisoner, he got on with his life with his faithful wife. After Zhou was born, they prospered in China until about ten years ago, when they moved to New York City. Zhou loves it there, and talks about New York City like I talk about my family.

1445 hrs.

Good afternoon, honey. Today is my first full day off since arriving here. I have to say it is nice to have some down time. I got up at 0600, but went to sleep again. I woke up again at 0800, and stayed up for good. I lay in bed for a while, and then went downstairs for a while to talk to Nick. He was already up, and we somehow came to talk about our children, and I could tell that he misses his dearly. The way he talks though, like he's a ladies man, I think just hides his pain over not being with his children. I am no stranger to this pain, and I suppose we all deal with it differently.

After that, I took the videotape you sent, and walked up to the MWR, where they also have a videocassette payer. Being the battalion's day off, and considering that most of the unit stayed up late watching the Super Bowl, it was no surprise that I had the whole MWR room to myself. It was short lived though, as people slowly found their way up there. I would have called you then, but the tape was taking me on an emotional roller coaster ride. I watched about another 1/3 of the tape, and was so amazed to see you. You're so beautiful my love, and your voice is like an angel's to my ears. I see our children as well, growing up in pictures and video, and it drives me deeper into despising this God-awful place even more by the day. I long to be by your side again.

It really is amazing what you can get used to, but just when I think I can get used to one more thing here, I start feeling as though I'm falling apart at the seams. It's like there's so much that goes into my head that it's swollen, and sometimes it just feels like there is no relief in sight here. And that's because the only relief to me, is you my love. You are the only one who can relieve this awful feeling that overcomes me every single day that we're apart. I know there will come a day after I return home, that we may act as though we are comfortable again, as if I were never here perhaps, however, I won't ever allow myself to be lulled into that kind of complacency. I swear it.

3 FEB 04 D + 107 0635 hrs.

Good morning my love. The men are up and at breakfast, and unfortunately, Rafael has opted to stick around here and make no sense as usual instead of going off himself. I got briefed already today that there is a new type of IED being found on the streets. This kind is a 155 mm round hooked to a pole, or a bridge trestle, with a cell phone detonator nearby. Hajji need only make a phone call to reach out and touch someone. Unfortunately, they are very difficult to detect. I'll brief the men when they get back, and make sure they're aware of what the latest and the greatest is. I swear there's always something new here and it's rarely good.

I feel for some of the younger troops sometimes. Not for their youth and inexperience, but for their complacency about life. Here, if you don't have any type of faith in God, and support from a strong and loving family, then you have nothing. We have each other, but I'd of course feel more comfortable if we were all on the same sheet of music. I know this is a tall order, and it's rare that it is ever actually that way, but I can hope.

I miss you so very much my darling. This morning, I woke up with thoughts of you, of course. I only wish that I could kiss you before rolling out the door today. There's a lot of fog out this morning, and we have to go over that damned bridge going to Champion Main. It's narrow, and the guardrails are only about two feet tall. Not very sturdy. I switched drivers out the other day, and pulled Simmons off night

ROT to drive for me. I feel more confident with him behind the wheel, and I know that you would too.

I'm going to start videotaping for you today honey. I hope it turns out okay. I love you sweetheart. I have to go and get ready now, but I'll call you when we get back from all missions today. Kiss you later.

NOON

We're back from the first two of three missions. We still have a Bridge Recon to go through. From start to finish, it should take no more than 30 minutes or so. We've gone over the plan three times so far, just to fine-tune it; because we're stopping traffic the entire time on a well traveled bridge. The LT and I are using our trucks to secure the upper bridge, so some hajji doesn't decide to throw a grenade or something down to the lower bridge where the actual Recon is being done. After that, we are still on a 30-minute string until we come off PSD. We still might have another mission to Champion Main this afternoon later. I'm very tired now. I didn't sleep well last night, and I got up again about 0230 in a panic. I'm not sure why, but that's not the first time it's happened. I don't really think it will be, but I certainly hope it's the last. I'm supposed to go and talk to the Doc again this week, but it will not be today. I'll probably go tomorrow. I'm not sure what time we'll be done today, but I'll make time to call you when everything is done.

4 FEB 04 D + 108 0830 hrs.

Good morning my love. Hopefully by now you and the children are fast asleep, getting some well-deserved rest. I got to talk to you this morning for a god bit because I woke up at 0330. I didn't sleep well last night, but I'm glad I got through to you. It didn't set well with me that you were so depressed earlier in the day when we talked. I realize that both you and I have our days, but I just wanted to feel closer to you than usual today. This feeling grows in me with each passing day. We spoke of your mother being ill again, and in between phone calls, I called Billy and Challas and spoke with them briefly. It was good to hear their voices as well. I miss visiting with them, and look for the day when we can again.

Well, we will see what today brings. I know we have at least one mission to Champion Main this afternoon, and I think we may have some training this morning. This is the time of the day when we wait for the LT to come back from his meeting and put out whatever is coming at us for the day. I actually got up and ate breakfast with the troops this morning. It actually feels better getting something in my stomach.

1945 hrs.

Hey honey. We had four missions today, and we were busy all day long. We went back and forth to Champion twice, and almost had another mission that would have lasted all night long, but someone finally had the smarts to realize that we wouldn't be worth a damn tomorrow if we did. I know that the mission comes first, but we're all very thankful for this break.

Well, we shouldn't have too many more soldiers that are taking leave. A lot of them are starting to opt for taking the 4-day pass to Qatar instead. Currently, the policy is you take either a pass, or leave, but not both. The passes usually only keep a soldier away for a week or so, and that helps things go a bit faster. I'm actually getting a little hope up for being able to take leave. After two more of my soldiers take leave, then I may get a chance to go, even when I get promoted. I really don't want to get my hopes up or anything, but I really can't help it. I already have an idea of how I'd do it, so I have to do some prior planning now as well.

Sometimes we know who's going on leave, or at least eligible, and when a leave flight is coming in, we may only hear about it about an hour out. That's too easy, because I can pack in about 10 minutes or so. Then we end up spending about 3 or 4 days in between BIAP and Kuwait before actually getting on a freedom bird back to Germany, and then the States. All flights are going in through Baltimore now, so I'd have to catch a connecting flight back to Kansas City. That's okay though, because before I ever leave Baghdad, SATO travel will book all my flights, even the return flights for me, and help me plan everything. So, I'd fly into Baltimore, and then catch my other flight to Kansas City. From there I'd catch the shuttle back to Fort Riley, and surprise you by showing up at home. I so dearly hope that I can do this my love. I can't wait to see you again. I just know that you'd be so surprised, and I'd love to see the look on your face.

5 FEB 04 D + 109 0715 hrs.

Good morning my love. Well, I just sent the men off to breakfast again, and I'm here with my coffee. We should only have one mission to Champion today. We had to go and get EOD yesterday to look at some mortar rounds that our guys dug up with some heavy equipment. You just never know from day to day what you'll find here.

We got mortared again last night, as well as one RPG round fired at Ogden Gate. They're testing us to see how far we'll come out to chase them down at night. They actually fired at our boys, but it was just a probe. The hajji's are trying to find new ways to mess with us. After the other day, when we got briefed on the new type of IED, I always try to be extra careful about going over bridges. I am already paranoid about going over them anyhow, because the last thing I want is to get hit by an IED, and then wind up trying to shed my gear underwater, and not drown in the Euphrates River.

Also, we got briefed again about sending our laundry out through the hajji laundry service. Apparently, the loyalists are stealing our laundry, and killing folks, trying to make it look like the Coalition is going back on its word. So I told the men the other day that we'll just send out socks, underwear, and t-shirts from now on. We will just have to go back to hand-washing everything else just like we used to. It's really inconvenient to do it that way, but if it helps with the overall resolve of the Coalition, then so be it.

1410 hrs.

At about 0830, we got the call to roll out into Ar Ramadi. There was a huge firefight somewhere in town this morning, and we listened to most of it. We heard an IED go off, and saw a huge plume of black smoke; followed by a whole lot of returned fire from a .50 cal. Somebody was really working that gun. Not two minutes later, we got the call to go, and then 10 minutes later we were told to stand down. We knew there was a firefight, and the adrenaline started rushing more than ever. I never saw the troops look so serious before, but they reacted just as they should, and right at one time, they all looked at me as if to say, 'well, what do we do?' I said, 'let's roll!' and everything exploded at the same time. Weapons were mounted, rucks thrown in the trucks; everything was in motion, until we stood down. We just took it in stride, and started unloading vehicles.

Around 0900, we were told to mount up again, and this time it was a go. The firefight from earlier in the morning was a remote detonated IED followed by small army fire on a convoy. We went out to investigate the scene of the ambush, and the crater from the IED. I took a bunch of pictures, and it made me angry, that the enemy was standing in the same spot as me not an hour before then. I scoured every inch of the site, and even branched out into a small village nearby to peek around a little. I wanted to get hajji so bad, but we were out too late. We poked around for a while, took pictures and came back. It was originally thought that there was a sand table on site, and that this was the headquarters for a terrorist cell responsible for all the anti-coalition activity in the area. I really wish that it had been.

6 FEB 04 D + 110 0820 hrs.

I finished your videotape this morning honey. I'm not sure how it came out. I have bags under my eyes, and I think I look terrible, but I still hope you like it. Now I have the videotape, the DVD that the company made, and I'm going to make an audiocassette for you too. I'm going to try and print out some pictures to send along with it as well.

I'm sitting here listening to our music while I type, and have come to find out that Zhou, my second in charge and bunkmate next door likes Martina McBride a lot. Every time 'There You Are' comes on, he just loves it, and says he thinks we picked a great wedding song. He's so funny how he gets all giddy about it. It's easy to see that the guys know how lucky I am.

We're all just waiting around now for the LT to get back and brief us on what the missions are today. It already came out that we are still doing the Champion run today, and then we'll probably get back around 1715 or so, get some chow, and then rest up for a little while before we take off again about 2200 for another all-nighter in downtown Ar Ramadi along HWY 10. No one is really looking forward to this one, and I'm doing everything I can think of to keep the troops motivated. They know that I'm not really excited about this one either, but they've shown us that they'll follow our lead whenever and wherever. No matter how heavy the load that the unit puts on us, we still have that here. I am confident that the troops are confident in me. I know that the troops are not *all* I have here, but it sure helps a lot in a crunch. I now have a briefing at noon, to go over the plan for tonight. Only the LT and I are required to go for some reason. We'll see how it goes.

2130 hrs.

We just got some intelligence from Battalion that told us that there is a VBIED threat downtown tonight. Apparently, hajjis thought he might just wander around town and look for Americans, crash a checkpoint, and do a suicide bombing. Since we got here, Brigade made perhaps the wisest decision yet by canceling our five-hour mission downtown tonight. When I first heard it, I think I was in shock because before he told us we weren't going out, my first thought was to brief my guys on a new game plan with heightened security for the impending threat. I suppose I just never thought for a second that with the new threat that Brigade would cancel the mission. I guess miracles really do happen.

We got cut off the phone earlier, and then the computer as well. No one got hit that I'm aware of, so I think I'll go back over there again in a little while to try and call you again tonight. I just hope that you don't worry much when things like the phone and computer cut out like they did today. I know that it's easy for me to say that from here, because I know that nothing immediately bad happened and you do not. I must admit, I'd rather be home and have you not worry about this kind of thing at all about me, but when I hear the concern in your voice it is of great comfort to me. I love the way you try to be strong, which you are, but the occasional worry or concern leaks out a little and I am exposed to a range of emotions from you. I have to say that I really miss that.

7 FEB 04 D + 111 0745 hrs.

Good morning my love. This morning someone asked me why I don't usually go to breakfast, and why I choose to spend the time writing instead. I told them that I haven't seen my wife in a while now, and that this may be the only time I get to give to her today. I don't think they really understand. We get busy most of the time, I mean really busy, and this might be the only time I can give you. I can't guarantee the phones or internet will be up, so I have had to make certain adjustments in my day.

We found out that we come off of PSD on 13 FEB and the Champion run that afternoon, which normally gets us back here at around 1715 or so, will signal the end of our time on PSD. That's the good news. The bad news is that around 1900 the same day, we take over Ogden gate guard again. This time, we have nights, from 1900 to 0700 the next morning. We are going to be so exhausted the morning of Valentine's Day. No one is looking forward to it, but again, we're used to it by now.

1830 hrs.

Hello my love. We got back a little while ago from a hunting mission on the riverbank of the Euphrates River. The sun was glistening off the crystal blue and green water of a river from Biblical times. There were children everywhere, and then the shots rang out from across the river. Immediately, all the gun ships rotated their massive .50 cal machine guns across the river, and just as fast as they showed up, the hajji's were gone. We didn't even see anything but some dust coming from the other side of a large hill. The children barely moved, and never stopped playing and laughing with each other. I was a little rattled, and am still coming off that unnatural high as I sit here typing.

As soon as we got back, the Battalion CSM came through to inspect the barracks and weapons. We were back no more than 20 minutes or so, and Nick and I got both barracks bays cleaned up, all the soldiers to completely clean their weapons, did maintenance paperwork for the weapons, vehicles, and still got the troops off to chow on time. We work really well under pressure, but not even close to the way you and I do. We're the best team I've ever known.

I sent you some pictures last night, and tried to call you but the phones were down again. They were up again this morning, but I didn't have the time to e down there. I wanted to see if you liked the pictures, and I will try to call you again tonight. The last couple of weeks have been very stressful here, and I have been very needy of you. I never knew it was possible before now, but it is actually possible to think about someone for an entire year. It never ceases to amaze my, my love, about how much detail I can recall about not only you, your scent, your hair, your voice, everything about you; but also just about every single day that we've had together. It seems like I can remember every dance, every song on a road trip where we held hands, just every little thing.

2315 hrs.

Well, I tried to call earlier my love, however you were taking Michael back to Brandy's house and I did get to talk to Kevin for about 10 minutes or so. He was so cute. He gave me the rundown of the entire night with Michael, and how he nagged to play some game even though you said no. I also talked to Grandma, and she sounded better. She spoke of how sick she was, and how much better she was feeling now, and also about moving out. This as you know has been a great concern to me. By the end of our conversation, I did feel much better about it. She said that it would definitely be better to have their own place, and the grandchildren could come visit at grandmas every now and then. I was actually relieved to hear this from her, because of everything she said before, when she was being mean to you and the kids. I'm not sure, but there just seemed to be certain wisdom about her opinion that I'll probably never hear from my mom. I think that mom just figures that although she's codependent on a lot of things, and she does know how to work her tail off, she still thinks that the world owes her something. I could have just as easily fallen into that trap as well, many times in my life. You could have too honey. I love that you are my wife, and the mother of our children.

I'm off to bed now my love. I have Escort in the morning, and I'll call you in the afternoon when I get off. I love you sweetheart. Kiss you later.

8 FEB 04 D + 112 0545 hrs.

Good morning my darling. I just got back from the MWR tent. I ended up leaving two messages on our machine, and got Angel's voicemail on her cell. I know I said I'd wait to call until I got back from escort, but I just couldn't wait. I was up anyway. I'm not sleeping very well these days. I will try again after I get off work at noon today.

I got a rather disparaging email from Darrin Numbers today. It seems that things are not going as well up at Wainwright as he might hope. I started to write him a letter on the laptop, because I wanted to be very careful about what I said to him. He sounds very depressed, and mentioned he wanted to choke out his boss about a dozen times last week alone. He also said that Natalie is going active duty, and heads off for Fort Rucker, Alabama next month to become a Blackhawk Crew Chief or something like that. She'll be gone in school for six months, and that will leave him with Tristan for the entire time. I'm sure he'll do fine. He also mentioned saving his frequent flyer miles, and coming to see us after I get home. Darrin also said how he misses us, and how amazing it is how you and I deal with adversity so well, seeing as how so much has happened in the last year. He's right. I know I have an amazing partner, and I do know how lucky I am.

1230 hrs.

Good afternoon honey. I just got back from escort, and I scored some stuff from an Engineer unit that's leaving next month. I got us a hot plate and an extra microwave too. Too bad I can't ship some of this stuff home. Anyhow, I got us some movies on DVD too, and I'll go by tonight and get that stuff. I have to turn in some boots later on to get replaced. They got charred pretty badly in that fuel tanker fire on HWY 10. After that, I'm going to go and try to call you. For now, I'm going to try and lay down for about a half an hour. I love you.

9 FEB 04 D + 113 1427 hrs.

Good afternoon honey. I got the opportunity to call you this morning, which started my day, and ended yours on a good note. I'm glad we've got the chance to talk so much lately. We still get cut off every now and then, but usually I get the chance to call back. I felt so close to you this morning. I also got to talk to Abigail for a bit. She was particularly chatty this morning. She sounds so sweet. I know she probably has her moments, but my absence is the reason for my lack of understanding.

We just got back from Champion again just a few minutes ago. That was mission # 36 for me, but who's counting? Our afternoon run got cancelled, because we're going out all night tonight. It's the mission that got cancelled the other night due to the VBIED threat. We're on our way out the door for the briefing on tonight, and Ill try to call you again before we leave. I love you sweetheart. Kiss you later.

1830 hrs.

We just had to go down to supply to get our long-awaited gore-tex desert boots. Many units had them since November, but I suppose better late than never. I am especially appreciative of them tonight, as we are going out on an all nighter. The men are a bit anxious, as we learned that the night before the last mission there was cancelled, some ICDC guys executed a rocket attack against coalition soldiers. The problem with them is the same as the Iraqi policemen that are crooked. The curfew in town is 2300 hrs. and only the police, the ICDC guys, and us are exempt from it. Therefore, if someone wants to join the Iraqi Army, or become a police officer, and their intentions are that of terrorism, it's really the perfect cover for them. They get our training, issued U.S. bought weapons upon graduation, and are not subject to curfews and other restrictions as the other locals. If they are dedicated, and many of them are, they will be patient and use these opportunities for terrorism and not for the rebuilding of Iraq. It's just a small part of the picture here, and unfortunately, something else for us to deal with. I just don't particularly like dealing with it from sun down to sun up in downtown Ar Ramadi right on HWY 10. I'm sure everything will be fine though, and we will all make it back in the morning a little more tired, but all in one piece.

It's times like these that I miss you so very much my love. I would give anything to hold you right now. I'd do anything to see our children just one last time. I don't mean to sound so morbid, but I can't help but think of the worst case scenario. If for some reason, whatever it may be, that I do not come home, and you end up reading these thoughts, please know this; that if today was my time to leave this life, then my last and lasting thoughts were of you, my love. There is not one second that your love doesn't fill my heart and warm the depths of my soul. I have missed you these last months, and have lived in an eternal emptiness away from you. I do, however, feel closer to you than ever, and dream of seeing you and being with you again.

As the days of this tour go by, I am reminded constantly of my own mortality; we all are out here. I have seen many people affected by the absence of their buddies, buddies who will never return home. I only hope and pray that I will not be among them this time around. I look at the young, energetic faces around me, and am confident in their abilities. After all, I trained most of them. Some are more mature than others, but as children from broken homes grow wiser at an accelerated rate, so do the young folks around me. They possess a certain wisdom that is earned respectfully, and in the hardest way imaginable. It's a weight to bear, but one that is a labor of love; love of country, pride in themselves, and the hope of a better life that the events leading up to all this will never repeat themselves.

I will sign off for now, my darling Helen, and write again tomorrow. I love you my sweetheart. Kiss you later.

10 FEB 04 D + 114 0315 hrs.

We just got back from the mission. Everything went really well, and all made it back okay. We emplaced fifty-two 11,000-pound barriers to create a roadblock with two search lanes. I got some really cool pictures through my night vision goggles too. Well, I am exhausted, and I'm going to lay down now my love, and dream of you. Kiss you later.

1100 hrs.

Good morning my darling. I didn't get a chance this morning to go over some of the details of last night because I was so very tired. I didn't have the strength in me to walk over to the tent to call you, and for that I'm very sorry. I was simply exhausted. As we were leaving the gate, we got a 'net call' over the radio. It's a tactic used when someone has something very important to put out to everyone. Anyway, there was an Iraqi woman in the area near where we were going that had apparently strapped a suicide vest to herself, and blew herself to kingdom come. That's the one though that we had to digest as we were in our vehicles, leaving the gate. Then, after being on site for about an hour or so, some other unit saw a vehicle dropping off another Iraqi, and the intelligence stated that one of them was another suicide bomber, this time in a car bomb (VBIED). They weren't sure which one was the bomber though, and they couldn't catch up with either of the vehicles. So, for the rest of the night, everyone on our mission was hyper-alert. By the time we got back to Ogden gate, everyone let out a big sigh of relief, and started to relax a bit. In the short five-minute ride from the gate back to the hooch, everyone was completely exhausted. You should have seen it honey, the looks on their faces. Everyone was just absolutely drained beyond anything I've seen yet.

I just got back from talking to you. I was down at the MWR tent, getting my squad signed up for correspondence courses to help them get ready for promotions in the upcoming year, so I thought I'd call. It was 0300 back at Riley, and I was hoping you wouldn't be totally exhausted. It was a really good phone call, and although it just happened, I remember thinking how lucky I am, and even at 0300 my wife is willing to wake herself up enough to talk to me. I have to be the luckiest man alive.

I feel really weird today. We got in so late, and then slept until late morning. We all went to chow together, and then went over to the MWR tent. The sun is shining, and everything almost looks normal today. It's almost as if we're back in the rear sometimes. It's hard to shift gears sometimes too. Just like last night, for example. This afternoon, it's not very difficult to imagine, but it feels so distant, the fear and adrenaline of last night; and we were just a short ten miles from here.

12 FEB 04 D + 116 0515 hrs.

Good morning, my darling. Well, we are off on another mission again. This morning will make # 40 for me; trips outside the wire that is. Today the command asked for just two trucks, so Nick and I are going. This time, we are not just pulling security, but were asked to bring some detection equipment with us as well. Intel suggests that there may be depleted uranium where we'll be going. We were joking last night how if we did actually find anything nasty out there, then it would support the President's theory, and DECON Platoon would be famous. There's always hope. I sent the troops off to chow already, and, if I'm hungry enough, I'll eat an MRE later on today.

I couldn't tell you about this mission because it is pretty sensitive in nature. We all have some pretty high expectations about today. We were joking about it last night, saying that if we did find some nasty stuff, then the President would allow DECON to come home for backing his rationale for invading Iraq. We'll see though. I miss you so much my love. I won't volunteer for anything crazy or anything like that, but if I can help get us home earlier than we thought, hey, count me in on it.

Well, my love, I'll write more later on, and surely call you after we get back some time. I have to take my soldiers out to the gate tonight to get ready for gate guard, which starts tomorrow night. This time we'll have the night shift, which is a bit of a relief for us. At least we won't b dealing with five hundred or so hajji's every day, but then again, we have no light either, and hajji is a slick little bastard. I love you honey, and I'll call when we get home.

1945 hrs.

Once again, the intelligence we got wasn't accurate, and the depleted uranium we thought we'd find was apparently not there. That's a good thing of course, but we were really ready for this one, and had all the gear and equipment we'd need for it, and it really would have been good for DECON. Oh well, maybe next time.

I got mission # 41 knocked out today. It was our last day on PSD though, for a while, and tomorrow we start the night shift at the gate. Nick and I each have two shifts of three hours each. I have the 2200 to 0100 shift, and the 0400 to 0700 shift. We can at least get back to some semblance of normalcy during the day. We'll probably get some sleep in the mornings, and then play catch up on maintenance in the afternoons. Dorelus is a squad leader now, and he's running a support squad. He wants to be in on all the 'hooah' stuff, but he knows that he's up and coming, and taking his licks in stride. I'm having a bit of a hard time letting go, so to speak, but I'll support him as best I can, even though he's got his own squad now. I suppose you inevitably have to let the chicks leave the nest. Now I have Zhou though, and although we've got a lot of work to do to get him ready for promotion, I'm sure he'll be just fine. He's a hard worker, and never falters when tasked with anything. He's very intelligent, and I'm glad to have him as my second in charge.

VALENTINE'S DAY D + 118 0145 hrs.

Well, we just finished getting something to eat after our first 3-hour shift at the gate. My squad has the 2200 to 0100 shift, and the 0400 to 0700 shift as well. The guys did well, but it was a little chilly out there. I'm very tired right now, and I think I'm going to try and catch a little nap before my next shift. I love you honey. Kiss you later honey.

1945 hrs.

Hello my love. Well, my other soldier came back from leave tonight, and my entire squad is back with me. We're about 45 minutes from our first shift, and I already have plans to take them over to the MWR tent to call you for Valentine's Day. I got to email you earlier, but it was way too early to call you. I know you say I can call you anytime, but I really wanted you to be awake already when we talk, and I figured the least we could have that if nothing else on the day that celebrates love . . . our day. I love you so much my darling.

15 JAN 04 2030 hrs.

Here I sit once again, looking into the computer screen, somehow hoping and praying that these words will reach you, even though I know all too well that you will probably read them at off moments, while I'm off at work or something, after I return home. The only thing about that is that I somehow feel that the words that I write in this journal are somehow more important now, than later. I miss you so terribly bad my love. I know these words have repeated themselves countless times throughout this journal honey, but I feel like I'm falling, and the only one who can catch me is you. And just knowing that that day will not come for a long time leaves me in a state of constant silent desperation. You are my soul mate my love, and it pains me deeper and deeper every day that I am away from you. Some days, I can't even imagine that the pain could be any worse, and then I wake up again a day later and realize that I was wrong. I hate to sound so desperate and depressed, but you are my strength, and without you near, I just feel like I weaken with each passing day. I know that I've told you before that you are my greatest strength and, at the same time, my greatest weakness. I have never known how true this could be until now, my darling. You truly are my everything, and I feel so blessed to just know you. The fact that I am privileged enough to be your husband is likened to the rapture of biblical promise. I truly do love you with everything I am. It's more than that though. You are me, and I am you. You truly are the best part of me, and without you, I would be nothing my love.

It's now 2110, and I have to start getting the men ready to go to our first shift of the night. After that, we'll go over to the MWR tent again, and I'll try to call you. It felt so good to get through to you yesterday, on Valentine's Day. That's the only thing I wanted yesterday, in the whole world, and I'm so glad that I got it. You're my universe honey.

18 FEB 04 D + 122 0225 hrs.

Good morning my love. I am sitting here in my hooch, and I just finished eating my first meal of the day. We all did. The Platoon just got finished being briefed on a Top Secret mission that is to happen tomorrow. We even got pulled off of Gate Guard for this one. Tomorrow, DECON is going out to Fallujah for a potential Decontamination mission. If this is in fact true, then we will once again potentially have a chance to break new ground, and possibly make history. We are ready. We've spent the last few hours loading up equipment, and packing our rucks and stuff very carefully. I am a bit nervous, but if this is a success, and not just another milk run as we've had so many times before, then a few things will happen. First, no one should mess with us anymore, because it will be great, not just good, but great news for the battalion, brigade, and division as well. It will of course be good for the President, and will lend credit to his policies, and pretty much get everyone off his back too. We all welcome this opportunity, as it signals one of the first big attempts to do our actual job.

The unit moved the C-6 package today. It isn't operational yet, but it should be within 24 hours or so. Unfortunately, we will not be here during that time. Our mission takes us to Fallujah, the most dangerous town in the world at present. I miss you so badly right now. We're loading up all of our equipment tonight, and getting the troops both prepared and mentally ready.

Anyway, I must close for now because we are to get up in just 3 ½ short hours. I love you my darling. Please know that in the event that anything happens to me in the coming days, either from being in Fallujah, or from the NBC agents that we might encounter, know that I loved you with everything that I am even unto the very end. Know that also, in the worst case, that your husband and soul mate did not die alone, but with you in my heart, warmed by your love eternally. I will love you forever, my darling. God will provide for us, whether together or not. Please don't ever lose that faith. It's one of your strongest qualities, and as a wife and mother, makes you a saintly woman in my eyes. I could never properly express my love to you my angel, however, please don't ever doubt that there was ever anything but absolutely true love in my heart for you, and you only. You're my everything, and always have been. Even before you and I, when there was only the promise of you in my life one day. You are the strongest person, woman, soul, wife, and mother I've ever even heard of my love, and with God by our side, our children will more than fare well in their lives, but flourish into fine young men and a young lady. I must sign off for now honey. I have to take this time to rest up, and God willing, there will be many more entries in this journal, and a warm homecoming someday over the horizon. I love you my darling, more than anyone or anything, and I always will.

22 FEB 04 D + 126 0445 hrs.

Good morning my love. Well, we made it back from Fallujah last night without incident. On the way out the other day, some hajji decided to throw a satchel charge (portable IED) off a bridge at our convoy. It bounced off the roof of one of our trucks, into the bed of the truck, bounced out of there, and detonated just as it impacted the road. We were all very lucky that day. We kept rolling through though, without stopping, because our mission was still ahead of us. When we arrived at the camp, we linked up with some Tech Escort folks out of Aberdeen, Maryland, who were doing the digging out in the desert for some suspected WMD. Nick and I set up a DECON line to get the vehicles clean, should they become contaminated. This was as real as it gets so far for us. The site that we were digging at was so hard and compacted sand, that the team thought it might have been buried there before the first Gulf War. The Tech Escort people, in this case are like the Special Forces version of the Chemical Corps. They decided to call it quits and deemed the area safe enough to stand down the mission. We ended up going back to the camp, and decided to stay overnight.

We would be there for the next two and a half days, waiting for an armed escort back. This gave the Platoon some well deserved down time. They had about 10 phones and 60 computers at this other camp, FOB St. Mere Eglise, which was run by the 82nd Airborne. I got to talk to you a lot on the phone, and even got the chance to see you and Abigail on a webcam for about 45 minutes one night, and with you again a little bit the next morning. I really enjoyed that a lot. Across the camp, there is a huge pond, complete with goldfish and minnows. There is a fountain in the center of the pond that arcs the water beautifully through the air. Around the edge of the pond is a small wooded area with lots of greenery. It's a sight for sore eyes and a welcome one at that.

When we got back in last night, everyone was talking about how DECON was attacked, and also how we were on AFN television with our mission. It was nice to see some actual genuine concern finally. But then we came back, and reality set in once again. Today our platoon has hajji guard, a rifle range, motor stables, barracks maintenance, and a barracks inspection from the Battalion Sergeant Major as well. Yes, we are definitely back at Junction City now.

23 FEB 04 D + 127 1440 hrs.

Good afternoon my love. Today makes a whole two and a half days off that I've had since the beginning of our tour. I was running the Escort yesterday, and it actually wasn't that bad. I think I am just becoming numb to it all, and I'm getting used to running on empty. I slept until 0730 this morning, and almost felt overtired, as if I slept too long. I finally went to sleep around 2330 or so, after two days with only 3 ½ hours of sleep. I think I just wanted to make sure that I'd go right to sleep when I lay down instead of staring into space for about an hour or so like I normally do. I took my first shower in four days last night, and my first hot one in over a week. The conditions are steadily improving here, but this chain of command is different than any one I've ever had before. When every other unit here got showers, internet, and running water to flushing toilets, anything that resembles a comfort of home, their soldiers got it first. Not so in our case. Our senior chain of command ensures that the staff and all seniors have these things first. Our hot water heater went out, and only two days later did the seniors decide that we could use their showers, and then only with an NCO escort for all the soldiers. I've really never seen anything like this before. Even down here in the ghetto, at our level, Nick and I make sure that all the soldiers have everything first. We made sure they got their Wiley-X glasses, free t-shirts and underwear, and desert gore-tex boots first. It's just what you do, plain and simple.

I went down to the internet café today, and got another email from Billy & Challas. I'm glad that they're so supportive. It really is a relief to see at least some family that even tries to understand our situation sometimes. All of this compounds itself over time. Not seeing you, the family overall, being here, and then having the chain of command that we do; it just gets very frustrating sometimes. Today, I am trying to be invisible. I just don't want to be near anyone, talk to anyone, or anything. I haven't even gone to eat at all today, but I will go to dinner tonight. Apparently, there are a lot of missions coming up, and we are taking the lead in supporting all of them in one form or fashion. I'm used to it by now, and although we always adapt to whatever the situation, it does get a little tiring. The commander has the people skills of a rock, and is of no help to anyone here. From what I understand, the word on the street has it that she has a boyfriend who's also in the Army, and she no longer wants to stay in, and she's apparently very unhappy about the whole deal. Her leadership, or should I say lack of it, shows this to be pretty much accurate. From her complacency on day one to her frosty demeanor, I haven't felt any sort of loyalty towards her as a commander at all. There are good units and bad ones. This one here is the latter I'm afraid. I just do the best I can for my soldiers, and I can pretty much deal with anything they can dish out if it means that I can come home to you, my love. I would not opt to ever come back to a combat zone with this unit. Had I known before what I know now, I would have fought tooth and nail to get into another unit. Their personal agendas are not mine, and most of these 'cherries' have no clue as to how to prioritize and lead properly in a hostile area. I am by no means an expert; however, my frustration grows with each passing day at the seeming incompetence displayed here. After all, it's only their first tour.

24 FEB 04 D + 128 0600 hrs.

Good morning honey. I just got off the phone with you. Actually, we were cut off, but we still got to talk for 47 minutes. I miss you so much this morning. When we were talking, Angel was over helping you with Kev's new desk, and Kevin is grounded at the moment for not listening to you, and Abby and Caleb are fighting. Believe it or not, it actually sounds like fun. I wish so badly that I was home to help you deal with everything.

We were attacked again last night. We had a couple mortars fired our way, and we had to turn all the lights off outside, and keep everyone inside as well. When that happens, we automatically account for everyone, and go get them if they're not here, and just hang out inside for the rest of the night. The phones are shut down, so there's no temptation to take advantage of the moment when it's not really busy there. After all the weapons caches and ammo supply depots we've taken from them, hajji still has mortars and stuff, and seemingly has a steady supply coming in. The intelligence guys still track arms dealers shipping stuff in from Syria and Jordan all the time. It's a weird way to live over here. Just the exposure to things you see and hear that are so far out of the realm or normalcy for most of us is just phenomenal sometimes. A few months back, for example, I'd never thought that I'd have a 10-year-old kid ask me if I wanted to buy 200 RPG's for $200 apiece. I think of Kevin and Abigail often, every day, and hope and pray that they never have to be exposed to anything like this. I saw a little girl Abby's age the other day, when we were outside the wire. She was running around near the road, and there are tanks and Hummers and all kinds of traffic all over the place. She was just outside playing, and not even acting like anything was out of place. That kind of thing just kills me inside. I just wanted to pick her up, and give her some candy, or my winter hat, or something, but I suppose once again that I've been desensitized to these things. I have to say, that that bothers me a bit. I know that I won't react like that when I get home, especially with our own kids, but even a hajji child is still someone's child. This place forces me to place different values on different lives, and sometimes I'm not sure what to make of that.

Well, the men are up now, and we are on our way out to Escort for the day. We'll be there for most of the day, and it should be better than normal. Today is my first day not running it, but just being a chase vehicle. It's actually a break for me in a way. All I have to do is sit in the truck and have my driver drive to wherever the hajji's need to go and work for the day, drop off an escort to stand watch over them for the day, and drive back to the Escort lot and do it all over again. There's not much actual work involved, however, it's about 30 to 35 degrees outside right now. I'll write more this evening my love. I'm sure I'll be cold and tired later on today, but I want to keep up this journal for you as best I can. I love you my darling. Kiss you later.

2010 hrs.

Hey honey. I just got back from the PX with Matt, and we caught up a little. He's on the day shift now, and he said he's starting to feel like an actual person again. Well, Escort wasn't actually that bad today. I got to be the 'pickup man'. I got to ride from the escort lot to the gate back and forth all day in a small quad-cab pickup truck. It was just me, and I listened to the CD you sent me all day long. I just put it on repeat, and I ended up going through two sets of batteries. It was worth it though. In between runs, I actually got pretty far towards your next letter, and it was almost like I had some actual time to myself, yet got to spend time with you as well, only you weren't there. Does that make sense? It was a nice change from the norm around here, and a welcome change for me. I should be able to do it again on Thursday, and if so, I'll probably be able to finish your letter, and listen to some more music again. It was almost like I had you right there next to me in the truck, and we were just going for a ride. I can only dream of such things right now.

I am so very tired right now, but Eason got a movie in the mail, and my Chinese guy, Zhou, wants to see a country movie. Tonight's movie is 'Cowboy Up'. So, I suppose we'll try to convert another one to liking some kind of country. I told them it would happen over the course of a year. I even caught Simmons singing along with some George Strait the other day, and Zhou just loves Martina McBride's 'Valentine'. It's working honey, it's really working. Well, I'm going to lie down now, and probably not finish this movie . . . again. You know me. I love you my darling. Kiss you later.

25 FEB 04 D + 129 0600 hrs.

Good morning honey. I just got back from the C-6 tent, and got an email from you. I am very worried right now. You mentioned something about your heart, and having some pain, and I am really concerned. Someone fried the generator last night, so the computers and phones are not all working properly. I am hoping to get in there sometime today when things are working better than they are now. I love you so much my darling, and it pains me to think that you're having some sort of ordeal that I can't help with. I wish so badly that I could be home with you right now, and just to be by your side.

As I mentioned before, I got to spend some 'quality time with you' yesterday, so to speak, and I look forward to potentially having it happen again tomorrow while on Escort. I am missing you so much these days. It's almost unbearable.

Today I have a lot of maintenance to do on our vehicles. I wish that I were prepping them to get ready to go home, however, they are just wore out from overuse. I also have to do three load plans for our trailers so we can be prepared for the next actual DECON mission that comes up, if there is one.

0730 hrs.

I just got off the phone. I could not get through to you, my love, so I called Uncle Steve and Aunt Nancy. I just cannot believe how much shit he gave me over that last email that I sent to Mom, about not respecting you, and enabling Jon. He was totally up my ass about that, and seemingly did not want to listen to any reasoning whatsoever. I told him that disrespecting my wife and children was unacceptable, and he kept repeating about how 'you're not home', and 'it shouldn't concern you right now', and 'there's always two sides to every story'. I've got news for him; the only side that does matter is my wife's . . . period. I haven't spoken to him in a couple months, and I'm still in Iraq, and I'm beside myself, seething mad right now because I can't believe that he had the balls to try and make me feel bad about all this. Well, unfortunately, there are two sides to everything. And in my book, if you're not with me, you're against me. He now falls in the latter category, and I'm sorry to say it, but this is not the first time that he's fallen from grace with me. As far a how he feels about my family, I could really care less right about now. He mentioned how any time there's anything on the news around our area on the news, she runs around the house crying and screaming. This makes no sense to me at all, and I'm not going to concern myself with it. I'm pretty sure that it's just part of the whole attempt to pace a guilt trip on me. Not gonna happen. Oh well. This is just another reason that makes me realize that my family sucks, and I shouldn't waste time or effort staying in contact with them. I'll try and call you again later on, and, if not, shoot you an email or something. I love you my darling and I need you to know that you can't do any wrong in my book. Some people might have things to say about that, but I really don't care about anyone's opinion but yours. I love you in God's way.

27 FEB 04 D + 130 0515 hrs.

Good morning my love. I just got back from the MWR tent where we got to talk on Instant Messenger for about a half hour or so. I miss you so badly honey. I both want and need so badly to be with you right now. You told me a couple weeks ago that you were having some sort of chest pain, and now you are on a heart monitor at home for God only knows how long. I know that you do not want to blow any whistles with the Rear Detachment; however, I did have to mention it here. I am sick to death worried out of my mind over this honey. It's all I can think about, and has been for some time. I never though that I'd look at that computer screen and watch the words, "I don't want to die" come from you. I suppose that it's just one of those things that you never think you'll hear. I was in a tent full of people, and all I wanted to do was scream. I am angry at myself for allowing myself to get into this deployment, and scared for you at the same time. I have no pride left in me, and will always put you first. I'm so very sorry if I have not done this. I know I haven't. I am a very selfish person, and I will not allow that to happen again honey. I am so very sorry my love. I will do everything within my power to get home at this point. It's not that I don't believe anything you have, or will tell me about all this but I'm also aware that you don't want me to worry 'unnecessarily' as you'd say. I just don't think that anything but seeing you in person is going to make this any better for me. I already got the men up, and now we have to go and pickup our hummers for PSD. I love you my darling, and hopefully I'll talk to you soon.

0740 hrs.

We finally got our vehicles signed for, and if it weren't almost 2300 back home, I'd try and get on the internet again with you. I really don't have the time for that right now, but I'd make time. I am really worried about you right now my love, and if I can't talk to you on the phone or on the internet, then I feel as though the least I can do is write in this journal to you. God forbid anything happens to me over here; the weird thing is that the thing I worry about most is not being able to see you again or spend the rest of my life with you. I know it sounds selfish, but if something were to happen to me, then at least you would know that I was thinking of you till the very last. I've given very specific instructions to about half a dozen people that if something were to happen to me here, then one of them are to send you this laptop, so you could have this journal and all the pictures and stuff. At that point, I know it wouldn't be much, but I'm sure you'd want to read this stuff. From here, even now, it's all I feel that I can give to you, and at that point, that being the worst-case scenario; I'm sure I'd probably feel the same way then as well.

I don't mean to sound so depressing or gruesome honey, but I feel so far away from you today, and I would do anything to feel, and actually be closer to you right now. As I have told you many times before, this is by no means my first tour abroad, but I sincerely hope it's my last. This tour is so different for me in so many ways, and the worst of it all is being away from you my darling. I'll stop rambling on for now, and get back with you later on today sometime. We're probably going to Champion again this afternoon, so we'll see how that goes. I love you honey. Kiss you later.

29 FEB 04 D + 132 0645 hrs.

Good morning my love. I just got off the phone with you a little while ago. We were cut off again, but we were having the discussion about the letter you wrote to the family about their disrespect and lack of support. I totally agree with you honey. As a matter of fact, I'm surprised that I hadn't written something like that sooner myself. Oh well, I'm very proud of you for that, and I'm all for you voicing your opinion my love. God only knows that you've taken a lot of crap from them in my absence, and at the very least you deserve to sound off.

Well, Dorelus was promoted yesterday, and I am very proud of him for all his efforts. He was a really good soldier when I met him, and he was always dependable and trustworthy as well. I really didn't have much work to do with him other than a little fine-tuning here and there, and he has always been willing to learn. He reminds me a lot of me when I was younger in my career.

1 MAR 04 D + 133 0530 hrs.

Good morning honey. Well, all the men are off to chow, and I am posted up here guarding the weapons and equipment so I can have one last chance to write you before our trip today. Today, we are going to Al Asad, about 4 to 4 ½ hrs. to the West/Northwest of here. Apparently, the camp is very nice, complete with an Olympic size swimming pool. We are picking up some equipment there, and transporting some Marines to and from. This shouldn't be an all-nighter, but I actually hope that it turns out to be that way. It's a very long trip, and the vehicles are beat down as it is, not to mention us.

Everyone is going today, and I think we all actually feel a bit better about this one, even though it's long and rough through the desert, simply because we're all together. That is the only comfort that I draw from being out here, and aside from our occasional conversations, the only comfort I need. The only thing that will make me feel truly better about any of this is coming home to you my love. You are my rock, my foundation, my everything. I feel as though my transition in coming home will of course be easier because of you, and I hold that sacred right now. I am still concerned about the children, in that coming home I may have changed some, and I sincerely hope that it doesn't hamper my relationships with them. Honestly, this may be a bit naïve of me right now, but my relationship with you doesn't concern me in the least honey. I believe it to be stronger than ever before, and even though we're going through all of this right now; things like the family still come up, the phone getting shut off, the van breaking down, and we still deal with it together as best we can. I truly applaud you for all that you've done, as well as how well you've handled everything. I couldn't have done it better myself, and every day I consider myself more and more lucky, and proud to be your husband. Well, I will end this session for now. I just took my prescription Zoloft, and I don't think I'll be so easy to set off today. We'll see. I love you my darling. If possible, I'll try to call you from Al Asad, or, at the very least, just after we get back. I love you so much my darling. You're my universe.

4 MAR 04 D + 136 0550 hrs.

Good morning my love. I just got off the phone with you. You and Angel took the kids to Denny's for dessert. I think that's a pretty good idea. I wish I were there with you. I just told you that we were on permanent PSD, and although I think I told you the other day, the fact that you didn't know really didn't surprise me at all. I think maybe I hinted towards it, but I'm also pretty sure I avoided telling you also. I'm not trying to keep anything from you, but I know that you'll worry about it. Today we will have mission # 60. Today's mission is an easier one than we've had. Our Platoon Sergeant isn't going with us, so the LT has him doing things like running our laundry for us and such. The other day, when we were returning from Al Asad, he turned his radio off on the way back and went to sleep. His driver told us this, and we told the LT. He was the trail vehicle in our convoy, which is usually the position that I take. It's a very important one, and you have to relay a lot of information up to the lead vehicle and the convoy commander throughout the entire mission. I took over as the rear communication at that point, and we thought his radio got jarred loose due to all the potholes in the road. Nick and I were so pissed off. The LT knows how we feel, however, he also knows that we can't get him moved right now. There's a new E-7 that came in just yesterday, and we're all hoping seriously that he will come to DECON. The LT knows that we don't trust him very much, and that's true now more than ever. He didn't just fall asleep because he was tired on a long trip; he actually turned his radio off intentionally and took a nap while on a convoy! Unbelievable.

Yesterday, we ran another two missions. One was to Camp Hurricane, and the other to Champion Main, where we all decided to take our showers from now on since we're there so much. The showers work really well and there's never a shortage of hot water. It's getting very hot outside now, so I found that if I take a shower as hot as I can stand, then it's not so bad when I go back outside. We usually only have just over an hour to wait for our package at Champion, so it helps pass the time, and makes it so we don't have to wait in line at night back at J.C. just to get a warm shower, if that. We do what we have to do to survive.

I'm really glad that you talked to my brother this morning, and it makes me feel a lot better that you two actually touched base. I know that he's sorry about how things worked out with the family, however, it's not his fault, and I am grateful that he still offers his support. I'm sure that you feel better about all this, at least Gary and Kali, and that makes me feel better as well.

Yesterday I got the chance to clean up my area in the hooch, and put my sleeping bag and blanket out on the laundry line to air out a little. They got some Febreze at the

PX the other day, so I bought a bottle. It really helps out around the hooch, and everyone loves the stuff. I know it doesn't sound like much, but it's a big deal around here; anything to take the stale, dusty smell out of the air. It usually doesn't work for long, but at least it's something. And out here, something is always better than nothing.

Well, I have to go and get some chow now so I'm not starving later on. We'll probably be back sometime after lunch, and I'm not eating another MRE unless I actually have to with nothing else to choose from. I love you so very much my love. I loved talking with you this morning, and I'll call again after we return sometime this afternoon. I love you so very much my love. Kiss you later.

I decided against going to chow this morning. It's quite a walk from the hooch, and most of the time, it's just easier not to go for me. Most of the time nowadays, the support Squad, which is Dorelus' folks, run up and get us 'to-go' plates and have them here for us after missions. It's really interesting how much we are turning into trolls when we're not outside the wire. Everyone just prefers to stay in the hooch; because it's the closest thing to being home that we have now. It'll be nice one day to not eat off of a plastic plate with flatware that comes wrapped in a little plastic bag complete with a napkin and salt and pepper. I know that it must be that way now, but I think I'm just getting a little tired of it. Even going to some place like Denny's, at least you get a real plate and steel hardware to eat with. That's just one of the things I really miss; one of many.

5 MAR 04 D + 137 0530 hrs.

I made a decision last night. It was a decision that might be a career-ending one for someone in the Platoon. After our Platoon Sergeant fell asleep the other day on the way back from Al Asad, and then his driver told us about it a couple days later, it was just eating me up. Last night I decided to tell the 1SG about it. I know that the LT already knew about it, but when I approached the 1SG about it last night, he obviously had no clue about it, so I knew it didn't go any further. He was very upset about it, and told me that he'd talk to the LT today and would tell him to do something about it. If the LT doesn't do something about it, then the 1SG would tell the Company Commander about it, and that the LT had knowledge about it and did nothing. I think that there are going to be some changes around here shortly.

I also told the 1SG that under no circumstances would I go outside the wire with that guy again, and that I also wouldn't put my soldiers in that type of situation again. I told him that I've never refused an order in my life, but this was unacceptable, and I couldn't in any good conscience do it again. I understand that sometimes these situations come up, and there are hard decisions to be made. The only thing that matters is how a man deals with them. I only hope to be able to teach my children thee things one day, and that they one day have the courage to stand up and do the right thing when it's time for them to do so.

I think the Zoloft is helping some, because when I found out I was of course very upset, but not nearly as much as you'd think I'd be. Maybe I'm just getting a little older and just deal with things a bit better than before. Maybe it's a little of both.

The phones and internet are down again. This time, it's something locally wrong with the C-6 package. I'm sure they'll be working on it today, and have it up by tonight. It's a bit of a disappointment to have it down, but also to be expected here.

Well, I have to wake up the troops in about 10 minutes or so, and then have a Squad Leaders meeting at 0630 because Rafael didn't want to have it last night because he was 'tired'. Our Platoon Sergeant's driver said that he slept yesterday while we were outside the wire, and didn't appear to be too concerned about anything. I can't say I'm surprised. Actually, I don't think that anything would shock me anymore. Oh well, I'm sure that something will come out of all this very soon, and when the dust settles, the Platoon will have a little more clarity about what is going on. I surely hope so anyhow.

In the meanwhile, we don't have any missions on the calendar today, but I'm sure that that will change after the morning meeting. It usually does, and at this point I don't even thing that it would bother anyone since it keeps us away from our fearless leader. At least Nick and I feel that way. We're just stifled by him, stifled as leaders. You can only flourish in the right environment, and when you're inside a box, like we are now, and it's because someone like this guy who doesn't know what to do, then it's very frustrating. We shall see.

2100 hrs.

Hello my love. Today we had two missions. The first one got cut short because some of the equipment from our package went down. Our 'package' is the passengers or group of vehicles that we are pulling security for. Also, while the engineers were excavating this area of land, they found some unexploded ordinance (UXO). There were HE and Illumination rounds there, and fortunately, they were removed without incident.

We have another big mission tomorrow. Now that we are permanently on PSD, it seems like we are running more and more outside the wire. Tomorrow we are going to an Ammunition Supply Point (ASP) the size of Fort Riley. Apparently there are at least 80 or so bunkers full of ordinance. We're going out because a UAV (Unmanned Aerial Vehicle) took pictures of a civilian car going in and out of the area, which is off limits to all civilians. This happens a lot, and apparently there are a lot of civilians who go in there to steal the ordinance to make the IED's they use against us all the time. There has been, however, a decline lately in IED and VBIED activity in the area.

I would love nothing more than to talk to you tonight. It's been very busy lately, and the phone was down last night, so it was a little disappointing. But I'm going to go ahead and go down there to try and cal you now. I love and miss you so much my love. I think of you every day, and you are my motivation for every decision I make out here. You're my everything my darling.

While investigating an Ammunition Supply Point for insurgents stealing scrap metal and minor explosives, one of my soldiers captured me on film pulling security on top of a bunker.

7 MAR 04 D + 139 1030 hrs.

Good morning my love. Today, so far, we actually have a day off. I can hardly believe it, but we'll see what the rest of the day holds for us. We found out last night that we're no longer going to be on PSD permanently, and this upcoming Wednesday we take over Gate Guard again. PSD was good because we were all together all the time, and I think in a way it served its purpose. We're all very tight now, tighter than before, and we work surgically together on the gunship escort missions.

Yesterday, when we went out to ASP 309 (south), we had a bit of excitement, and it was quite the rush. As we pulled up to the ASP, we saw two hajjis on a motorcycle making a run for it. We took off after him, and lost him in the dust. With three gun ships hauling ass through the desert, it creates a lot of dust, and although we did end up losing him, it was really cool. It was almost like the old show 'Rat Patrol' from the 70's, which was about a combined unit of American and British troops rolling through the desert in gun ships similar to ours. We ended up finding a lot of ordinance, but not as much as the cache we found before and we got the EOD guys to blow it up. All in all it was a good day, and although it was one of our better days on PSD, I'd still rather be home with you any time.

As promised, I talked to my brother this morning, and we got cut off after about 10 minutes or so. I had enough time to ask about the kids and Kali, and get a firm reassurance that all is still well between us as well as he's still backing us when it comes to matters of the family. I think he still doesn't want to make waves, and sometimes appears to be evasive when making comments about the family, actually to them, however I can plainly see that he knows right from wrong without creating any disloyalty. In some ways I think that that's a gift that I don't have. I can be diplomatic when I have to be, but especially out here I usually don't keep my mouth shut very often. At this point, I think DECON and the chain of command both count on that. Oh well.

I'm going to try and call you later on my love. I still don't like to call when I know you and the kids are probably sleeping, but I promise to call later on this evening. I know that it's Sunday at home too, and you deserve as much time to rest as you can get. I love you my darling. Kiss you later.

2225 hrs.

Good evening my love. I just got back a little while ago from talking to you on the computer. I was going to call, but when you logged on, and we started talking, the line got longer, so I will try again later on, probably in the early morning hours for me.

Well, today was something new for all of us. I actually took a nap today, after I watched our video, and I watched some more of it just a few minutes ago as well. The wind is howling outside, and our one window is rattling. It reminds me a little of the day it rained in North Carolina. I will remember that day for the rest of my life. We just lay in bed the whole day long. I'd give anything to be able to do that with you right now. It's Sunday, and a great opportunity to do something like that. Maybe one day we can go for a drive out to the middle of nowhere in the truck and have a picnic just you and me, and lie in the bed of the truck and just be together. I think that would be nice.

I think that more and more nowadays I think of the things I'd like to do when I get home, because we're over the hump now, and although it seems like we have a long time left, the clock is still ticking and every day is just a day closer. I'm still miserable without you my love, but the thought of coming home keeps me going, and I look forward to doing everything with you all over again. This is the longest that we've been separated and I know it's hard at home as well, but God will guide us through it, and everything will be just fine when I get home. I just know it.

Well, I'm going to lay down now my love, if I'm to get up early to call you. I just can't wait to hear your voice again honey. I'll pray for you and the children tonight, that God may keep you all safe and not too overburdened until I get home. I love you. Kiss you later.

8 MAR 04 D + 140 0630 hrs.

Good morning my darling. I just got of the phone with you, and although I slept through my 0330 alarm this morning, I'm really happy that I got through to you. I'm glad we talked about everything going on back at home. It really makes me feel good, almost apart of what's going on even though I'm not there. You told me about taking the kids swimming, and about what a ham Abigail is being.

Abby was very talkative this morning, a pleasant surprise on my end. Usually she doesn't talk too much, except when she's fighting with Caleb or Kevin while we're on the phone. Today she was really talking so good, and for the first time I got to see how big she's really getting. It's a blessing, but at the same time it really tugs on my heart strings making me wish so badly to get home to you all. I really do hate missing everything that I have. But I know it has to be this way right now, and I keep telling myself that we're on the back side of this tour, and everything will be done and over with before we know it. I love you so much my darling.

The troops are getting up right now. I put the Trace Adkins DVD you sent on, and that usually does the trick waking them up. Most of them don't like country, but I caught Simmons the other night in absolute darkness after lights out singing 'Then They Do'. He has a really good voice, and I think he must have thought that everyone was asleep, including me. Too funny.

1230 hrs.

Today I sent a soldier to mental health. Before he went there, he went to the Battalion Aid Station to get a referral first. After the questionnaire, his weapon was confiscated and I had to inventory all his ammo and knives and such. I really don't think he's quite over that edge yet, but however he answered those questions led somebody to believe otherwise. He's usually one to shoot his mouth off before a whole lot of thought behind it, and I'm assuming that that was probably the problem. He has to go back to Combat Stress again this afternoon to see the actual psychologist, and probably get some meds. My soldier is ADHD, and I suggested Wellbutrin, and the referring NCO agreed. So until then, I have to escort him everywhere. The soldier also mentioned that he's always worked better as an individual, and has a hard time concentrating and focusing. Yes, this sounds very familiar. Wellbutrin is the medication that the doc gave me in Alaska to effect my ADHD, and it seemed to work, if only for a short while. It's challenging to deal with, because I seem to be the only one who is even trying to understand him at all. All the leadership is frustrated, including me sometimes, but I'm trying the most though. It's very difficult with no support though. I can see how Kevin might feel a lot, and I won't be the one who makes him feel like that. Maybe I had to step outside my own world for a while to get some perspective on this one.

9 MAR 04 D + 141 0720 hrs.

I fell asleep last night with the laptop in my lap. I'm sorry my love. I was so exhausted from working on trucks yesterday, and when I actually got done with our late night meeting, the drama kind of just wore me out. We confronted the LT last night, and told him that we, as a Platoon, wanted to talk to the 1SG without the Platoon Sergeant. We're tired of all his crap, and the only way we can see to deal with it is to talk to him. After we were done with the LT, he came outside to talk to the Squad Leaders, and told us that the 1SG approached him yesterday and wanted to talk to him, as well as told him that the platoon wanted to have a chat as well. He just now, last night, apologized for falling asleep on the convoy. What a jackass. He told us he was waiting to get counseled from the LT before he talked or apologized to us. I have never not trusted someone so very much in any unit that I've ever been in, not once in my entire career.

Since he was asking last night, we told our Platoon Sergeant that he was probably the most unapproachable person that we've ever met. He seemed a bit surprised, and just kind of played it off. When he asked what we thought the troops thought of him, I think he liked that even less. We told him that they "couldn't stand" him. Everything to never wanting to go outside the wire with us, to falling asleep when he did, to sleeping during the day when the whole PSD team was on a mission, to going to the internet and phones while we're all prepping for missions. It's one thing if a leader isn't strong, or won't always lead from the front, but doesn't bother showing up at all prior to a mission, or late is another thing all together. Oh well. I really can't wait for our meeting with the 1SG to hash out some of this stuff. The 1SG told me yesterday that he already has two counseling statements on him, and is just waiting to pick his moment. This is no environment to have a complacent or uncaring leader. If it weren't for our troops, Nick and I both told the 1SG that we would rather be reassigned to another unit. He said he feels our pain, and is working on it. We'll see.

I love you so much my love. I can't wait to come home and be with you again. We were talking to some of the Marines at Hurricane Point yesterday, mission # 69, and they were telling us how they're only deployed for either six or seven months. If we're due to come home in six months, and they are too, this can't possibly happen. This is so because we will all be leaving at the same time, with no transitional force on hand here in country. So, in reading in between the lines, me, Nick, and LT were talking last night, and we are presuming that we'll be home or at least leaving somewhere near July as best we can guess for now. So at this point, we're not really even looking at September, much less October anymore, and we figured that we probably have about 4 straight months of work left before we start packing it up and shipping our vehicles out. That's one of the worst parts, packing up and cleaning vehicles, but I'll gladly do it if it gets us home just that much faster. I love you my darling. I'll be in the motor pool most of the day today, changing tires and getting my trucks ready. The LT, Nick and I want to get them as mission capable as possible as soon as possible so when we get the movement order to pack it up, we don't have to jump through our ass to do it then. This is all purely on our own speculation, however, it can't hurt to do it sooner than later. Every time I get frustrated and don't want to be in the motor pool any more, I think about how much closer it gets me to coming home to you. I love you my darling. I'll write more later on. Kiss you later.

11 MAR 04 D + 143 0825 hrs.

Good morning once again my love. I was fortunate enough to talk to you again this morning, and the children sounded well which is always good. Kevin sounds so good; I was really glad to hear it. Abigail sounds as ornery as ever, and is talking so much now. It really is still such a shock for me to hear her talking so much. I suppose I knew that she would all along; however being here has made me out of touch to a certain extent. I can't wait to get back home and get back to normal.

Well, it's back to the motor pool today. We'll go out to the gate for a little while to transition with the other company that's out there now, and then head back to the motor pool again. We are ordering parts like crazy now, and absolutely killing ourselves to get new tires on and everything working right. We are running these trucks into the ground out here. I've had to order three new engines and a new transmission since we've been here. The dust, dirt, and heat are absolutely killing them. But every day that we go out and bust our ass in the motor pool gets us a little closer to home. I keep telling the guys that, and it seems to be working to keep them motivated. We should finish up one truck today, and start another. I have four trucks and I'm hoping to get all the new tires on them by the end of next week. It takes about two hours to do a single tire, and the electric impact wrench is broken now, so we have to do it all manually. Each tire has ten nuts on it, and most of them are very difficult to break, plus the tires weigh about 100 pounds each. I never thought that changing tires would be such a pain in the ass. I also never though I'd be so excited about getting tires done either.

I hope this guard schedule isn't going to be so difficult on our time schedule. We have it from 1000 until 1300 hrs, and again from 1600 to 1900 hrs. The later shift is easier because the gate closes to all inbound traffic at 1600, so the only people we should see during that shift is our own convoys, and maybe a few informants. The Iraqi's like to come into the gate under cover of darkness, so they're not seen by the other Iraqi's. Sometimes, if they're seen, other locals try to kill them for helping us out. When this happens, we have to get them inside very quickly, and call for an interpreter as well as the intelligence guys to try and figure out if they're lying or not. If their information leads us to a good catch (a captured bad guy, or weapons cache), then they're eligible for a reward. Most of them come to the gate thinking we're just going to hand them out some cash on the spot no matter what they tell us. They're not too bright.

I miss you more and more with each passing day my love. I cannot express in words the way that I love and care for you so deeply. I would do anything to take away the loneliness that we feel without each other by our side. It's a feeling that we've both known before, and unfortunately, not for near as long as now though. We'll get through this as best we can, with God guiding us, and I'm sure everything will be fine in the end.

The Battalion Command Sergeant Major tells us that we are due for a rotation to NTC out near Mojave sometime in April, but we'll cross that bridge when we come to it. I've never been to the training center before, and the closest I ever got was visiting your mom. We'll see.

12 MAR 04 D + 144 0845 hrs.

Hello my love. Well, today starts our first day of Gate Guard again at Ogden Gate. We did our left seat/right seat out there over the last two days, and they've finally implemented the Standard Operating Procedure that I wrote in December, after our first tour at the gate. I am pretty proud of this, and am glad to see that the chain of command has also made some force protection improvements as well. We've got more concrete barriers for walls, and as I suggested before the traffic lane is narrower and slows things down considerably as far as hajji accessing the gate.

The Platoon knows their jobs like the back of their hand right now, and I am not at all concerned about that kind of stuff. We also have a new tower built for our heavy machine gun. The .50 cal was introduced into the Army inventory during World War II, and it's still in use today due to its ability to stop a moving vehicle with about two rounds into the engine block.

I am at the very furthest forward position today with Eason. We will be controlling the flow of traffic for the vehicle and personnel search teams. We're also about 200 meters outside the wire, and closer than anyone to Route Michigan (Highway 10). It's a living, I suppose, but not for much longer. We haven't been told yet, but I think we're on the gate for about two weeks. At the rate that things change around here, I wouldn't doubt if we were kept there for a month or so. It gets truly exhausting doing it for that long, but at the same time, it does help to pass the time. That's all I'm looking to do right now; that and get home.

I would have called you this morning, but there is a media blackout again. Yesterday, two soldiers from Bravo 1/34 Armor were killed in an IED attack. Also, one soldier from our Battalion fell off of a 20-foot ladder while coming down from the machine gun tower at Ogden Gate. I must have climbed that ladder over a hundred times to check on my gunners up there while on gate guard. No one's ever fallen off of it before, but accidents happen, and there's always a first time for everything.

1500 hrs.

Well, our first shift back on the gate was certainly uneventful. Friday is hajji's version of Sunday, and I think maybe we searched five vehicles during the entire shift. I'm glad that today is slow, as it gets everyone back in the groove slowly, and not at an alarming pace. Some of the local contractors still remembered us, and as far as I can see, pretty fondly. One guy came up and hugged me, saying, 'welcome back my friend'. The other normal sights were there as well; the herds of sheep moving slowly off the south gun tower in the early afternoon, and the kids begging for candy and such, trying to sell the soldiers anything they can. I put in a standing order for some Iraqi bayonets. I told my brother Gary, and Darrin that I'd try and get each of them one. I have another that I got earlier in the tour, and I don't carry it around or use it, but thought I might have it engraved later on for Kevin or something like that. Just a thought.

The internet and phones are up again, so I'm going to try and call you tonight my love. I certainly hope to get through, as I've been unable to talk to you over the course of the last day or so. This is bad business lately, and I want to make contact with you as often as possible. I love and miss you so much my love, and cannot wait to be with you again. I know I keep repeating myself in this journal, however, I feel that I simply can't say it enough. You're my everything my love.

13 MAR 04 D + 145 0715 hrs.

Well, I got in touch with you this morning. I fell asleep last night still dressed, and about 0200 I woke up not being able to sleep. I was really tired from Gate Guard, but since I was up, I put a pot of coffee on, and tried not to wake up anyone in the process. It's amazing how aware of your surroundings you can be in absolute darkness once you're used to it. I used to pop a chemlight every night by my bed to find my way around, but I don't even have to do that anymore. It's almost as if your senses are always hyper-alert. I suppose that will wear off a bit, slowly after we get back home again.

I'm really glad that we got the chance to talk this morning my love. You, Angel, and the kids were at the Rally Point for family night, and it sounded like everyone was having a good time. I really am glad for that. It gets all of you out of the house, and not so prone to going stir crazy. You told me of Abigail being in a high chair and not wanting to eat a PB & J sandwich, and how she's so much like you in eating so healthy. She is so much like you, and I've always thought that. It is a blessing, and she will come to know that in future years, and God willing we'll live long enough to see it.

Well, today is command maintenance day, but seeing as how we're on gate guard, and we spent four straight days changing tires and ordering parts for my trucks, I won't feel too bad in missing it. Besides, we'll be on the gate anyhow. Last night, we were about 20 minutes from getting off of our last shift of the day and we heard four consecutive explosions. They came from Highway 10, and right outside the gate. Someone had apparently set off four daisy-chained IED's. They sounded big too, like 155 mm rounds wired together. There's a large wall next to my forward position at the gate, which surrounds the glass factory, so I couldn't see them, but it shook the air around us, and I really felt for whoever got hit last night. Apparently, no one was killed or hurt, because the phones were still up last night, and this morning as well.

When I asked this morning, I was told that we're on the gate indefinitely. Usually there is a time limit of only two weeks, or in our case last time, a month. That was a long stretch, and it rarely happens, however, we're all hoping that that is not the case now. Although we have two pretty good shifts, it still gets old, and we still get tired of it. Last time we had it for a month, we actually looked forward to taking over the PSD mission again. Since this last time though, we were told that the PSD mission was dissolved, and no longer a necessity since the 82nd left, and we do not report such things to the Marines anymore. Oh well, the worst we can do is pull guard duty until we leave. If this happens to be the case, I have to say this now, as I'm sure I'll get tired of it fairly soon; but we really do have two good shifts.

I got to speak with my brother this morning, about four hours after I called you my love. I asked him if his arms had been amputated, as I've not seen a letter or email from him in over a month. He said that you and Kali had talked for a while about a week or so ago, and I was of course glad to hear of that. He also mentioned that the kids were both doing well, and he looked forward to a visit after I got home. I told him that I had a bayonet for him, and he was of course excited about that. Boys will be boys. Oh well. I'll write more later on my love, as always. I have to get the troops motivated this morning. I think the new shift work is already taking a toll on them a bit, even after one day, and I need them to focus on what's important . . . getting everyone home safely. I love you.

2230 hrs.

Hello my love. I just had 'our time' out on the porch with thoughts of you and me, and a few songs. I still do that even though I am dead tired. I just want to make sure that you and I get our time even though we are still apart. I think that that will make the transition to coming back home easier as well. Actually, I don't even know what we'll do with all the time we'll have when I get back. I hope that me coming home isn't difficult for you my love. I've really had to bring my mentality down to a basic level over here. Back home, I don't ever really even think about this stuff like this, but over here it's different. Over here, all I can do is try and stay alive from day to day, and try and remember to eat when I should, and get to the phone and internet at every available opportunity. Things won't seem so 'desperate', I suppose, when I get home, but I swear that I'll never take you for granted. You, as my wife, the love you've given me, and the support you've shown me always my love are things that I hold as the truest and most valuable things in my life. I love you so.

I suppose that it only makes things worse right now, but all we all keep talking about is coming home. We've all but planned the trip home in our minds. Someone sent a Junction City newspaper to us over here, and the front page had an article about soldiers from 3rd Brigade returning home, and how nice it was. I can't help but be jealous of them, and at the same time consider myself lucky in advance, if the good Lord blesses me by allowing me to return home in one piece. God only knows how many guys have returned home missing pieces and parts, and are changed forever. I pray every day to be with you my darling. You're all I need, and all I'll ever want. I love you so very much.

14 MAR 04 D + 146 0422 hrs.

Good morning my love. I just got off the phone with you a few minutes ago, and I'm still so very excited. Before I called you, I checked my email, and I got one from Ft Riley with my new promotion orders attached. I'm so happy for this. It could have never happened without you my love, and this is but one more of our successes. I've fallen off the horse many times during my life, and just when I thought I didn't have the strength or the will to get back on it again, along came you, and I feel like I was reborn again. You truly are my greatest strength my love. I always want to do right by you, and you are always so very supportive and enable me to do so. Even when the chips are down, and things just seem like they're never going to work out; then they do. I have you to thank for so many things; my renewed faith in God, for being the love of my life, for adding so much to my life and helping me to be the man I am today. I am forever in your debt, and you have my eternal gratitude. I love you more with each passing day; more than yesterday, less than tomorrow. You are and always will be my everything my love.

15 MAR 04 D + 147 0655 hrs.

Good morning my love. I was fortunate enough to be able to talk to you again this morning. Abby was sick yesterday and last night, but sounded well while I was on the phone; hyper as ever. I was however very sad to see you so depressed when we talked. We eventually got cut off again, but the phone cuts out at 47 minutes of talk time anyway, so at least we talked as long as possible. I came back to the bay and sent Eason off on his overnight mission to LSA Anaconda, and got Legary ready for his PT test. After hearing how sad you sounded this morning, that was just the icing on the cake today.

I tried to be really strong this morning and I think at this point in this journal I should mention that I was pulling it together this morning on the phone only because you sounded so rough. I know that this tour has taken quite the emotional toll on all of us, and that can't help but sneak out but every once in a while. The truth is my love, that I really am hurting right now, more so than ever. I miss you terribly. I know I tell you this all the time, but each day that goes by, there is a hole in my heart bigger than the day before, and some days I wonder if I'll ever survive this. I have to turn to God, and just know that He will take care of us, and bring us together soon. I love you more than anything my darling; you're my whole world. I miss your touch, being next to you when I wake up in the morning, and holding you when I go to sleep. This place is so cold hearted, and I've never seen such concentrated evil in my whole life. These people don't know you and me, and could care less if we lived or died. They are callous, and I'm so glad that you and I and our children don't ever have to live in a place like this.

0825 hrs.

There are so many moments throughout my day that I just feel like screaming because I miss you so much. I just get so frustrated because I can't talk to you at that exact moment, or can't be in the same room with you, or something usually like that. The Zoloft is helping curb my urges to go off on hajji for the most part, however, when they really upset me about something, I can still feel the anger but I don't lash out like I used to. I think the chain of command is actually helping a bit too. They're still getting micromanaged from the top, but being as far into the tour as we are, I think they're feeling a bit better about a lot of things too. It's sad to say, but I think at the company level, they're just used to it by now, and more tolerant to this type of thing. It's now the 'norm'. I also think that we're like that now as well, but I can tolerate a lot as long as I keep remembering that every day now is a day closer to you my love. You're my salvation, my every hope and dream, and the sole reason for everything that I do here. Every decision I make, every choice I make outside the wire, and every prayer that I pray goes with it my thoughts of you. I feel substandard sometimes as your husband. Sometimes, here, due to the way I feel when I'm down; I still absolutely love you with everything that I am, but I sometimes just don't feel like that's enough for you. I want to give you everything my love. I am absolutely yours, and I could not desire, love, want, or be more happy with you. I do know how truly blessed I am, and thank God every day for you. Again, you're my life, my everything.

During days like today, when you're not feeling so happy, I think about it all day long. I long to hear your voice again, and pray that your day will get better. I wish so badly that I could hold you and make your day better. My days would be better simply by being able to do this.

2206 hrs.

As I lay here tonight my love, my special time with you is being interrupted by a barrage of both inbound and outbound fire. The radio net has been buzzing with an information exchange for well over an hour tonight, and it seems as though the threats of last night's mortar attack were off by a day. We were expecting all this to happen last night, however it never came. Apparently, hajji can't keep to an accurate timetable of his own attacks, or he's intentionally trying to throw us off. As I sit here typing this, my body jerks every time there is an explosion; praying that the next one doesn't have my name on it. They're getting closer, and I think some of the local workers, no matter how good we treat them or give them steady employment, will try to exploit our kindness, and take it for weakness.

I'm glad that we're planning our reunion already. I've so enjoyed our last few days discussions about what to do when I get home. Honestly, I don't even think I know what I'd like to do first. No matter what it is though, I know one thing for sure, that I want it to be with you. I love you so much Helen, and my love for you is indescribable. You truly are my everything, and I don't think I could ever truly or accurately describe this to you. I do know however, that I'd like to spend the rest of my life trying.

2217 hrs.

The explosions have been constant for about an hour now. Apparently, hajji has decided to launch a major offensive tonight, and the artillery boys are matching them round for round. I stepped out onto the porch for a minute amongst the confusion in time to see the boys from 1/16 rolling out in their Bradley Fighting Vehicles. The Brad's are huge tank looking things, and can really take a hit as much as give one. Just last night in Ar Ramadi, a suicidal hajji rammed a Brad with a VBIED. The car exploded in a hail of fiery shrapnel, instantly killing the driver, and I don't even think that the driver of the Bradley would have spilled his coffee. The entire crew was safe, and injury free. That's always a good thing.

It's funny sometimes that throughout my career in the Army some things have seemed to have come full circle. Today, for example, while on the gate, I stood only a few feet from where SSG Cutchall was killed. Cutchall was a member of the Brigade Reconnaissance Team that was killed just outside Ogden Gate by an IED before I deployed over here. I remember taking the remaining and newest members of DECON over to Morris Hill Chapel, just a few blocks away from our home on Riley for the memorial service. There is no evidence of that incident left on the street today. The streets are rough, laden with trash and debris of an uncaring and dirty society. If someone hadn't told me about that exact spot, I would have never have guessed that there was even an attack there. I remember being at that memorial service; seeing his wife, children, and mother in as much distress as they could stand, probably more. I remember thinking that when I finally got over here I'd do my best to not ever place you and the children in those shoes my love. Thus far, I've been very fortunate. I've survived two IED attacks and harassment fire at the gate from small arms on numerous occasions.

There is still a part of me that, no matter how deep the hurting inside from missing you and all things from home, tells me that I was born for this life of service. I used to say that I lead a charmed life, and it disturbed you every time those words came out of my mouth. I no longer believe that my love. I have certainly been blessed though, and through our faith in God, each other, and the strength of our love for each other, I truly believe that all things will be okay.

2242 hrs.

The incoming fire has now stopped, and the only sounds heard are the fighter jets overhead in the dark. I saw some Little Bird's from the 160th earlier, and it once again gave me great comfort in their presence. Tonight was the longest barrage of the tour thus far. Earlier today, PFC Eason returned earlier from his mission to LSA Anaconda. About six miles off post, his convoy was hit by an IED, and I was instantly paralyzed. It was as if one of my own children was out in the war zone, and vulnerable. I was extremely relieved to hear of his safe return, and filled with sympathy for those who received small injuries in the attack. No one was killed, thank God, however, the Marines told the convoy commander that they were not continuing on with the mission, and even though that what protocol calls for with only minor injuries, the convoy couldn't continue without their additional gun ships. They're going to have to get used to the idea of being shot at every now and then, if they are to make it through their tour here. Oh well, everyone has to be a cherry sometime, and I suppose now is their time. I must sign off for now my love. I have to get some rest if I'm to get up early tomorrow and call you. I love you my darling, less than tomorrow, more than yesterday. Kiss you later.

16 MAR 04 D + 148 0804 hrs.

Good morning my love. As usual of late, I started my day with a phone call to you. You had great news for us, as far as the boys go. Apparently, a custody agreement wasn't integrated into my divorce, and there's a shot at getting some real time with our boys. At the time, I suppose I wasn't thinking straight, and it appears to have been a blessing in disguise. Of course, this opens an opportunity for us, and them, to do the right thing by them, and of course what's in their best interest. I'm really glad for that, because we've been unable to do that by no choice of our own for so long, but we've made preparations for them as always. Our home has always been ready for them and open to them always.

This really started my day off right today. I love hearing good news, and coming from you is always a blessing my love. I'm listening to our music again as I type this morning, and it somehow always makes me feel closer to you. After all, that's how we met, and loving the tunes like we both do, it's always been a part of our life. I'm really glad that our kids love music as much as they do. I think it helps to make them more well rounded. I just hope we show them the right example. I don't have any doubt that this is the case, and it just amazes me how lucky that not only do I have the best partner wife, best friend, lover, and soul mate that anyone could ever ask for, but that we also are blessed with so many children that we get to share our love with. Sometimes I get all deep with stuff, I know, but it awes me to think that God made the universe, all of us, and still thought to give me a life like the one I have. I haven't always known that, but I suppose getting older does that to you.

This tour has been a test thus far, about how much one can take in awkward and distant circumstances. It's been a test for the both of us, and I am so very proud of you honey. I know that we have both had our moments where we have been weaker than others have. Those moments of depression, angst, and sometimes loneliness are all natural; however still a tribute to our love. My darling, I could not want anything more than I have in my life right now. You're it. You're my everything, and I am the happiest man on earth.

17 MAR 04 D + 149 0815 hrs.

Well, this morning's conversation was one of those that I have dreaded forever. I never thought that Tracy would have ever been so callous and heartless, especially since she's getting married soon, but I can't find the words that describe how badly I feel for you my love. I can't believe that she would have the nerve to tell you that you can't possibly love or care for the boys. After driving to Tennessee, and then staying in a hotel with Kevin for two whole days because she wouldn't let you see the boys. And then there's paying out so much for plane tickets because she wouldn't' let us pay a little extra for Gary to fly unaccompanied to come see us, which, incidentally, we still paid child support that month. And then let's talk about all the hundreds of missed phone calls and missed opportunities.

My love, you have been more supportive and loving towards the boys than anyone could or should ever expect you to, especially with al the interference that Tracy has tried to block you with. Why there are obstacles from her I'll never know. I remember when she was dating Wayne, and they were talking about getting serious, Gary told us that his mother told him that that situation presented "more people to love him". I suppose that those words only apply in Tennessee, and then only when it's convenient for her, even though we've been together about 12 times the amount of time as her and her current man. I'm just venting here honey. I'm sorry. I just can't believe that she'd tell you those things after all that we've been through.

We will watch our every move, pay attention to detail, and build our case. I love you so much honey, and I can't wait to come home and be with you again. I know that all these issues would be so much easier to deal with in person and together. Our day will come my love. Our love for all of our children will eventually prevail. I only hope and pray that they know how much we love them. They have to my love. This has got to be some sort of test, and we shall not fail. I love you my darling. Kiss you later.

2305 hrs.

Good evening my darling. Well, today was interesting enough. On the way out to our first guard shift, I rolled my left ankle, and I ended up going to the clinic for it. I was just going to tape it up, but it started shooting up into my leg. I got checked out, and was told that it was a Class 2 sprain, just a tad less severe than the one I got before I left. I was given a shot of Torredol, a painkiller. The only catch is that the shot had to be in my ass so the muscle could absorb the medication faster. It was supposed to make me drowsy. Damn did it. It burned at first, and then when I went back to the hooch to lie down at about 1600, I didn't wake up until 2100 hrs. I was a little tired too, but that thing really knocked me out. I also got some pills to take through the next week as well to keep the pain down. You were right; perhaps I should have gone back to physical therapy before I left. I damn sure don't need something like this affecting me at the gate and stuff.

I was thinking about today a lot. I know that what Tracy is doing makes no sense, and is cruel, however, I'm quite sure that this will come back to bite her in the ass in more ways than one; legally, and the stigmatism of being a bitch in front of the whole family. But the most important thing is that when Gary told you that he loved you, it probably shot her right through the heart, and what she was doing was a defense mechanism. She's prone to lashing out like that, as she always has. She's even lied to her father before, and over things that would be much easier to tell the truth about. I am praying that this whole situation improves my love, and that one day everything will be as we like it. I surely hope so. I know this though; that God will not give us anything that we cannot handle. Of this, I'm sure.

I love you so much my darling. You really are my everything, and I'm so very proud of the way you've handled everything thus far. The thing I am proud of the most is that you are my wife. I couldn't be prouder, for sure. I'm going to try and call you in a little while my love. Kiss you later.

19 MAR 04 D + 151 0645 hrs.

Good morning, my love, or should I say, good evening? I just got off the phone with you, and woke you up. Sorry about that. Apparently, you're getting up early tomorrow morning so Angel can drop off the kids and get to the hangar for David's return. I have to say, that is very exciting, and I can't help but be a little envious right about now. I never wanted to leave this place so much as I do now.

Last night at the gate, our second shift couldn't get over with soon enough. About 1730, this guy shows up and says he's got VX nerve agent in his trunk, along with a CD-ROM with plans on it on how to build a nuclear device. He also told us that these 'people' he knows have plans to build a hydrogen bomb, and other WMD; something about some bad guys having some weapons grade uranium. This just might be the big break we've been looking for. God only knows the last mission we had was a 'dry well'. This guy actually had a sample with him in a vile, covered with a plastic bag and sealed with a rubber band. He also told us that these bad guys have about 25 kilograms of this nerve agent.

I just stared at that car for the longest time last night. This guy had a late model Dodge Intrepid, an American car, and I just stared at it for the longest time. He was seemingly very willing to help, however I just couldn't take my mind off of that nerve agent. What if the car was rigged? What if he wasn't who he said he is? A million questions went through my mind, and for the first time in a while, I was genuinely concerned if we would al love through the night. Nerve agent is a very scary thing. That was the same stuff that we witnessed when we went through the CDTF at BNCOC. This was just as real to me, however, we didn't have our gear on this time, and I don't think anyone could have expected it. This place is so evil, I hate it.

1500 hrs.

Our first shift went well. It was uneventful and slow as it often is on Friday's. Today is their holy day of the week, and the only ones working are the greedy ones. We came back and finished off our CTT testing for yet another year, and we're all relieved to be done with it. The testing really messed with our lunch today, so I made a cup of noodles, and I'm okay with that. At least it's finally over. Everyone was stressing over it, because it's just another thing to worry about; as if there isn't enough out here already. Now, the only stuff I have to worry about is gate guard and getting promoted on 1 APR 04. I can hardly wait my love. We *all* deserve this so much. I wish I could tell you how proud of you I am my darling. I really am.

2120 hrs.

Good evening my love. It's an early night to turn in tonight, but just as well because we are taking the other two-day shifts tomorrow. All went well this evening; at least there wasn't any nerve agent. I keep thinking about that guy last night, and how poorly he stored that stuff. Tupperware would have been better than how he had it packaged. If he'd only hit one bump in the road the wrong way, if the rubber band was any more loose around that vile, anything could have happened. We're told that he's supposed to come back sometime this weekend to talk to the SF and Intel guys again. I'm not looking forward to that visit at all.

The good news is that we finish our last shift at 1600 tomorrow, and will be off until 1000 Sunday morning, when we go on shift again. We still haven't been told when we'll be off the gate, but I suspect that it won't be for a while, perhaps a month or so again. We really do have a great schedule right now, but even so the platoon pretty much agrees that we'd rather be on PSD again. We're outside the wire a lot with that, but every single me member of the platoon is together then, and no one is left behind. We've already survived two IED attacks on the road, but then again, we've been shot at while on the gate as well. Either way, this is a bad place and there are no "safe" jobs anywhere, so we'd just rather do something that we at least enjoy a little bit.

I think we look at the whole PSD mission like the old World War II show called the 'Rat Patrol'. These allied American and English soldiers would race across the desert in their gun trucks just going and going, mission after mission. There's a certain ambiance about racing through the desert, day or night, with huge machine guns mounted on top, and then sometimes rolling through a small village throwing candy to the children. Maybe I've just been here, doing this job too long now. Oh well, what seems like fond memories now will, I'm sure, be nothing more than just plain old memories after I get home. I'll just save the cool stories for the kids and stuff, and leave the gory stuff out of it.

Well, my love, I'm going to try and get some rest tonight. We've had a busy couple of days lately, and I'll try and call you tomorrow morning. I love you my darling. Sweet dreams. Kiss you later.

21 MAR 04 D + 153 1930 hrs.

Hello honey. I just got back from the C-6, and I had to leave messages on both the boys' answering machine in Tennessee and ours as well. The internet wasn't running too well, so I decided to leave it for later. I understand, you can't just stay at home for a year, and I sincerely hope that you don't worry too much about missing my call. Actually, I'm glad you're out of the house doing something.

Well, we have the rifle range this morning and then straight to the gate. It doesn't really matter to us anymore about having any down time on Sundays, because we're used to this kind of thing now. No big deal. I keep telling myself that I'll be getting plenty of time off when we get home. I am very tired though. These last days have been very frustrating.

Hajji is getting very bold nowadays. Yesterday, there was a daylight attack. We're told that hajji actually believes that with the huge influx of Marines, that we're gone now. We have big artillery guns from 1/5, and they can reach over 20 miles away. Hajji was mistaken. Yet another Marine convoy rolled through the gate yesterday during our afternoon shift with more wounded. I'm not sure if they're acting complacent, however, they're trying to reinvent the wheel, and with not much success. No one here understands how they're attacking this whole mission, and apparently, they are reluctant to tell anyone. They're another service, and of course do things a bit different than we do, but there's no explanation, or even casual small talk. They just walk around acting superior, and wonder why we aren't doting over their few minor casualties when we've got over 20 KIA's and over 100 WIA's in the Brigade so far. Hajji makes it very easy to become a statistic around here.

I miss you my darling, more than ever. I catch myself at least once or twice a day thinking about what I'd like to be doing at home, and then realize that I still need to focus on what's in front of me so I can actually make it home. Yesterday for example, that guy who brought the VX nerve agent to the gate was back with his wife this time. They both seemed educated, and spoke pretty good English. We started swapping pictures of family, and they both made particular note of how beautiful you are. The old woman said she wasn't ever that beautiful, not even in her hey-day. We al laughed for a minute, and for just a moment in time, I felt like I was having a normal conversation with another human being over here. No never mind that they were Iraqi's, or that they knew who has a whole lot of nerve agent, or the fact that I have to talk to them while outside in the daylight wearing about 50 lbs. of extra gear to make sure that if I do get shot at that I don't get killed, at least right away. It's a weird world we live in over here. This truly is the worst place on earth. I pray every day that we al get to come home, and soon, and take us out of harm's way.

Well, my love, I must go for now. I have to get the troopers up and going, and get them ready for chow. We're going straight from the rifle range to the gate, with no break in between. We'll be off at least from 1300 until about 1530 and then again after 1900. I'll probably try to call you then, providing the Marines aren't hoarding our MWR tent again. I surely hope not. It seems lately the only time I can ever call you, use email, or even take a shower are between the hours of 0300 and 0530. And most of the time, I'm just too tired to get up that early. Oh well, I will keep trying to get in contact with you today nonetheless my darling. I love you more than words my darling.

22 MAR 04 D + 154 0650 hrs.

Good morning my love. I got up early this morning, but the internet was down, as were the phones. Well, when I spoke to you yesterday afternoon, I wasn't too concerned with our upcoming guard shift; after all it was only three hours. I couldn't have been more wrong. At shift change, as we were about to get off for the night, a call came over the net that Trooper Gate had between 80 to 100 semi-trucks loaded with cargo, and all had to be searched. Now, we're good; hell, we're great on the gate, but even with us it takes about 15 minutes to thoroughly search two semi trucks. And with that many coming into our gate, we were going to need help. The oncoming shift was the first night shift, so they only brought five people, normal for the night shift. One of the officers from Battalion showed up and asked what we need. At the same time, Nick and I said, 'more bodies'. A half hour later, a bunch of Marines showed up, and relieved us. After all, it was their equipment showing up, so why shouldn't they come help. Anyway, we finally left about 2100, two hours after our shift was supposed to end. The good part was that they all didn't have to be searched, and the escorts that they did have were from a National Guard Transportation unit out of Georgia. When I stopped them at the front gate to get their information, they gave me four cases of Moon Pies. If I only had an RC Cola . . . dare I dream? I told them we were from Riley, and one of these hillbilly's asked, 'hey, in Kansas, ain't Moon Pies they own food group?' I'm from Louisiana, and even I couldn't help but laugh out loud.

When we got back to the hooch, we found that the LT had bought a case of near beer, and SGT Dorelus had already made a chow run. Last night they had Mexican shrimp over rice, fish fillets, and steak . . . real steak. I couldn't believe it. It was by far the best meal that we've had here yet. Usually we only get fed really well like that either before a major offensive, or right after we take casualties. I don't think that many people notice that, but I do. Mike, my buddy at Brown & Root and I go way back to my Kosovo days. B & R is under no contractual obligation to do this, but Mike does it out of the goodness of his own heart. He's a good guy, and if there's anyone I'd like to see running the chow hall during a deployment, it's him for sure. He's good people.

Well, the troopers are allowed to sleep in until 0700 this morning, after the long afternoon and evening they had yesterday. After all, we did wake up at 0530 yesterday to go to the rifle range too. Damn, these days are getting longer.

I worked on your poem some more this morning. I think it's coming along rather nicely. Sometimes I just have no idea how these things pop into my head, but I'm glad this one did. It's so basic, so real for me, and I just wanted to share the thought with you. When it's finished, I will of course send it to you, and I'll keep it in this journal too. Maybe one day our children will read this, and feel at least a little bit of what I feel for you my love.

As I sit here writing you, I am enjoying yet another fine meal of a cup of Puerto Rican coffee and two vanilla moon pies. Two fine meals in a row. This is the best I've had it since I left home. I can't believe that I'd ever think something like this. I really do miss your cooking honey. There surely is nothing like it here.

I'll write more later on my love. I've got to wake up the troopers, and get them ready for chow. The guys tend to be slow movers in the morning, and the tour is wearing on them pretty well. They're doing well overall, but we'll all still be glad to get home. I love you.

1430 hrs.

Some things never cease to amaze me around here. When we got back from our first shift, we found out that we'll be off the gate on Thursday, and be picking up on PSD again. The PSD mission was supposed to be dissolved and no longer existing because we're now working for the Marines. I'm still not really clear on what one has to do with the other. Anyhow, most of the guys are looking forward to getting back on the road. The stagnant nature of the gate leaves a lot to b desired, and although dangerous the road offers movement and adrenaline; both of which help to pass the time.

Then, just a few minutes ago, some Marine Warrant Officer comes by the hooch, and tells us that we're getting new equipment, and that the Marine General doesn't want any vulnerability, including Hazardous Materials incidents/Fire liabilities. I of course told him about the proposal I drew up for the battalion a few months ago, and how it was shot down because of no imminent threat, even though we had three fires inside a week. He said he would shoot me an email, and I could then shoot him back my proposal. Good deal for DECON.

Of the new equipment that we're getting, he mentioned the FALCON DECON System. The Decon tanks and hoses are just like fire hoses, and come mounted on a trailer which is towed by a Ford F-350 pickup. I don't think this could get any better. It sounds good for now, and a little hope is better than none at all. We'll see how it all turns out. I don't think that the battalion has the vision to see the potential in things like this, and would much rather use us as the 'go to' platoon as always. Again, we'll see.

23 MAR 04 D + 155 1415 hrs.

Hello my love. Well, for some reason I feel particularly alive today. Everything seems to be going well, although it's over 90 degrees out today. My interpreter told me it's nice for 'Spring'. Yeah, something like that. The days are a bit repetitive now, but the battle rhythm is going well in the battalion, and we are definitely doing our fair share, probably more. That's the norm for us though.

Today is the one year anniversary since American forces came into Iraq. The hajji's have some religious martyr name for it, but I can't pronounce it for sure. Anyhow, we're expecting a lot of resistance today. We have extra people on the gate, and a few extra heavy machine guns. Good stuff, at least for us. We'll see how it goes.

I sewed some of my new rank on a uniform and a couple of hats last night. I have to say it looks pretty good. None of this could have happened without you, all your love and support my love. You are the best thing that ever happened to me, and certainly the best part of us. I love you so much my darling.

I found out today that the Marines want the Artillery guys to stop lobbing illumination artillery rounds over Ar Ramadi at night. When a unit is outside the wire at night, if there is little to no light, they call the artillery boys over at 1/5, give them a grid, and they lob an illumination round over their position to give them about 5 minutes or so of light. Apparently, the Marines think that this is harassment to the 'good' hajjis in town, and want it to stop. Half the town rarely has power, especially in the slums, so I can't honestly see how the locals would mind having a little light at night, even for a short time.

The other thing that disturbs me about the Marines (among many) is the fact that they got hit with an IED the other day, and when they stopped they continued to receive incoming fire in the form of an RPG, which killed one, and wounded a bunch of others. This unfortunately is not abnormal here, however the Marines' response was. Out of about 20 Marines, not one of them returned fire with so much as a single shot. I couldn't believe it when I heard that. I remember thinking that surely someone was joking, as if they only returned a few rounds and didn't hit anything, but it was actually true. The Ammunition Consumption report proved it. It really makes me wonder about how disciplined they really are. The few, the proud . . . the trigger-shy pussy cats. Oh well, at least we're still here.

Well, I have guard mount in another 45 minutes my love, so I'm going to lie down for a few minutes before we go out into the baking sun again. My lip split due to dryness the other day, so I'm going through Carmex like it's going out of style. I'm just trying to keep it from getting worse. I don't want to stand in front of the battalion in nine days to get promoted with a bloody lip. Oh well. I love you my darling. I'll try to call later on.

24 MAR 04 D + 156 0600 hrs.

Good morning honey. It was so good to talk to you this morning my love. I know that we talked a bit last night, but when I talked to you this morning, you'd received the box I sent, and I am so glad it finally got there. I'm glad you liked it. I thought it was so funny how Kevin was so excited when he got it from the mailbox. I can just see him running across the courtyard yelling. It sounded cute, but also a little sad about how Abby reacted to the tape. I could picture it just how you described it to me. I also thought it was cute how she'd been playing outside all day, and just came in and fell asleep on the pillow on the floor. She's so adorable. She's so you honey.

I absolutely loved the picture you sent in my last email. You're so incredibly hot honey. To me, that picture was just as hot as any other you've sent, and I know you know what I mean. Your hair was pinned up, and you had a little makeup on, and your neck was looking so sleek and sexy. Your eyes look great, and you always have a great smile. I love your cheek bones honey. When you smile, they make your whole face light up. I am so blessed with such a beautiful wife.

Well, today is supposedly our last day on the gate. There was some confusion between Rafael and the LT over which day it actually is, and we still, after two days, haven't got any clarity on that one but we're pretty sure it's today. Anyhow, we're all looking forward to getting off the gate, especially since hajji is getting bolder. We have a 100% success rate for not letting a single thing get past us while on the gate, and we want that to continue. About a month ago, one of the units allowed a cell phone and a Molotov cocktail to get through the search pit one day while I was running the Escort. Yet another unit was letting cell phones through the gate without even thinking that it would be wrong. The reason we don't allow cell phones, pagers, calculators, and such through the gate is that they could be used as a detonation device of some sort. I know it seems like a stretch, but it happens every day here outside the wire, and we take absolutely no chances on the gate. And we're the only ones who have a perfect record out there. Everyone hates that we're that good. It's really not being cocky, it's just true. And as you know, any time there's a situation like this, the good guy always becomes a target.

Well, I have to get going my love. We have out 10% inventories today with the commander. Just another task in the never-ending list of crap to do around here. I love you my darling, and I'll try to call you tonight if possible. Kiss you later.

25 MAR 04 D + 157 0545 hrs.

You mentioned how the kids are getting on your nerves, and that is absolutely understandable. I can only imagine how frustrating it must be to have them repeatedly not listen to you, or talk back, and stuff like that. I'm sorry that these times are so tough on your end honey.

Well, we had our last shift on the gate last night, and we start out on PSD today once again. Today, we have a 'Lioness' mission. Lioness is the codename for female, and it just means that apparently we have to escort a female somewhere to either talk to, or search Iraqi females. Males are strictly prohibited from doing this, and to even have another female do these things requires approval from the Brigade Commander. Male and female interaction of any sort is a very touchy subject in the Islamic culture. I don't want to search any of them, to be honest. They all need a shower in the worst way, and last December, after a month of gate guard, I had to burn a pair of gloves. Even after soap and water, and a little bleach, it still didn't wash the stink out. Oh well. Today is mission # 70 for me. I'm still not trying to rack up numbers, but I think the mission will do that for me anyway.

0800 hrs.

Hello again my love. This morning, the whole platoon played flag football for PT. I don't know what got into me, but I was really sporting some moves out there. I scored two touchdowns, and was faster than I thought I could be. I think taking off 16 lbs. really has helped me out a lot. It's funny though, I haven't really noticed it a lot, but I don't eat near as much as I used to. I usually eat only one meal a day now. I snack throughout the day, and I know I'm not eating really healthy, but this environment doesn't always allow for that either.

I wanted to say again how great it was to be able to hear your angelic voice this morning my love. I can't tell you what that does for me. Even when you're not having the greatest of days, when you're venting, upset, or the kids are just driving you crazy, it's still great to hear your voice. I will always be your sounding board my darling. You truly are my best friend, and I love you more than anything on this planet. You truly are my everything, and without you I would be truly lost honey. I consider you a gift from God, and will love and cherish you forever.

With every mission outside the wire, it seems as though I go into this time warp. Everything seems faster, the time, the driving, everything. I think that's why I don't mind being on PSD so much, because it allows me to pass the time so much faster.

I realize that you probably won't read this journal until after I arrive back home, but it really feels like a lifeline to you sometimes. This morning for example; it may seem kind of silly to a lot of people, but because you're my best friend, even after I talk to you on the phone I still want to come back to the hooch and write you about our conversation. Does that make sense? Well, it does to me, and I really get excited sometimes when I get the time to write you.

I know it may seem as though I've bitched a lot throughout this journal, but even here, typing this journal and staring into this screen, you're still my sounding board. I do so love you my darling Helen. You truly are my everything.

1850 hrs.

Hello my love. I just got back from supper a little while ago. Just like every day, they had chicken again. I do love chicken; actually, I love your chicken. The Indians that cook the food at the DFAC must know about 200 different ways to cook chicken. It's better than MRE's, but it does get old after a while.

I was thinking tonight about family. I told myself that I wouldn't allow my family to bother me anymore, especially here. I was thinking about it today though, about Gary and the twins. Both my parents didn't have much involvement with me when I was growing up, and I think that has everything to do with this stuff. And now that they've become accustomed to being so distant from me, I suppose I can see how they see no problem with treating us like they have. I still can't believe my mother, taking advantage of us like she did, and then treating you and the kids like crap after I left. My Dad, not having ever seen Abigail, or coming to our wedding, and then going to

Tracy's wedding and staying at her parents house. I think that you and I are the only ones who can see the irony and absolute disrespect and malice caused by all this.

I'm not so upset about all of this stuff anymore. I almost started to think about what was so wrong with me to make my parents treat us this way. But then I thought about how I must have some worth because you chose me my love. Not only that, but God has blessed us with five beautiful and healthy children. Remembering this makes me feel better about everything. I love you so much my darling.

2125 hrs.

My darling, I was just outside playing with a new toy that I traded a knife for from a buddy of mine, and I met up with Nick. I told him that I got a heads up from the LT that we were on for a mission tomorrow afternoon for PSD. He told me that he had already heard about it, and was briefed by the commander the other day when Rafael and the LT were out on their mandatory cache search. The command did this because of people like Rafael who don't realize how rough it can be outside the wire, and so they get in touch with what their soldiers are going through. Good idea, but I don't think it made any impact with him. Anyhow, apparently tomorrow's mission is classified, and Nick said that he was hesitant to tell me for no other reason that he was sworn to secrecy due to the vital nature of the mission. I probably shouldn't even be writing about it in this journal, but I do because if the worst should occur, I want you to know everything that I could possibly tell you . . . in person or not.

Tomorrow, the coalition is releasing between 300 and 400 insurgents that have been captured and such by the Coalition. Apparently, they're having a big 'get out of jail' party, and our intelligence guys found out about it. We've been slipping our people out to the other camps for days now, strategically placing them in tactical locations to get ready for this offensive. At a specific time tomorrow, the EOD guys are going to do a controlled detonation to simulate an IED strike by the enemy. When that happens, we'll roll out the gate to 'simulate' rolling out to investigate the IED. Also at that time, our other forces will converge on this 'party' simultaneously with the appropriate agencies as well to get whatever intelligence we can get. It's a Classified, but high profile/high importance mission at the same time. I'm just glad to be a part of it, and we'll be doing what we do best out here. The hunting team rides again.

Early in my career, I used to only dream about doing things like this. Nowadays, I only look forward to things like this due to their strategic importance to our mission as well as the fact that if they're successful than it may bring us a bit closer to home. I can only pray that it will. I used to think that even above family or anything, defending our country was the most important thing ever. I still agree that it's very important and I still believe in it very much; but it's not the most important thing in my life anymore. I can assure you of this. You and the children are the most important things in my life my darling. I suppose that I used to be a bit misguided or 'brainwashed' as most would call it. I know I always thought that I had a higher degree of dedication to the Army and the country than most, and I suppose I also thought that one would compliment the other; family and duty. Now I realize that they can compliment each other, and even coexist peacefully with one another, but in moderation.

I write this to you now my love because I want you to know this is what I believe. Please always know that no matter what I have to do to provide for our family, I surely will, but nothing, repeat nothing will ever supercede you and the children. Being away from you for this long is the hardest thing that I've ever had to do. It is the test of all tests of my life thus far. I love you my darling Helen, more than anything on this earth, and I always will. There's no doubt in my mind that tomorrow will be dangerous, especially when the cat's out of the bag, and it becomes obvious what we really left the gate for. I can live with this, especially if it gets us home a little sooner, or takes care of some horribly bad people. Either way, I know it will have an inevitably positive effect on the safety of my family in the long run, no matter how small. I love you my darling.

26 MAR 04 D + 158 2020 hrs.

Good evening my love. Well, the highlight of my day was that I got to once again talk t you my love. I still feel a bit awkward about calling you at around 0400 your time. I had some down time today, and quite honestly I think I was just very lonely. It was great to hear your voice honey. It soothes me, and comforts me in ways that I couldn't begin to find words for.

Today was actually mission # 71 for me. It was a short and sweet little observation mission to the bridge that we use to go over to Champion and back. We were actually back within an hour. The whole deal with the SF guys apparently went down okay, but the need for us didn't come up thankfully. In all reality, if we'd been called out for this then it most likely would have been a full-scale battle. Thank God for small favors.

Tomorrow, we're going out again, this time to an area called the Snake Pit. It's a small outpost on the outer fringe of town. We're escorting some engineer equipment there to help build another ICDC facility. After that, we'll start planning our trip on Monday. Early Monday morning we leave for LSA Anaconda to escort a supply and logistics run. It will be the longest PSD mission yet. It's 4 hours one way, and we'll also be spending the night there as well. Everyone is looking forward to getting away for a day or so, and I think it will do the platoon a lot of good to get away from the norm, as it were. We've got rehearsals on Sunday for the trip, and we'll be on the road a lot during the next week. I pray that everyone is safe, both here and at home, and we get through everything incident free. I love you honey. Kiss you later.

27 MAR 04 D + 159 0520 hrs.

Good morning my love. I just got back from the tent. I was only able to talk to you for about 20 minutes or so, but it's better than none at all. You were at one of the girls' house, having a barbecue. I really am glad for that, in that you're able to get out of the house. I really appreciate you forwarding the house phone to your cell phone too. You always take such good care of me. I feel so lost and lonely right now. I need you so badly my love. I told you on the phone this morning that I really can't even imagine what it would be like to be home right now, and not have to worry or concern myself with al the things that I do now. I will tell you this though. I can't wait to find out what it's like.

I have to get the guys up in about 10 minutes or so, and get ready for today's mission. Our first mission is for PSD. It shouldn't last too terribly long, although any time outside the wire makes you get old fast. When we get back, we're supposed to help out the same Engineer unit do some work on the softball field that they're building here. I think it's absolutely ridiculous to build a softball field here, but then again, they really are trying to turn this into a garrison post.

The Marines are renaming all the camps in their AOR (area of responsibility). After today, we will be called Camp Ar Ramadi. Our mailing address won't change; it's just another little thing the Marines are doing to show that they are now running the mission. They're really starting to get on my nerves. Oh well, I suppose after all we've got accustomed to in the last seven months, a few more months of this won't kill us . . . . I hope.

Well, the men are now up, and they look like stir fried crap. Everyone I constantly tired, and although we had half a day off yesterday, I think everyone was actually bored, and is looking forward to today's missions. I am looking forward to Monday, because the town of Balad is the only town on the route to LSA Anaconda, so the trip will be mostly through the open desert. It will be a nice opportunity for some pictures I hope, and I'll get some to you a son as I can. I love you my darling. Kiss you later.

0645 hrs.

Hello my love. I haven't stopped thinking about you this morning at all. Not that I ever do, but after we got the trucks ready early, I sent the men off to chow, and decided to stay back myself and eat some pound cake that Simmons got in the mail from is aunt. Really good stuff. I know I'm not eating nearly as well as I should, and I do feel a bit depressed today.

I miss you and the kids so badly today. I miss dancing a lot today. I've been listening to our music a lot lately, almost to the point of being a distraction. I miss dancing with you out on a hardwood floor, and dancing Abby to sleep at night. At the rate she's growing, I have my doubts as to whether she'll even remember the song. I remember dancing out on that ball field at the Missouri State Fair with her as Jeff Carson sang our song for us live. That was a miraculous event for me, and as a father, I was filled with so much love, pride, and sheer joy.

I must have told the story of our first dances at the Palomino, the night you gave me your number, about a hundred times now . . . the last time being this morning. As

I sit here writing to you, I am lost in my own reminiscence and our songs bring me closer and closer to you from across the miles. I love you so much my darling. I have to go now, but I'll call you after we get back.

2330 hrs.

Hello my love. Well, as I sit here writing, I am literally exhausted from the day's activities. The temperature was 90 plus, and then I had two missions outside the gate as well. Our first one went really slow, but really well. I define a mission going well as getting everyone backs in one piece. The whole platoon went out this morning, but only Simmons and I went out on the last one.

We were briefed that we had less than an hour to get ready to go downtown Ar Ramadi to distribute water to a nearby village because their main water line had broken, and the water they did have was tainted somehow. The desert is no place to be without water.

I can't tell you honey, how it just tore my heart out to see those kids. A lot of the kids that come to the gate to sell us stuff live in that neighborhood. It was somewhat nice to see some familiar faces, and it surely was for them as well. There's one little boy named Ahmed, that comes to the gate just about every day. He brings knives, lighters, and cold sodas, but not until after school and helping his mother out. I sincerely believe that he's a good kid, and I was pleasantly surprised when he ran up and gave me a hug in the middle of the street. For the first time since we've been here, I actually saw the innocence of a child. He introduced me to his mother and sister. It was almost as if he was proud to have me as his friend. I slipped him two dollars in a handshake before I left, and his smile was as big as it could be.

Ahmed is an exception, for sure. The impoverished neighborhood that we walked through yesterday was full of kids that were all glad to see us, but most were less fortunate than my little buddy Ahmed. As Simmons and I walked down the street, carrying heavy buckets of water for the older women, the children would cling to us like a moth to a flame.

There was another little girl, whose name I don't know. She ran alongside the truck as we went from street to street delivering water, and stayed right by us when we stopped. She was absolutely adorable, and had a smile that you wouldn't expect to see from a child living in the slums. She had no shoes, and she was very dirty, with a torn shirt and a little ponytail. She asked me for some water, and I gave her the bottle out of my own pocket. Under all that dirt and dust, there stood a beautiful child and I saw the hope of an entire generation in her smile. Obviously, I was very touched, and I smiled politely when she kept asking us for some chocolate, but we had none to give. We usually carry a Tupperware container full of candy in our trucks for the kids we see along the way. Due to the fact that it was a last minute mission and the truck was not mine, we didn't have any with us. We're not too used to any Iraqi's smiling at us, so her smile was a welcome one. I felt so bad, and I think I wished nothing more than to have been able to have given her a piece of chocolate. I think the water helped more with our image and public relations than it did with the actual water problem.

Although there were a few moments of joy, it was still very, very sad. I don't think that I'll ever forget the images I saw, nor the hope of a nation in their smiles. I pray that things do get better here, and that their future is brighter than their present.

I find myself getting emotionally hardened because of my environment here. I miss you and the children every day, my love. I found myself with my eyes watering for about four hours after we got back. I didn't notice it until this evening that my eyes weren't watering because of the sun and dust, but because I was crying. Not crying like you and I might normally think of it, but silently, and minus a few ears, not even outwardly. It's the first time I've ever experienced something of that magnitude, and my inner sadness crept outside with no apparent help from me.

Today was one of the most rewarding . . . and saddest days of my life.

The Steel Horse – My gun crew and I were incredibly tight after a year of combat together. We were fortunate not to lose a single man, however we did have a few minor injuries over the course of the year.

29 MAR 04 D + 161 1845 hrs.

Hello my love. I have to tell you that so much has happened, which, by now you already know of course. Today was a busy day, and after the firefight, we are all very fortunate to be alive. On the way to LSA Anaconda today, we ran into an ambush. The enemy was very well coordinated, and more aggressive than I've ever seen. They've really been getting bold lately, and today was the highlight of that new mentality. All in all, our men did really well, and although we had three casualties, they were minor, considering they could have been so much worse. SGT Nuin, a buddy of mine had a bullet rip through the steel door of his Hummer, and all kinds of shrapnel get into his hand as he was closing the door. The other two were from DECON. SPC Kongsy, who was a gunner today, had a bullet rip through the back of the truck, ricochet off of a metal cot leg, and graze his leg. It was a flesh wound, and although it bled quite a bit, he held his tongue. I told him to squeeze my hand for the pain, and that he did. He damn near cut off my circulation, but I'm just glad that I could be there for him. PFC Valencia had a round go through the window of the door behind him, cut through the top of the headrest on top of his seat, and impact his upper left shoulder, and then ricochet up and tag his ear pretty good. His shoulder has a huge bruise where the round impacted, and he's okay for the most part. He wasn't sitting up straight at the time, thank God. Our guys did absolutely great today. I couldn't be more proud of them.

I got to talk to you a little bit today after we got back. You were at the psychologist with Kevin, and I certainly hope that the Doc isn't giving you any crap and genuinely wants what's best for Kevin. I suppose we'll see.

I love you so much my darling. All I could think about today was getting home to you in one piece. After the battle, which lasted about 30 minutes, I really had a little time to reflect on what had happened, and when you have a great life with great people, like your best friend who love you, and then it makes it a bit easier to fight, even when it's fighting for your life.

1 APR 04 D + 164 0555 hrs.

Hello my love. It's been a few days since I've written here, and I've been unable to call you since just after the ambush on our convoy due to the phones being down. The day after our ambush, we heard of the Marines getting hit just about a mile outside of Ogden Gate. Their convoy hit an IED, and when the vehicle was disabled, they finished off the truck with an RPG. Just yesterday, we took a huge convoy to Habbaniyah to escort the Battalion leadership there to see Bravo Company. Yesterday morning, an Armored Personnel Carrier hit an IED in the center of the road while on patrol. Not so unlike our ambush with a sustained fight ensuing, this IED was different. The explosion was absolutely huge, creating a crater about 8 feet wide and 10 feet deep.

The armored vehicle was hurled about 50 feet forward, and completely destroyed in an instant. The five soldiers inside the track were killed instantly, bringing the total for Bravo Company up to 9 KIA since our arrival here. This is what's known as a 'catastrophic kill', which means that the vehicle and everyone in it has been killed and/or destroyed. This is an absolutely terrible thing.

The first thoughts that raced through my mind were of Matt, Mo, and Kurt, who are all in Bravo at Camp Manhattan in Habbaniyah. Once we got there, I found the guys right away, and I found Matt sitting on the floor in the middle of a pile of gear and personal stuff. He was taking inventory on one of the fallen soldiers' possessions, and getting it ready to ship it back home. It was a very silent and solemn time, and I've never seen Matt like that. I begged him to stay out of a line company and just stay at Battalion working with staff. Shortly after that, I ran into Mo, and he could hardly speak. At the time of the explosion, he was in a track behind the one that blew up, and was going too fast to slow down in time. His track couldn't stop in time and drove into the crater. Now stuck, he and his men had to dismount and go forward on foot. I saw a sadness in his eyes that no one should ever have to experience. Three of the five that were killed were in his old squad. He told me of how he promised them all when he got there that he'd bring them all home. I did my best to console him in that it was in no way his fault. He still felt terrible.

So, that was our first convoy for us after our worst convoy. That's always a tricky one, because the last thing that most people remember is how hairy the last one was, and they're constantly wondering if it's going to happen again. Thankfully, yesterday we convoyed to Manhattan, then Champion Main, and then back to Camp J.C. So, with three missions under our belt now since the worst one for us, I'm hoping that our guys are getting their confidence back about being on the road.

We changed the truck assignments around, and now our Platoon Sergeant is in charge of my truck. This isn't such a bad thing though. The assignment that I now have is the one that he wanted, and he's very bitter about it. But his motivation was false motivation, and although he said that he wanted it, I doubt very seriously that this was true. My new assignment is the NCOIC of the dismounts. We no longer call them passengers in vehicles anymore, they're dismounts. If we come under fire from snipers, hajjis in a building, house, or palm grove, then all my guys, of which there are eight, dismount their vehicles from throughout the convoy, and assemble on me. I split us up into two teams, Alpha and Bravo. At this point, we maneuver on foot over the terrain, city, whatever it may be, and go hunt down and kill the enemy threat. I realize that you would probably have a heart attack if you knew this right now my love, so in a small way it's a blessing that the phones are down right now. I only say that for your sake honey; I actually wish the phones were still up and running because I have missed talking to you so desperately over the last couple of days. These last days have been so rough here, I can't even tell you. I can write every detail in this journal, but the emotional load that comes with it cannot be described. I just don't have the words.

2300 hrs.

Hello again my darling. Well, I finally got to talk to you tonight for a little while. I consider us fortunate to have the opportunity again. When the phones go down, and then come back up again, everyone and their brother is waiting to get on. It's a real pain with all the Marines here, but there's no getting around it. There used to be only 1650 troops here, and now there are upwards to 3000. The space doesn't get any bigger, but the lines certainly do. Oh well, I just wanted to write a little something before I turn in for the night. I love you so much my darling. You're my best friend in the whole world my love.

2 APR 04 D + 165 0645 hrs.

Good morning my darling. As you now know, I got up at an un-Godly hour this morning, about 0330 to call you. I haven't slept very well without you, and after Monday's ambush I haven't slept at all. I get up at all hours of the night, dreaming about the firefight and trying to fine-tune the battle in my head. At least everyone made it home in one piece.

I was so glad to hear your voice this morning my love. You told me of Abigail starting day care tomorrow. I'm actually glad that we found this, because it will enable you to get some 'Helen time'. I know by now that you must need that pretty desperately at times. Our baby girl in daycare . . . I can hardly imagine that. I can hardly imagine a lot of things these days, however, I live for the day when I can again. I won't have to imagine anything then, because I'll be home again.

I also talked to you about receiving the Easter box that you sent. I loved it honey. It was so nice of you to think about al the little things that you know I like. I must confess though, that I did dive into some of the chocolate already. As you know, there's nothing like that out here, and to be quite honest, with as much as we're outside the wire these days, I just want to make sure that I'm still alive to enjoy it. If I'm at home right now, and you're reading this, you'll probably be thinking something like, 'don't say that, that's terrible!' If I'm not, then you know I was right about the chocolate. I certainly hope that I was wrong.

Well, I must get going right now my love. I have to get the soldiers outside to check our trucks out and start the day. I love you my darling. Kiss you later.

1100 hrs.

Hey honey. It's about a half an hour before lunch here, and I'm bored out of my mind. I got the guys up early this morning, and we've checked out trucks, cleaned the hooch better than ever, fixed up our personal areas, and got water for the entire platoon for the week. I heard this afternoon that we're doing some drills for our new

POD teams to get everyone used to working together. I split up my dismounts into two teams, a primary and a backup. If I go down, or if my whole team goes down, medics will automatically come to our location and get them out, and I will continue on with the backup team. Most of the soldiers don't have any experience in dismounted patrols or ground tactics, so here's where I really get to shine. I want to get them trained up so that we can minimize our risks and prevent casualties. We can't train for every scenario, but I'll do whatever it takes to make sure that I get as much of what's in my head into theirs. All I want is to bring everyone I go out with home in one piece, one mission at a time, and then eventually home.

2245 hrs.

Tonight, my love, I have truly seen the face of my enemies. A buddy of mine gave me a captured video of terrorists planting IED's in the road. It even shows one of our tanks being struck by one of them, as well as them burying the one that got our five troops this past Wednesday. I made my troops watch it tonight to show how dedicated the enemy really is, and to give them a small but valuable insight into hajji's mentality. It really made me a bit ill to watch one of our tanks getting hit, even though no one died in that particular attack. What tore me up the worst was the one video of the enemy burying a huge IED that must have been about 300 lbs. of PE-4 (hajji version of dynamite), which was eventually the one that killed our boys this week.

I don't look forward to seeing Matt and Mo tomorrow, as they were close with all who lost their lives. I also don't look forward to hearing the roll call and Taps, which are synonymous with memorial services. It's saddening to even think about it really.

I'm going to try and get on the phone in the morning my love, to call you before we leave for Habbaniyah for the service. I love you honey.

3 APR 04 D + 166 0620 hrs.

Good morning my love. I just got off the phone with you, and it was so good to hear your voice. The kids were acting up while we were on the phone, and I could hear the 'tired' in your voice. I wish so badly that I could be home with you.

I'm afraid that I can only tell you now that something that I said this morning wasn't exactly true. I told you that I wasn't worried about anything happening today. I really didn't want you to worry in light of all the bad things that have happened recently. We are taking Highway 10 again today. The Battalion Commander likes to take it because the route is only 25 minutes, as opposed to the longer two-hour route that is much safer around TQ Air Base. I'm not really sure why he likes to take this route consistently, but it bothers all of us. I'd rather leave two hours early and ride through the open desert than through the city. On the route to Camp Manhattan in Habbaniyah, we have to go through a town called Khalidiyah, which is where we got hit with that IED that injured Simmons this past November. There are known terrorists in that town and it is believed that they have terrorist training camps there. It just doesn't give me a warm fuzzy to drive right through there just because it's faster.

Regardless of the route or the mission today, God willing we'll get promoted tonight. I'm not sure how I feel about that today. I'm supposed to stand there and accept accolades and be happy about a promotion just hours after I attend a memorial service for five of our fallen brothers. The memorial, in my mind, is the only thing that matters today; laying this ordeal to rest so to speak, and moving forward.

Last night, about 2330, hajji shot a bunch of mortars into the camp. They struck some of our vehicles and we pulled all of our guards out of there for the rest of the night. I ran outside to see what was going on because these wee the closest ones to date. They've never hit so deep inside the camp before. I think hajji is still testing his own capabilities, and getting intelligence from some of the day workers about where they may have hit.

The bay is very quiet right now, except for the sounds of my typing. Most of the men are sitting in their chairs with their eyes closed, taking a peaceful moment before the inevitable convoy. The convoy alone is a huge ordeal for us, coupled with the stress of attending the memorial. I suppose no one likes to be reminded of their own mortality. I can't wait to get home, around you and the children. Then and only then will fearing for my life on a daily basis be a distant memory.

4 APR 04 D + 167 0830 hrs.

Good morning my love. Well, as I thought before, we did get hit yesterday on the convoy out. There's just a certain irony about hitting an IED while on a convoy to another camp going to a memorial service. I don't believe that these people will ever stop. The good thing was that there were no casualties, and we got the trigger men. I cuffed them myself, and turned them over to an armor crew to be taken to a detention center.

After we got to Manhattan, we had to go fill out statements to send these guys to court with. There's even politics in taking POW's, but it's worth the paperwork to keep them out of our way. We finished up at the detention center just in time to make it back for the very end of the memorial service. I would have liked to been there for the whole thing. I saw Brian Mohammed and Kurt Mollenkopf, and they were both pretty down. I can imagine.

After we got back to Camp J.C., we had about two hours before the awards formation, so I sewed rank on another set of DCU's, and laid down for a little while. At the ceremony, everyone in the battalion must have stopped to shake hands. It was a very simple ceremony, and all I could think about was the five soldiers we bade farewell to just a few hours before. Once again, it really puts things in perspective.

LT Pirtle and LT Ebdrup gave me a present for my promotion, a Benchmade switchblade knife. It costs about $160, but they got it for nothing from a buddy in supply. Good stuff. I have lots of respect for those two LT's. I never thought the day would come when I would be able to say that, however, we've always ridden together out here, and there's a bond that blurs the officer/enlisted barrier. I've seen this before, but only with senior NCO to junior NCO, and it's very refreshing to see. Good stuff.

Well, I must lay down again my love. I got up very early this morning to call you, and I'm glad I did. Another Marine was killed from injuries received in an attack in Ar Ramadi last night. Apparently, an RPG was shot, and it blew his arm off. They kept him alive until they simply couldn't anymore. When he finally expired, the command decided to shut down the C-6 package, which, quite inconveniently, was in the middle of our phone call. I was glad, however, to have been able to get a few minutes with you while I could. After that, I went to take a shower and went off to eat breakfast with Murph. With him working in the TOC, and me being on the road all the time, we rarely have a chance to share a meal or just hang out, so it was nice. Then I hunted some materials down to put some training together for my hunting team. It's a really weird business we're in, and I'll just be glad when it's over. I love you so much honey.

5 APR 04 D + 168 2030 hrs.

Good evening my love. Well, we didn't hit the road at all today, but of course it was too good to be true. As I sit here typing this tonight, Operation Wild Bunch is ready to launch out of our camp. It's a Brigade-wide mission designed to hit multiple targets in the Ar Ramadi area. The PSD is now on standby to support either a sustained offensive operation including taking down three houses out in town that are chock full of bad guys. Most of them have been released recently from the coalition's custody in order to be used as bait. There is a mosque adjacent to the neighborhood where we'll be heading into, and it's not really a mosque at all. It's actually an anti-coalition stronghold, and will be watched like a hawk tonight. The mission kicks off around 0200, so we shouldn't be called until the wee hours of the morning.

I am very tired today. We trained very hard today, and had rehearsals for the mission for hours. That has become standard now, and it will be a long time before we get another break. Oh well.

I love you so much my darling, and absolutely cannot wait to be with you again. I'm going to try and get a little sleep tonight, so I can be as rested as possible for the mission tonight. I love you my darling. Kiss you later.

6 APR 04 D + 169 0630 hrs.

Good morning my love. Well, I can hardly believe it. I'm not sure what happened last night, and I probably won't find out until Dusty comes back in from the cache raids with Charlie Company, but we didn't get called last night. This is the first time in a long time that the PSD hasn't been called in over 24 hours. Operation Wild Bunch must have gone really well last night.

I sleep with a radio next to my head every night so I can get a jump on whatever is going on, especially if we get called. If I hear that the C-6 is going down in the middle of the night, then I just head over to the TOC to see Murph, and try and find out if it's one of our guys. It's certainly no way to live, surely if you like sleep, however, I can't sleep that well nowadays anyway, and I can't just lay there if I don't know if all of our guys are okay. Most of the time nowadays, it's the Marines that are getting killed left and right, and that's usually why the C-6 goes down. Too bad.

I am missing you more and more these days my love. I can't even find the words. I think that the level of depression that I'm experiencing is so deep rooted that sometimes I even find it hard to recognize. I watch the video that you sent al the time, and my wall behind my bed is laden with all sorts of pictures of you and the children. I still take time every night at 2200 hrs. to have a little 'us' time, even when I'm tired. It's funny, because even if I was at home right now and I was tired, then at least I'd have you right beside me, and we could be tired together. Sounds funny, but it's all the little things I miss.

The last picture you sent was a really good one honey. Your hair is getting so long; I know you must be happy about that. I think it looks great. I know that you've worked hard going to the gym while I'm gone, and I'm proud o you for that my love. You know it doesn't' really matter to me, because I love you anyway no matter what. I am, however, glad that it makes you as happy as it does.

Well, it's almost time to get the men up for the day. I'm not sure what's on the slate for today, but I'm sure we'll find some kind of training to do. It's all good in the end, and as a team, we are getting better by the day. It's great to see the troops evolve, especially after becoming battle-hardened through IED attacks, ambushes, and grenade and mortar attacks. Usually, some of the younger ones will retreat into their childhood mentality when that happens, but not our guys. They all seem to be doing really well. I'll get going now honey, and write more later on. I love you. Kiss you later.

0735 hrs.

Hey honey. I just found out that the mission apparently didn't go so well last night. The enemy, upon seeing our convoys heading into the Faruq neighborhood, a particularly bad area of Ar Ramadi and the site of the raids, shot up signal flares to their forces to signal our arrival. It's very similar to Somalia where the enemy would start burning tires to signal our helos arriving. This is such a bad place, I can't even tell you. It's looking worse and worse every day for the coalition, as far as the danger goes. These people have been fighting for centuries, and us being here isn't going to make the Sunni's and the Shiite's get along.

I honestly believe that if we pulled out al of our forces tomorrow; inside a month the whole country would be fighting again, and the Sunni's and the Kurds up in the mountains of northern Iraq would be all but eliminated due to genocide, and Iraq would be annihilated back to the stone age. It's very sad, especially for the children. I try to save an ounce of compassion, at least for them, but it's getting harder and harder for me to feel that way. I really am losing anything that I may have once had for these people. I just want to come home and be with you and the kids.

As I sit here, in this place, I am even starting to question my own moral character as far as my dedication to helping Iraq rebuild itself. This whole place is going to hell in a handbag, and I really don't think I care anymore about it. My dedication nowadays is only to getting my men home in one piece and being with you and the children. I love you so very much honey.

When I found out what happened last night, I decided not to go to breakfast, but instead 'tell' you what happened. I know there's a huge difference in being able to tell you in person, and writing to you in this journal, however, these days I'll take what I can get. I of course, can't mention this kind of thing over the phone right now, and it does give me great pains to not be able to do that. One day, we won't have to worry about the internet going down, or getting cut off on the phone, or waiting forever for the mail. I can't wait for that.

7 APR 04 D + 170 0015 hrs.

Good morning my love . . . early, early morning that is. Today was a very long day. We just finished escorting five detainees over to Hurricane Point for further questioning and to be turned over to the Marines. The five detainees were captured today in what was probably the bloodiest day of the war for us so far.

Last night operation, Operation Wild Bunch, was apparently not a complete wash. It was just prolonged until this afternoon. The Marines ended up getting pinned down at several locations all over the city, and we had to send in our M113 Armored Personnel Carriers with heavy machine guns to pull them out. We, the PSD, stayed on standby the entire day, and we ended up sitting in our trucks in front of the TOC listening to the battle unfold over the radio. When it finally came down that we would not be going out, we stood down, and went back to the hooch. We got a late supper, and tried to wind down for the night.

Tonight, we were introduced to Operation Reebok, which is designed to cordon off a certain section of the Faruq neighborhood, and try to do a snatch and grab on some local warlord. This is the neighborhood where most of the battle took place today. We heard later on in the day about how these fights were taking place as far away as Baghdad.

2010 hrs.

Hello my love. Today was another long day. We staged over at the 'Snake Pit', a small outpost of Marines on the outer fringe of town. We staged a task force of Armored Personnel Carriers, Bradley Fighting Vehicles, and armored humvee's over there for about five hours or so. It was a long, hot day to be geared up for so long, and it ended up with us going home again, without getting into the fight. The same thing happened yesterday afternoon, but the only difference was that we never left post. Many Marines died yesterday, and our Battalion had to go out and save their asses. We took no casualties, and from what we are told, our guys did really well.

Yesterday morning, we received information that one of the local clerics in the area declared 'jihad', or holy war on all coalition forces. By definition, a jihad is supposed to last 100 days. The last two days have been pretty bloody, and have lived up to the reputation of a middle-eastern brawl. Hajji has put up quite a fight, but we have given more than we've received. This local fanatical leader is fanning the fire between the coalition and an already unstable government. We think that he believes that if he causes a big mess and calls it a holy war, and then all Iraqi's will give up any kind of hope of rebuilding Iraq, and join in the fight against the coalition. It's a real mess over here right now.

I know you're not much for watching the news honey, but if you have lately I can only hope and pray that you're not worrying too much. This I certainly hope for, my love, but with an unrealistic expectation. I can only imagine what I would be thinking if our roles were reversed right now. I would probably be going out of my mind with worry.

The phones have been down for many days now due to the twelve or so Marine deaths yesterday, the six or so today, and a few more the day before yesterday. I'm not sure if I'll ever understand the Marines philosophy on fighting an urban war. They believe in fighting hand-to-hand, and house-to-house, no matter what. We even cleared our people out of a square kilometer grid yesterday so the artillery boys could start lobbing rounds in and take out anything that moved. The Marines denied our request to use artillery, even though our Brigade Commander told the Marine General that we were unnecessarily losing lives and blowing all our ammo away for no reason. I'll never understand that.

Tonight, we actually got to go to chow instead of getting plates to go like we have a lot lately. I should get to sleep soon because we have another mission kicking off at 0400, which means I'll probably have to get ready around 0230. This schedule never gets any better. Today's mission was # 86 for me. Every now and then we have a 'milkrun', something close to post and relatively easy, but it doesn't matter to me. It's all still outside the wire.

As I sit here typing to you, we're taking inbound mortar rounds yet again, the second time since 1800. They are coming just about every night now. It's sad, but nobody hardly gets up or even turns their head anymore, because it's so commonplace. The closest to our building that they've got was about 250 meters or so last week, and again last night. The enemy is getting bolder too, as they're firing a lot during the hours of daylight and deeper into the camp. I pray every day my love that this all ends sooner than later.

8 APR 04 D + 171 1900 hrs.

Hello my love. Today, this journal serves as a lifeline to you, though you'll not read it until after my return home. The phones have been down now for five days, since the holy war was declared on us, and the bloodbath started. There have been firefights every day throughout Ar Ramadi and Fallujah, and the Marines are running shifts, surrounding the city of Fallujah in order to squeeze the bad guys out. They've literally surrounded the city, and their efforts are continuous.

The OPTEMPO around here has been non-stop, and the men are always tired. We're constantly on standby, or on the road, or escorting EPW's from camp to camp. It's exactly what most people picture a war to be like. I've seen this before, and have prayed many a night that I might not again. However, the Marines and the Army do not share the same doctrine, and the Marines all seem to have ADHD. Although I can see some of the practicality in their tactics, I do not appreciate that we now fall under them. They don't seem to mind sacrificing their own, so we're sure they'll have no problem sending us out to slaughter. We've already bailed them out three times now. You'd think they would get the point.

On three occasions over the last five days, hajji has used mosques as firing positions. Obviously, these are not devout Muslim people, and are willing to use the sanctity of a holy place to store weapons and explosives.

I keep telling my men that they have to understand and respect the dedication that our enemies have. If our enemies were wise, they would do the same, however, they do not. Our dedication and resolve are still unwavering, and I am still proud to be here. I still, however, do not have anything for Iraq or its people. They are a mix of religious zealots, terrorists, and Saddam loyalists; there isn't' any hope for peace any time soon. We can't honestly expect to come in here after millennia of fighting and try to stop it inside a year.

These days are so lonely my love. I am missing you terribly, and sometimes fear the worst; that I might not lay my eyes on you again. This troubles me greatly, and I try not to think about it as much as it comes creeping into my head. PSD missions used to be short and sweet for the most part, though still outside the wire. Nowadays, we've melted into something they're now calling the Battalion Quick Reaction Force. Unfortunately, I have a lot of experience in these matters, and I've been told on many occasions about how people are glad that I'm leading the dismount (hunting) team. They say that I have the 'right mentality' for it, whatever that means. The men follow without flaw, and are getting really good at our tactics. I see the hunger in their eyes as the radio calls out to us every day. They're sometimes exhausted, and still get really pumped up about going out. I am really proud to be associated with these men.

2210 hrs.

As I lay here awake, again, I am finding it very difficult to sleep at all. We are on standby yet again for another night mission. We're expecting another VBIED somewhere in the city tonight, and are on standby along with the Engineers to provide security for the impending rubble removal operation. I lay here thinking about something that has yet to happen. It's really weird, but an expected threat nonetheless.

I also think about the battles yet to be fought. I am reminded every day in the eyes of the three soldiers in our platoon that have been injured, and the off the cuff stories I hear bits and pieces of about the ones we've lost already that I never knew. I listen intently to those stories, as if to somehow gain an understanding about them, yet I'm also denied in knowing anything further because they'll never be back with us again.

Tonight, I'm thinking of you and the children a lot my love. Since the day you told me about losing your father as a little girl, I've always felt some sort of regret in that, and so much sympathy for your mother as well. I wouldn't want you, Abby, or the boys to ever have to go through that; however it is getting really hairy around here lately.

My thoughts are as choppy as my writing tonight my darling. My mind is going in a million different directions, and it always leads back to you. You're my salvation, my love. You're my anchor. You are the very roots of my life, and as I cannot tell you right now, I must at least write you that I am clinging to you as much now as ever. I love you with everything that I am.

Last week, at our ambush, I think I felt something different in battle than I ever have. When I took aim and killed that guy out in the field, I really think I shot so well not so much because he was trying to kill me, but because if he were even slightly successful, then it would have hurt you my love. Don't get me wrong, I'm glad that I dropped that guy. I would do anything for you my darling, and as twisted as it may seem, I'd even kill for you. I already have, and I'll do it a million more times to make sure that I come home to you. You're my everything and you always have been.

I got to pick the movie for the night tonight. I'll give you a clue what it was. Do you know why I wanted to marry you? So I could kiss you any time I want . . . I love you honey. Kiss you later.

9 APR 04 D + 172 2010 hrs.

Hello my love. I'm so glad that I got to talk to you this morning. I know it was brief; however I was definitely thankful for the opportunity. I could tell by our conversation that we now have something else in common, and that is a deep rooted depression caused by the separation. I have never needed anyone or anything so much in my entire life my love. You are my soul mate, and my heart longs for you across the world.

So much has happened here lately; so much it's hard to even write it all down. After we spoke this morning, another Marine was killed out in town, and the C-6 was shut down again. Everyone was of course disappointed; however, unfortunately this is becoming a routine thing here. I truly hate all the losses we've had here. I don't care about the politics or the influence . . . just getting home to you in one piece my love.

2210 hrs.

I just returned from the shower, a nice one too. It was my first in five days, after an exhausting schedule of being on the road and battle planning, training the dismounts, and basically being in a reactive mode even more so than when I was a firefighter. I am simply worn out, and you and the children are all I think about anymore honey. I have had to train my mind to prioritize my entire life as if I'm fighting for it every single day . . . because we are. With each new day brings a new opportunity to be in harms way. I'm being sarcastic of course; it's no opportunity at all.

Earlier this evening, we were returning from mission # 87, a short haul just outside the wire to escort some bulldozers doing some excavation work. On our way back in, we were actually on the camp, well inside, when a mortar was shot at the camp and landed not 20 feet from my truck. The dozer operator in front of us must have been scared because he stopped instantly, giving us nowhere to go. It was only seconds later, but we were moving again, and got back to the hooch unharmed. We were all a little shook up, but none the worse for wear.

10 APR 4 D + 173 0420 hrs.

Good morning my love. We just returned to the bay after mounting the trucks and moving out to our staging area for the latest big mission. Today, the whole Brigade is involved. We are hitting weapons caches, two mosques, and a few homes of some of the bad guys. We have been temporarily downgraded to REDCON (Ready Condition) 2. This means that we are on a 15-minute string, and although we are allowed to lie down again, we must remain fully dressed. Everyone is exhausted, as we spent most of last night tailoring our trucks for today's mission.

One of the possible scenarios that we may be called upon for is to recover the dead and wounded, in conjunction with an ambulance escort into the hot zone. We were issued body bags this morning for this ominous task. Myself, and the rest of the leaders handled this one, as most of the young soldiers have mixed feelings on this. I do understand it, as I was in much the same position many years ago. Back then, each soldier was issued his/her own body bag, and most of us made hammocks out of them. Looking back, this was probably a defense mechanism in making light of a serious situation that no one wanted to think about. Seriously though, combined with an inflatable mattress a body bag makes a great hammock.

Well, we'll see how the day goes. I just checked a few minutes ago and the C-6 is still closed. I suppose the Marines aren't as quick to make notifications as we are. I hope we're on nothing more than standby today, and that all missions outside the wire go well to the point that they don't need us. All of us have been under fire, and in a lot of pretty hairy situations lately. I could surely do with one less. Tomorrow is Easter, and even though they despise Christianity here, I'm going to try and get up for the sunrise service, as long as we're not on mission. I'd really like to see Easter come and go without any bloodshed.

It's now 0500, and after getting only 2 ½ hours of sleep last night because of the incident with my soldier, I'm going to go lay down now my love. I did wake up dreaming of you this morning, however. We were walking down our street, hand in hand, and it was so nice. It was one of those weird dreams though. We looked up in the air to see a helicopter, and the sound of a Blackhawk outside is what inevitably woke me up today. My dreams are mixing with my reality. Weird, huh? I wish being at home with you were my reality now my love. I'll write more later my darling. Kiss you later.

1900 hrs.

After lying down again, I crashed pretty hard this morning. About 1000 hrs. we were downgraded to a REDCON 3, which is still a 30 minute string, but better than a 1 or a 2, to be sure. After that, I made a cup of noodles for lunch, and then went to the PX to get you a Mother's Day card. I couldn't find any birthday cards for the twins, because the PX doesn't carry any. I went back to the hooch, and, still being hungry, ate an entire jar of Tostitos salsa and a bag of Frito Lay scoops. It did take a while, and of course I was stuffed when I was done with it, but it was nice to lounge around for a few hours and do absolutely nothing for a change. Then I got to take a nap, and fill out your cards. If I had the opportunity, I would have called you. But of course, the C-6 is still down. We didn't hear much about the battle today. The radio was pretty quiet, at least the three or four times that I went out to the truck to listen in. The Marines had a few more wounded, and a guy from our Battalion fell off his tracked vehicle when an RPG was fired his way. We heard that he just landed hard on his ass, and was not injured due to the RPG at all. Finally . . . good news.

2055 hrs.

I am missing you so very much today my darling. I know I keep repeating myself, but I cannot stand it today. Today is one of those days that we have an unusually large amount of time by ourselves, and unfortunately, a lot of time to think. These days are very long for me, as I think of you and the children constantly. Today is the first day in nine straight days that I can actually sleep in my PT uniform, because we have planned PT tomorrow. Otherwise, I'd be sleeping in my pants and brown t-shirt just like usual. I have slept in my clothes for seven months now, and I can't even imagine crawling in bed wearing nothing. Believe me though, I'd like to, for sure. I look forward to all the things I want to experience with you again my love. I really do. I just hope that I don't disappoint you in any way. I already know that you are different, and this tour is different as well, so I'm sure the homecoming will be different as well.

Other than that, the day was pretty uneventful, and it will all change of course tomorrow. We have OP Guard, which is like the PSD (QRF), except we go just outside the wire, about 100 meters or so, and with only one or two gun ships. I'd like to say that it's at the very least relatively safe, but after the mortar almost tagged us just yesterday, I'll have to think twice about that. I'll pray tonight about it, and hope that the phones are up again tomorrow. It won't be a complete loss tomorrow, because after platoon football for PT, my OP shift doesn't start until 1115 hrs., and ends at 1400 hrs. Then, I can relax a little, and hand wash my laundry. I acquired an antique washboard, and the platoon already has buckets, so it shouldn't take too long. Ever since the jihad started the other day, no contractors have been allowed to come on post, including the laundry guys, who currently have about half of my clothes. Oh well, maybe I'll get them back by the end of the tour. I'm going to try and get a good night's sleep tonight, so I can be on top of things tomorrow. I love you my darling.

11 APR 04 D + 174 2125 hrs.

Well, I did get through to you this morning, even though the phone connection was broken up and there was a lot of interference. It does at least make me feel a little better knowing that you know that I'm okay. I worry that you fear the worst when a few days go by without me being able to call. I know that this is war, and you know that I've seen this before but this is really bad lately around here. It's the Wild West around Ar Ramadi, and I can't wait to get home to you my love.

12 APR 04 D + 175 2315 hrs.

Good evening my love. I can't tell you what an absolute pleasure it was to hear your voice today . . . . twice. I was listening intently on everything you said today. How tired you were, how your work day was going to be short, and how Kevin and Abby were better behaved in pictures than they were on video. I love hearing all the little things about your day my love, all the things that I'm missing right now. I know you have different shoes to fill than I right now, but I do sincerely admire you for all you do, and al that you are. I miss every little detail about you my darling. I miss it all, from the way you open your eyes halfway with your face half buried in the pillow when I get up too early, and then lay next to you staring at you hoping you'll get up sooner than you want, to the way you walk out of the house with such confidence when you clean up and do your hair and we're going somewhere. I miss the way your perfume smells, and the angelic sound of your voice when we're lying down for the night and you tell me that you love me. I don't know if you can tell, but I am missing you a lot today. There is so much going on at home right now, and I hate to miss even one second of it. Then again, there's so much going on here right now too, and I would give my life to shelter you and the children from any of it.

13 APR 04 D + 176 2140 hrs.

Hello my love. Today was an extremely long, hot day. I'm glad we had the opportunity to share pictures and talk on the phone as well. The Marines didn't have any missions today outside the wire, so of course the C-6 remained open all day. I'll probably get up early to call you again tomorrow morning. I would do it tonight, but in addition to pulling security for the construction engineers who are building the new gray water sums for the used shower water, we're also on standby for a raid tomorrow morning at another bad guys house. There are so many out here. It just seems to never end.

Even with all the crap that comes with this place, and the daily stress that compresses in so many areas of my life, the comfort of your voice and the promise that it gives me is comforting beyond words. It gives me solace in the many stressful times of my day.

There have been many days lately honey that, although I have prayed about it many times I have actually doubted that I might make it home. The dangers in this place are many, and around every corner. I just don't understand how these people don't pick up their kids and move away from here. There isn't much hope among the locals here, just trying to survive from day to day . . . just like us. There is an evil here as well, my love. I really can't put my finger on it, but overall there are so many people that are Muslim, of course. Christianity is a severe minority here, about .001%. That's even more than I would have thought of, but surely not enough to make a difference here. They believe in Allah, their God, and preach peace; however they rule this land by waving a gun.

I can't tell you how much of a relief it is for me to know that you and our children will never now this as a way of life. And if me being here for a year or longer ensures that things stay that way, then I'm okay with that. I could never write you enough or send you enough pictures to show you the poverty, disease, violence, and uncivilized and degrading human treatment that go on here every single day.

My darling, I love you more than anything on this earth. And even though I do have my moments of doubt as to my own survival over here, I want you to know that you are always the first and last thing on my mind . . . . always. You are my life, my everything, and I love you with all that I am. I'm going to get ready for bed now honey. We have another long, hot day ahead of us tomorrow, and I have to start drinking more water, which there is a shortage of right now. Hajji is hitting our convoys and blowing up bridges to interrupt our supply lines, and we're starting to feel it lately. Anyway, I love you my darling. Kiss you later.

14 APR 04 D + 177 0700 hrs.

Good morning my love. I got on the internet this morning, and got another bullshit email from Emily. They keep talking about me coming home in July, and I corrected them, yet again. They just have no clue. They said there's another box on the way, and I told them with the way things were going right now that hajji probably had it by now. I also mentioned about how the phone and internet goes down every time there are casualties as well as the food and water shortages right now due to hajji hitting our log convoys and blowing bridges up.

It's now 0710, and our new LT just walked in and told us that someone just got killed, so of course the C-6 is down again. Nothing new here, unfortunately. I wonder who it could be, and just hope it's no one in our unit. There were two operations that kicked off this morning about 0500. The first one was Operation Nike, which was to take down a house not four or five blocks from Ogden Gate to find some bad guy. The second was Operation County Fair III, an operation designed to raid a certain portion of the Faruq neighborhood. That place has a huge soccer stadium near it, and is terrorist central. Throughout the States, there are some bad neighborhoods, but nothing like this at all.

Well, today we're still on Operation Dog Watch, providing security for the engineers again. It's long, hot, and boring, but it keeps us busy. We've only got about another 90 to 100 days or so, if all goes well, until we start packing it up to drive down to Kuwait. I can't even imagine that day, my love. It's about a three or four day convoy, and I can almost picture every mile. I'm sure it will be liberating in a way, however, that's a long time to be on the road. The last convoy . . . one day.

Well, I have to go and start the day now. All the troopers are off to breakfast now, and I actually have a little time to myself, a rare commodity nowadays. I have some reheated coffee on from last night, and I'll put the notes out to the soldiers from last nights leader's meeting as well.

15 APR 04 D + 178 0200 hrs.

Good morning my love. It's very early now, and we just got back from a mission that came up last minute. It was Operation Rawhide (North), about two hours away from here. It seemed like the entire Brigade was out there, and I've never seen so much armor and tanks in one place in my whole life. I'm really glad they were with us though. When we first rolled up to the area we would be in for the next 16 hours, the first thing we saw was three dead Iraqi's. Zhou said, 'It's looking good here already'. Zhou is my second in charge (2IC), and always throws these little jabs out there at the perfect time. He keeps me laughing. Then we rolled out to the field where they were killed earlier in the morning by the Infantry, and found a pretty elaborate bunker that they used to operate out of. That's when we did the rest. It was a very long day, but well spent I thought, overall. We did a lot of damage to the enemy today. I think the overall picture is that we are trying to send a message that we're not wiling to take this shit anymore and also that we're trying to take a proactive role in clearing he supply lines/routes as well. We have no choice, as failure is never an option here. If we fail, we will simply starve ourselves inside this hole we're in. Hajji is learning as much from us as we are from him, and he's learned to take advantage of it. To his credit, this has been very smart to exploit these vulnerabilities; however, we just have to continually counter them.

16 APR 04 D + 179 2015 hrs.

Hello my love. Well, today was a busy one. We started with change of command inventories with the new LT, 1LT Ratcliff. He's our new PL, sent over to us from 1/34 Armor in Habbaniyah. He's got some road time, but not as much as we do. I still think he'll be alright. He's originally from Anchorage. He's a paratrooper, and now all the senior leadership in the platoon are jumpers. Leaders . . . . jumpers . . . . coincidence, I think not. You know me honey, any excuse to take up for the Airborne.

After a short morning of inventories, we had a mission to Shark Base, the Special Ops compound just off Camp J.C., about halfway between J.C. and Champion. We met some really cool guys that had some weapons that even I've never seen before. They were SEAL's, Special Forces, ODA (Delta) guys, and CIA. They were more down to earth than I would have expected, but not different than the guys I used to know back at Bragg. I was talking to one of the Delta guys, and when I told him that we are the only Decon Platoon in theater, he mentioned that one of their contacts lead them to a place where they located some blister agent in large quantity. I told him that we haven't had the chance to do much actual Decon work, and he should get with Brigade to assign us to the task. After all, that's what we're supposed to do; find the bad stuff and go kill it whether it's toxic agent, or hajji. We escorted the engineers out there to beef up their security outside their camp a little.

After that, we returned to camp, only to find out that we had yet another mission. It was now 1500 or so, and this next one would take our guys all afternoon, until about 2000 hrs. to complete. That's not the unusual part. The weird thing about this mission is that it was to complete the softball field. Yes, for reasons unbeknownst to me, the chain of command built a softball field in the middle of the camp, and has really got a lot of effort, man-hours, and resources poured into this thing over the last month or so. Most of us think that it's utterly ridiculous to have such a thing here anyhow. None of us want to play softball, which you know I love, in 100 degree plus heat. The entire chain of command, I think, is really focused on this whole softball project in order to give us something else to focus on. The intentions are good, just bad timing I suppose. The morale isn't very high around the camp right now, and I honestly don't think I could get very motivated or excited about much right now, except maybe getting a definite date to go home.

I miss you so much my darling. The only thing I care about now is getting home to you again. There are so many things to worry about here, and I know I can't come home again until we've dealt with all of them.

Right now, there are only five days worth of food left on the camp, with none inbound in sight right now. Our supply lines have suffered great losses recently, and hajji is gaining ground in some areas. Our boys are out every day taking the fight to the enemy as best we can. Water is at a premium as well. There is a natural well just outside the gate, and we have a water purification team to purify it. It's not bottled water like we're used to, but it is still a bit rough. We're saving every bit of bottled water we have left for our QRF missions, and using the purified water from the well for drinking only. Then, we're using our water distributor trucks from our platoon to provide water for the entire battalion to do their laundry. There are no civilians allowed on post, still.

The only thing we still have is the port-o-jons, and the contractor lives on post with us as well. They remember us from the gate, and the escort lot, and they do seem to be nice. They're not hajjis though. There are no nice hajji's. The contractors for the port-o-jons and the trash are from Hungary. Their leader is a guy named Jonas. They're crazy rock and roll blaring Hungarians. Jonas, or Jon, as he likes to be called, and I have talked frequently over the last many months. He is a father of two, and is very happily married as well. He visited his homeland for two weeks a couple months ago, and seemed like he couldn't wait to get back to tell me about his wife and boys. It's nice actually having an adult conversation about things that mean the most to me, even if it is with a crazy Hungarian who loves American rock n roll. It's just nice to see that even in a place like this; other fathers around the world can still express their fatherly nature amongst each other, even if they're not from the same country. It's one of the few things that I have to look forward to here.

18 APR 04 D + 180 0700 hrs.

Good morning honey. Well, I only went to sleep a short five hours ago. It was well worth it though, as I got to talk to you for about 23 minutes the first time, then almost an hour just after that. Yesterday was about the worst day of the tour for me, emotionally that is. It was a long day of maintenance and repacking our QRF vehicles. The Brigade had a barbecue, and held a softball tournament with about ten teams playing. I do love softball, but for some reason not out here. It was very depressing for me, and instead of partaking in the festivities, I opted to take my squad over to the motor pool to play so well needed catch up. The afternoon was a bit slow with only a walk through of the barracks from the Command Sergeant Major. After that, everyone started to hibernate. I didn't even go to chow, but instead made a cup of noodles in our microwave. I really wanted to be home yesterday more than anything.

The first time we talked last night, I think that you and I were both trying to get everything out so fast that we just thought we might not have more than about ten or fifteen minutes to talk. That's when you told me about Dave having his accident, and him borrowing our truck. At first I was a bit jealous, having never driven it myself, but then irate when you told me they were driving it all over the place. By the time I called you back about thirty minutes later, you had already called Dave and Brandy, and told them that you wanted the truck returned as you and I agreed. This made me feel a little better, as it made me feel like you and I could make a decision together. Besides, Dave and Brandy haven't exactly been the best of friends since they got to Kansas. They don't have the type of marriage that we do, and they're users. Oh well, hopefully they'll see that and take care of that one day. Not our problem.

Apparently, you had quite the day with the kids yesterday. You told me of how you took them to Manhattan for the day, had ice cream, and pretty much wore them out. Good idea. I was a bit envious though, I must admit. But I'm glad that you had some quality time with them yesterday. I'm sure with everything going on since I've been gone that it was well needed and even much appreciated by the kids. I so wish that I could have been there.

I felt a lot better about my day though, as I came back to the hooch and started to lie down for the night. Talking to you, my love was the only thing that could have made me feel better yesterday, and I'm sure glad that I did. I love you so much honey. You told me about a song called 'Letters From Home', by John Michael Montgomery, and the words along had us both tearing up over the phone. That was the closest that I'd come to crying since leaving home. I tried so hard not to, but the tears just kept coming. It was good though, for both of us I think. It was yet another experience together, albeit an emotional one, but a rare opportunity nonetheless to share something in common. I love you so much my wife.

Well, I'm going to get up and enjoy a little bit of 'Ron time' before all the troopers get up. I love you honey. Kiss you later.

20 APR 04 D + 182 2130 hrs.

Hello my love. I haven't written for a couple days. Please excuse that. We have however spoken about three times in as many days. Between our talks, and hearing your voice; my spirits have truly lifted a lot lately. I miss you so much honey, and I long to be with you again. I felt bad for waking you up last night, as you woke to hearing our computer at home beeping to let you know I was online. I love to hear your voice when you first wake up. I can't wait until I can wake up to you again my love.

We just found out that tomorrow we're supposed to refit our vehicles and do rehearsals in preparation for a 36 hour mission. It's very similar to the one we went out on the other day. This time, the whole Brigade is going. Everyone has a piece of the pie, and our piece is still escorting engineer equipment, but it's more on the patrol and hunting team side of things this time. My men are already asleep, and as I look at them sleeping as peacefully as they can, I dread telling them that we'll be off post for 36 hours straight. No walls, no wire, just each other. We've done this before, but not for this long. Just when I think that we've experienced all there is to do here, something else comes up, and reminds me that it can, in fact, be worse.

I don't really mind though. I hate to say it, but today was rather boring and the men will probably look forward to getting out. I have seen it in their eyes, and it does concern me a bit. I have seen the taste that they crave. Most of my men have killed at least one enemy since our arrival, myself included, and after recent events I see the men craving to do it again. It's not a sadistic desire to kill, but, I believe, a means to an end. The end of the tour. It's almost as if we believe that if we kill all the enemy, then we'll get to go home. Our tour is still a year long, and if all the enemy were somehow eliminated tomorrow, we'd still be here trying to rebuild this God-forsaken place. It's almost surreal at times. I'm sure with all the news at home, the public has to be asking itself why we're still here. Funny thing, sometimes we do too.

When people ask me what kind of day I'm having, I still tell them, 'another day in paradise'. I still think of you and the children when I say it, because even here, in the worst place on earth, you are the guiding light that is the only true light of my day. I love you so.

Well, I have to get some rest my love. I'm going to bed here shortly, and have a busy day of checking and rechecking our gear. I love you so much and always have you in my heart.

21 APR 04 D + 183 1945 hrs.

Hello my love. I spoke to you a couple of hours ago, and was glad to get in touch with you. I was sorry to hear that Kevin wasn't' feeling well, but I'm sure he'll feel better with you home with him today. It was, as always, great to hear your voice honey. With tomorrow's big mission, the biggest so far for us, it's always great to hear your voice. It gives me just that extra bit of confidence. It really does seem to help. I told the men to bed down tonight before 2000 hrs., even if they're not sleeping yet. As I lay here now, I am starting to wind down a little from the briefings, packing the trucks, weapons maintenance, and everything else.

But now I have a few moments with you, my darling. I am missing you terribly as always, and am counting the days down as best I can. I am actually starting to see a light at the end of the tunnel now. I am trying to be optimistic, but it's hard sometimes when every day is a new opportunity to take a bullet. We're all just trying to survive one day at a time.

Well, I have to get up at 0100 hrs, with a rally time of 0200 hrs., and we'll actually leave the camp around 0400 hrs. We should be gone anywhere from 24 to 72 hours. I don't like these missions, where we basically 'circle the wagons', and sleep in shifts while most of my guys and I pull security wearing night vision goggles and don't get much sleep at all. Oh well, it can't last forever. It's hard for me to imagine how life will be in the rear. The War on Terrorism will still go on, but the first part will be over for us. Our Brigade has taken heavy losses, and it's not over until it's over. I just want to bring my men home in one piece. I'm going to sign off for now my darling. I love you so much honey, more than anything. I'll call as soon as we get back. Kiss you later.

23 APR 04 D + 185 0845 hrs.

Good morning honey. Well, our last mission was an apparent success. The route we were supposed to clear was in fact just that. Charlie Company went out earlier than the QRF, and we staggered the unit's times for leaving to keep a continuous flow of Coalition traffic on the roads. Dusty Sinkes told me that upon arrival to Objective Sheriff, the enemy was in place, waiting for us. What they didn't expect was for us to arrive in force with such large numbers of armored vehicles. The enemy ended up running, instead of staying to fight, and our guys found two IED's in place, which were then detonated by us instead of on us.

We left early and stayed late, but it ended up being worthwhile because we got 35 refrigerator trucks through to our camp by days end. Food. It's something that we normally take for granted, that it will always be there. This, of course, is not always the case. It was a big relief to see a full spread for breakfast this morning, so my troops tell me. I decided to hang back again, and have my usual coffee and have a little time to myself.

This morning, I sent out most of the troopers after breakfast for a rehearsal. Today's rehearsal is for tomorrow's Combat Patch ceremony. The Brigade is holding this ceremony as a matter of pride for the soldiers who are by now very worn out. A soldier is authorized to wear the combat patch after 30 continuous days served in a combat zone. We have surpassed that by leaps and bounds, however, I think the Brigade has been saving this for a time when the soldiers are starting to see a light at the end of the tunnel. Most of our guys are really worn out now, and most have expressed to me that they don't really care about sewing on a patch for their uniform, even a combat patch. I caught two of my guys up late the other night, though, sewing their combat patch on. As I walked by late to use the bathroom, I gave them a wink as they proudly continued their sewing. If anything, I hoped that I've fostered their pride in not only themselves, but their service as well.

Well, I finally finished your poem. It's taken me since December when I started it to put the finishing touches on it, and I believe it's ready for you my love. While on gate guard at Ogden Gate, there isn't much of anything to look at, except a lot of sand, and trash filled roads and wild dogs running around all the time looking for scraps of food. In the middle of this, possibly the world's most horrible place, are these tiny flowers of purple and gold that by some miracle seem to survive the wind storms, torrential rains, and tank tracks crushing the sand around them. It's a tiny little detail in the big picture here, but for some reason they caught my eye on more than one occasion. Anyway, you my love, and these tiny flowers were my inspiration. Here is your poem.

Ogden Flowers

Far away from home
And surrounded by the sand;
This place is my home for a while,
This flower dotted piece of land.

This place is not beautiful . . .
Maybe just a little piece,
But at times reminds me of us,
I have that at the very least.

In this desolate place
Where nothing seems to grow,
I've learned one thing
That perhaps you didn't know.

These flowers so strong
That stand as a pair;
Their tops so golden,
Just as your curled and flowing hair.

Patches of lavender flowing
As the breeze blows by,
Stained by the colors of sunset
Sent from a velvet desert sky.

They stand watch with me
And look so small.
These little sentries
Will outlast us all.

These long stemmed soldiers
With helmets of lavender and gold
Stand shoulder to shoulder,
Outnumbered but bold.

A light breeze on my face
Offers me comfort for a while;
A lighter moment it gives me
As if I were a child.

I see you in my dreams
Yet awake all the while;
Staring into the horizon . . .
I can hear your smile.

They are my allies
Waving bravely in the wind,
In this place consumed by evil
They have no sin.

As we stand our post,
No comfort of a cool morning dew,
I wonder which of us stands watch,
And who is watching who.

At day's end
With the setting of the sun;
Still standing tall
Together, they have won.

1730 hrs.

Hello my love. I regret that I didn't get a chance to call you back again yet today. I hate that so many things come up in this environment. By now, I expect it of course, but it's still irritating nonetheless. Well, I hope that you like your poem. I'm sorry it took me so long to finish it. It's difficult out here finding moments of inspiration.

As long as the C-6 is open later on, I'll try and call you later on. I know that Mike is supposed to arrive today, so it must be somewhat difficult today for you. I just hope that you and the kids can get through this visit without too much stress. It isn't stressing me as much as I thought it would, but then again, I haven't had too much down time to think about much else. I love you so much my love. I'm praying that all is going well for you, especially in the coming days.

2215 hrs.

I just got off of guard, which is pretty simple for us seeing as how all we do is sit on the front porch and watch the gun trucks parked outside. Nick and I came up with that, and our soldiers have no other details to perform. Motor pool guard, shower guard, gate guard, and a few other trivial taskings are no longer in our lives, and the soldiers are grateful for it.

I have had a little bit of time to think about things tonight, and I've decided that I'm not going to worry about Mike's visit. Sure, it helps with his grandfather being there, but that's not the only thing that I'm concerned about. I'm concerned about your nerves, and how stressed you already are about all this, and that's without him even being there.

I'm also concerned about Kevin. This is a very fragile situation for him, and I pray that Mike understands this before he arrives. I love Kevin as my own, because that's what he is now. I suppose I have a certain anxiety that I will never be able to control because Mike is his biological father, and I am not. I guess that that's one thing that Mike will always have over me, and it kills me to see him take that for granted. I really do hope that Kevin has a nice visit with his father; however I also hope that neither Kevin nor Mike expects a red carpet to be rolled out for him either.

As I lay here, the sand fleas are jumping all over the place, making me itch like crazy. Some people actually had to get medical treatment for them last year because they were so bad. I certainly hope that that doesn't happen to any of us. They say that they're really bad during the extreme heat, and usually around the ankles and belt line. Doesn't sound like too much fun. Well, I suppose my body is finally playing catch up with me, and I am very worn out from yesterday's mission. My ass is sore from sitting on a Kevlar panel, which is harder than our helmets, so it doesn't give very much room to give. My body feels drained now, and I have spent all day drinking about six bottles of water. I am rehydrated now, as are all the men. We surely needed it after wearing all of our gear for over 20 hours yesterday. Well, I'll sign off for now my love, and try to get some rest before PT tomorrow. I love you my darling. Kiss you later.

24 APR 04 D + 186 0430 hrs.

Good morning my love. I just got off the phone with you, and you sounded better than I expected for having Mike upstairs in our home playing XBOX with Kevin. I must admit, I suppose that I had a tad more anxiety about the whole thing than I let on, but not more than I can handle. I am surprisingly cool about the whole thing for some reason. I know that we have to put a certain amount of effort into this, in order to facilitate their relationship, but not foster the father/son relationship. That's Mike's job. However, I am sincerely hoping that this whole experience has given him a wake up call of sorts. I wrote earlier about how I thought that I was envious of Mike in one regard, and that's due to him being Kevin's biological father. This may be true to a degree; however, after talking to you this morning, and hearing of them having time together, I think that bothers me more than anything else about this whole deal. I wish that I could be home playing with Kevin right now. I will do my time though, and come home and have my time as well. It's just harder when I'm here, and not there. It always has, and it always will my love.

When I get home, there are a lot of things that I'd like to do, but there is something that I definitely don't want to do either. Last year, I was packing, and getting things ready to come over here, so I couldn't afford a lot of personal time with you and the kids when it came time to going to things like the Apple Day Festival on post, or checking out the post museum, and stuff like that. I am really looking forward to doing all that stuff this year. I just don't want to miss a thing my darling. I have missed you and our kids in this way for far too long now, and I have to say that I do not like it very much.

Well, I do have PT today. The platoon is playing flag football, and this old man is going to get beat up as usual. These young guys are brutal on me. After that, we have the combat patch ceremony, and maintenance, and then a G.I. party in the barracks for the Battalion CSM's walk through in the afternoon. By the time he actually comes through, we will be done with everything, and pretty much sitting around cleaning weapons. After he comes through, we'll be done for the day, and God willing, have some down time tomorrow as well. Just a chance to sleep in until about 0700 would be nice. We'll see. I love you my darling. Kiss you later.

2140 hrs.

Good evening my love. As I sit here writing to you this evening, the day has gone well overall, however there is a sense of irony in the air today. This is one of those weird days for me, as I've had a couple already like this since the beginning of the tour.

These days are bittersweet for me, and although they are not overly taxing to my heart and mind, however they still stand out as being unique. There is no battle involved, no enemy to fight, no wounded to care for, only the inner struggle that is my own. It is my struggle to accept things that invade my mind, and present an irony that I can't explain. The day of my promotion was one of those days. As you know by now, it started off with an IED filled convoy, and my team capturing the trigger man en route to a memorial service. After our return from Habbaniyah, we had the promotion ceremony to show the unit, so the commander says, that we will endure and still recognize excellence even in the wake of our tragedies.

Today was another such day. It started off simple enough, and although I was filled with joy to hear your voice again, however Mike was in our home. I have no fears or concern of our marriage my love, but as I also mentioned before, my envy for the time that Mike has with Kevin and around all of you as well. I make jokes, but in my reality here, I do empathize with his injuries, and shutter at the thought of facing you and our children with such horrific disfigurement. It really does concern me. I just pray that we all make it out here in one piece.

2345 hrs.

Hello again my love. I regret to make this entry this evening, especially at this late hour, as I have hurt you, which is the last thing that I would ever do willingly. I have felt like a caged animal these last two days, with the visit still in progress. I take great comfort in our marriage of course, but I wonder what Kevin is feeling right now, with his mother and father in the same place at the same time. I can only imagine that, as a 30 year old man at my brother's wedding, when the same thing happened to me, I felt some sense of relief, gratitude, and even at that late time in my life a false sense of hope that they still had a chance to be together . . . improbable as it may be. I know now, as I knew then that this was an impossible thing, but I think the reality of having them both there at the same time hurt more than even I could have imagined.

I feel that I may have been a bit selfish with this visit, and although Kevin must be overjoyed about his father's visit and showered with gifts, I certainly hope that he still knows what we've instilled in him. I pray that he still knows what is truly important, and that it's not material things. I'm sure he does, but in this short term fantasy of his, just as in mine years ago, I can't imagine that he wants to let it go. And when it comes time for his father to leave him again, I hope the reality of the situation doesn't come crashing down on him as it did me. I know all too well though; that whether it happens immediately after the conclusion of the visit, or months down the road, it will indeed happen. I feel for our son, in that although with divorced parents he must go through these trials, they are a necessary evil for him to see the truth and the reality of the situation we are all in together. I only pray that this doesn't hurt him too badly, but give him a sense of closure on his past. I pray that Kevin sees this without stumbling too badly, and endures as he has before. I love him so much. And even the thought of him feeling that kind of pain, however brief it may be, troubles me. I'd do anything to take it off his shoulders, but at the same time still know that he must endure this if he is to get past it. Kevin is a survivor, like us, and I'm sure he'll be fine.

I suppose what upset me the most is knowing that Mike has always had hidden motives, and with that in mind, it upset me greatly knowing that he was not only in our home, but in our friends home as well, and then going swimming with you and Kevin as well. Not only is this stressful for you, but God only knows what for Mike in his mind, and also potentially damaging for Kevin due to the reasons that I mentioned earlier. I may be way off base here, but it is a possibility. When I visited with the boys after leaving Bragg, I went swimming with the boys, as Tracy looked on from poolside. The twins were confused due to their young age, and even Gary looked a little puzzled at times. At that point it became awkward for me as well, and we all decided it was time to go. I speak from whence I know.

I know that I already apologized over and over on the phone already my love, but I feel that I must do it again here and now because I would never second guess your judgment. My darling Helen, you are my love, my partner, my everything, and I know that you would never put yourself in a situation where you or I would be dishonored by each other. I know this in my heart of hearts, and I would never doubt you. I simply allowed the stress of this whole deal here on my end to spill over and lash out a little. I do apologize. I have tried all day to keep it to myself, and I have failed miserably. Although our discussion got a bit heated due to me, I have to say that I feel so much better about this whole thing now. I vented to Nick earlier about this, but it only felt better when I ran it all by you. I'm sorry again my love. Please know that I would never intentionally cause you pain or question your intentions. I love you with everything that I am.

Well, now it's after midnight and I've got to get some sleep. I love you my darling and I pray that you have sweet dreams. Kiss you later my love.

25 APR 04 D + 187 0950 hrs.

Good morning my darling. I hope you had a good night last night. When I woke p this morning, I remembered that most things that may not look so good usually look worse at night. I'm thinking that this is probably the case now. I don't feel so bad now, other than being upset last night, and adding to your stress.

I finished my laundry a little while ago. I had a lot of laundry this week because we've been so busy. Now, everything I have is clean. We ran out of powdered detergent that was sent to us, so I had to use my vanilla shampoo instead. Some things are so primitive here. I think I'd kill for a washing machine right about now. The simple things ate the ones that I miss the most. Sometimes, it just gets very old living off of port-o-jons and to go plates. I miss eating with a fork that doesn't break off in pieces when cutting into a piece of mystery meat. Of course there's none of that at home. I miss your cooking so much.

1815 hrs.

Good afternoon my love. Well, we did get a little down time today. I did laundry and then relaxed for a while. I also got a brief on tomorrow's mission. This will be mission # 100 for me, and we'll be escorting EOD out to the desert to blow some captured weapons and ordinance. I always like these missions because they get a lot of potentially dangerous stuff out of enemy hands. Also, these missions are always pretty low profile. With six gun ships going out along with the package, we're not pegged as a soft target and shouldn't be messed with too badly, if at all.

2240 hrs.

I just got back from talking to you on the phone, and as you might suspect, I am a little upset. Apparently, Mike wasn't behaving himself very well last night, and disrespected you. And the fact that it was around Kevin and a friend of yours as well makes it worse. I'm glad that you immediately told Cathy what happened, but at the same time I don't believe that it will change anything. I can't believe that he didn't even offer to pay for gas or anything. This is the first and last time that anything like that happens again. You were perhaps overly generous, and understanding beyond belief; more so than I would have been to be sure. My anger about all of this stems from one simple thing, so fundamental that even a monkey could understand it. When he disrespects you, it's not just you. It's us, all of us. Our entire family. I hope he enjoyed the visit, because this is the last time that he'll enjoy even the slightest bit of anything resembling hospitality, or so much as a ride across post without giving up some money up front for the gas. We are above all this honey, and although it is upsetting now, I'm sure Mike is hurting even as I type this, as he travels just a couple hours down the road. At this very moment, he's not even out of Kansas yet, and if he's got a shred of decency or compassion towards Kevin at all, this should be killing him to drive away. Also, I would like to think that there is some kind of guilt there for only making an allowance of two whole days for Kevin while he sits on his ass at his mother's house for another five weeks. Between his reenlistment bonus and his mother, he could have stayed much longer, rented a car, and even flown back to California at his leisure. But once again, I knew I could count on him to screw this up too. He came in like a bat out of hell after 3 ½ years, tried to 'buy' Kevin, and due to his lack of planning for the trip, denied both Kevin and himself more quality time than they did have. It's too bad actually, for Kevin anyway. And the sad thing, which I certainly won't mention to Kevin, is that our son probably considers himself lucky to have had the little time that his father was actually willing to give him. Mike knows this, I'm sure, and is counting on it. Or maybe he doesn't even realize this, and that is truly sad. Oh well. I don't believe he'll be treating you like that again.

Well, it's getting late now my love, and we do have a mission tomorrow. Simmons has an early guard shift, so he's waking me up to call you about 0400 or so. I love you my darling.

26 APR 04 D + 188 0530 hrs.

Good morning my love. Well, I just got off the phone with you, and luckily we got to talk for over an hour this time. I had Simmons get me up at the end of his guard shift, at 0400, and apparently that's the best time to go. I got right on the phone, and there was hardly anyone in the tent at all. Other than being a little on the chilly side this morning, it was very nice. When I called, you were at a barbecue at a neighbor's house. They live in our quad, and apparently are very nice. From what I could hear, Abby and Kevin play really well with their children. I really am glad to see that at least some of our neighbors are considerate and understanding of you, in seeing that their husbands are home already.

Well, Mike's visit is now over, and I really hope that he enjoyed all the things that he took for granted this time around, because rest assured that it won't happen again. Now we can all move on to better things. It was so nice to talk to Kevin last night, as he told me that he wished it were me that was home instead of his father. Hearing Abigail's sweet little voice just kills me, and I long to be home to see her growing up in person. She's getting quite the little personality.

I'm not sure what I want to do first when I get home, but I've rally been thinking about that kind of thing a lot lately. There are so many things that I want to see and do that I couldn't possibly even begin to name them all. One thing is sure though, that I don't want to do any of them without you my love. I don't think that I want to visit anyone except the boys while on leave, unless they come to see us, and that's only after we have some time together.

I'm absolutely dreading one thing about the day we actually get home. After the formation, or whatever deal they have at the airfield, then there's weapons turn in, getting barracks rooms for the single soldiers, and God only knows what else. I really hope that the Rear-D has their stuff together by the time we get home. They really need to be on point, *especially* on that day. We'll see. Well, it's time to wake up the men now, and get to chow. All my men and I slept in DCU's last night. That's standard for a night before a mission. It just saves time in the morning. Okay, I really have to go now my love. I'll try and call if the phones are up after we get back from today's mission. I love you my darling.

0745 hrs.

We just got back from breakfast. Not too bad this morning. Well, I suppose that I've developed some rituals since coming here. Before I go out on every mission, I listen to our wedding song, for one. Everyone knows this by now, and when it's playing, they also know that it's wise to not interrupt me. Also, I watch a portion of the video you sent. I'm surprised the tape still works these days. There's this one portion where Kevin looks so happy, and Abby says, 'I love Dada!' I absolutely love that. When Abby says the word 'love', it's possibly one of the sweetest sounds I have ever heard. It's so pure, and I think it really captures an innocence that as a father, I wish would last a lifetime. I've rewound it a thousand times at least, and I can't get over how happy the kids look.

Well, we're staging our trucks in about 45 minutes or so, so I'd better get going now. I love you my darling, and I promise to try and call you as soon as I can. Kiss you later my love.

2100 hrs.

Hello my love. I called earlier, but you were at work, I assume. I left a message on the machine so you knew we made it back okay. I spent half my time dialing and redialing the phone due to a poor connection, so I didn't have time to call your cell. Anyhow, I hope you're having a great day with all your kids on your end.

I'm not really sure what I'm feeling today. It's really weird. First of all, we were at the gate about to leave for the mission this morning when we heard a loud 'boom'. It was an IED going off just outside the gate. A Marine was injured, but not fatally. We were turned around at the last second, only to head out of Trooper Gate which took a little longer to get to our destination, but not by much. We loaded about 100 confiscated rocket motors, which weigh about 100 lbs each onto our cargo truck, along with some other munitions, and moved out. I remember thinking that hajji had to go to a great effort to obtain such materials, as they are not easily hidden, nor available. Upon reaching the middle of the desert, we downloaded the munitions, and let the EOD boys go to work. They used blasting caps, det cord, and a lot of C-4 to set the charge. After the big boom, we mounted up and came back home.

I've been feeling a lot of strange feelings today. I think it scares me a bit because I don't quite understand it. Another convoy escort, another mission, another day to get shot at. I'm not getting complacent, and I'm certainly not bored, but I guess certain things just don't bother me as much as they used to, or cause so much concern.

2200 hrs.

I'm back honey. I was on the porch pulling my guard shift. What I was talking about earlier was that I'm in this state of mind that our good luck streak has lasted so very long now, and although we've had no more than minor casualties with non-fatal injuries, no one has this long of a streak with luck this good. I know that God is on our side, and is watching over us and guiding us, however, the evil that men do is sometimes unspeakable. Take the last casualties that the Battalion had, for example. That was a catastrophic kill, and I don't think I could fear two words more. By all accounts, the soldiers probably didn't feel anything because it happened so quickly, but it still scares me to death. The thought of being snuffed out in an instant without ever holding you or being with you again scares me to death. I pray all the time, and suppose I can only pray for guidance from God, and ask that I live to see you again.

27 APR 04 D + 189 1015 hrs.

Hello my love. I just got in from Champion Main, now known as 'Blue Diamond Headquarters', the Marine headquarters that the 82nd used to occupy. The street sign reading 'Ardennes' is the only visible sign left that the 82nd was ever even there. The Marines are cocky like the Airborne, with less than decent justification in that their tactics, strategies, if you can call them that, justifies such an attitude. Oh well, perhaps they'll learn when enough of them are killed. What a shame.

1920 hrs.

Hello once again my love. Today was a meat grinder. We made three trips to Champion, six trips over the bridge that I hate the most. The rails, if you can call them that, are about 1 ½ feet tall at their tallest point, and made of cheap scrap metal screwed together by hand. After getting the construction engineers home safe and sound for the final trip, we relaxed for about an hour. We thought we were done for the day, in seeing that we have an all day mission tomorrow. Wrong. The call went out, and a VBIED exploded just outside the main gate to Champion Main. We had been in that area six different times today, and we were all instantly thankful to still be alive. We went out to do the blast assessment, the investigation to learn more about the stuff hajji is using against us. We spent about an hour and a half exposed, pulling security and sifting through debris looking for evidence of wiring, explosives, and the like. We found two sets of wiring, and some shrapnel from at least three 155 mm high explosive warheads. What a hell of a day. After we got back, only my sleeves were dry, and many people commented on how drenched in sweat I was. Hell, I changed t-shirts twice today already. I've also been told that I'm getting a little red. The sun is high all the time now, and doesn't go down until around 2000 hrs. or so. Normally, I would probably think that later in the evening is pretty nice, except for the fact that I'm so tired by then. Oh yeah, and that I'm still in Iraq. I think that I'm actually starting to see some light at the end of tunnel, so to speak. It may be a little warm still when I get back home, but it's okay too if it's starting to get cool with the onset of fall. I know that I'll just be so glad to be home that I won't even know how to act.

I just miss you so much my love. I am so very tired lately, and it seems as though I can fall asleep at the drop of a hat, only when I'm supposed to though. I really do though. I miss you so much sometimes that I actually get tired due to thinking about it so much. Thinking about home these days is very exhausting. There's got to be about a million and a half things that I want to do when I get there.

2130 hrs.

Hello my love. Well, tomorrow's mission just got cancelled, and I have to say that I'm more than a little relieved to hear it. I was even happier about it when I found out that the Marines would actually be executing the mission tomorrow in order to learn more about our area of operation. It's about time. All of us agree on that one. Instead, I will take Simmons and Zhou with me and go to the CSA for the day. Escort Duty. I can hardly believe it. It's not nearly as bad as it used to be, plus, I won't be running it, just a participant tomorrow. Lately, with all the action in the area, and the lack of civilian traffic coming on post due to their contracts being finished, it's been a lot easier to deal with. Although, I haven't been out there in so long I couldn't tell you how much easier it is. Dorelus went out there last week for about four days, and slept most of the day. When I told the squad that we had the CSA duty tomorrow, they just about broke their arms volunteering for it. Any chance for some well-needed rest. I think I'll take my notepad out there and catch up on some letters and post cards. I always feel better when I get something out in the mail. Then again, I always feel better when I receive mail too.

I got both of us a sweatshirt yesterday at the PX. I thought you might like it for the fall and winter. I think I'm actually looking forward to seeing some cooler weather for a change. The winter was cold here, but only because of the extreme weather changes from day to night. Some of the days were cold too, but not too many. I know that I'm just babbling tonight. It's been a very long day and I'm so tired.

Our Platoon Sergeant is being an ass tonight. He's upset because the dismounts got rave reviews from the Battalion Commander today on the VBIED site, and he's not a dismount he wasn't as involved as he would have liked. Oh well, he eventually took my truck, but I don't have it because I'm in charge of the dismount team. I'd rather have what I have now. My dismounts are very loyal, and each one of them would take a bullet for me, as I would for them. I'm not trying to sound morbid my love. I just realized once again, as have all my guys I'm sure, that if you're in a position where you might only have a couple of minutes to live, then it's for your buddies, the man next to you. It's not that family isn't important, but I can only imagine that in those final moments that we would all go down with a fight for each other just as much as we would for ourselves.

28 APR 04 D + 190 0630 hrs.

Good morning my love. I just got back from talking to you on the phone, and although it's never as long as I'd like, we did get more time than we should. I love you so much my darling. You told me of your epiphany, and how if ever I felt the need to be unfaithful to you that you didn't want to know about it. I respect you my love, your thoughts, you feelings, your everything. But I have to say that it still makes me chuckle a little from time to time when you come up with things like this. There's nothing in this world or any other that could ever make me even feel the slightest bit different than I do now about you and our marriage. I love you more than life itself, and that will never change. You're so funny sometimes.

Well, it's off to the CSA today for a long day of not much. Today is a high threat day because it's Saddam's birthday, and also the first anniversary of the initial riots in Fallujah. If it was up to me, then I'd shut the gate to any and all inbound traffic, especially in light of yesterdays VBIED attack. Oh well, I'm only in charge of so much. I just have to trust that the powers that be know what's going on and are doing the right things. I have to go and get dressed now. Last night I actually got to sleep in my PT's, a rare treat for me. I didn't get a chance to grab a shower last night, so I'm glad I get to relax a little today. I'm definitely going to grab one tonight, even if the water is cold. I can't wait to take a long, hot bath when I get home. It's ridiculous to even think of it out here, but I can barely remember what it's like to have a tub of hot water all to myself. Okay, I've babbled long enough this morning. I need to get ready now. I love you honey. Kiss you later.

2130 hrs.

The CSA was no big deal today. As I thought, it was much better than when we started it, and the day, although hot, was over before we knew it. When we got back, I found out that we'd be going to ASP 309 again, the site where we chased those guys on a motorcycle stealing ordinance a couple months ago. Apparently the area is secure now, and we're going there to see what engineer support can be given to fortify the place. Now, the ASP might be secure, but since we'll be traveling on Highway 10 so early in the morning, the route will not be. There has been an IED in every 500 meter stretch of that road in the last few weeks. The command feels that the enemy is regrouping after all the attacks, especially in Ramadi and Fallujah lately. The roads are heavily patrolled nowadays, and hajji doesn't have time to dig in like he used to. They can't afford to sit out all night digging holes in the middle of the road, so they're leaving hasty IED's on the side of the road now. They might disguise the explosive in an old tire, burlap bag, or the carcass of a dead animal. These are things they've been doing all along, but more so nowadays due to time constraints. This place really is no fun at all.

I have to tell you honey, I am becoming increasingly concerned with all this time outside the wire. It's very old now, and there is nothing exciting about it, nor something that I enjoy. I don't think anyone likes getting shot at. I'd hate for anything to happen on any day, but I just don't want to get shot tomorrow, on my birthday. I haven't mentioned it to anyone, and I really don't care about it either, not this year. I'm more concerned with getting all my guys back home in one piece tomorrow night.

I really wanted to call you tonight, but the phones are down again tonight. All the guys wanted to call their families tonight. We've all talked about it, and in taking the fight to the enemy by rolling out so much, we just increase the risk of someone getting hurt. I am almost numb to it myself, as I lay here thinking the worst sometimes. I realize that it's a defense mechanism, and although we can all sit here and talk smack about how it wouldn't be that bad to give our lives for God and country, I know the pain it would leave in its wake at home would be unbearable. I really do try not to think about it, but it's always there, waiting in the wings. Those words 'catastrophic kill' keep ringing in my mind. I pray that it never happens, but then again, look where we're at right now. I long for the easy going days back at Riley, nailing pictures just so on our walls where you like them. I also miss so very much everything that I'm missing, with you, the kids growing up so fast, even down to the changing of the seasons that I've yet to see in our new home. I want to get the truck all washed up and take you out on a date in the worst way. I haven't had any means or reason to get dressed up nice for anything. And besides, I only have a whole lot of brown and tan to wear anyhow. Oh well, we'll see how tomorrow goes.

2330 hrs.

I just got back to the hooch. I was woken up by a buddy who has to go and get 12 new soldiers flying in tonight, one of which is coming to the platoon. I had to go and get a truck to transport them, assist in setting up the landing zone (LZ) for the inbound chopper, and set this kid up with a bed. While all this is going on, our fearless leader of a platoon sergeant is snoring so loud that I don't know how anyone can sleep. I'm so glad that he's so dependable. Well, my love, I have to get up in four hours for the all day mission tomorrow. I love you more than words could say.

MY BIRTHDAY D + 191 1600 HRS.

Hello my love. We just got back from Habbaniyah, TQ Air Base, and FOB Killeen. Today was very nerve-wracking for me, as I really was praying to not have the same date twice on my headstone. I know it sounds a tad morbid, but then again, look where I'm at.

2115 hrs.

Hey honey. The phone lines are pretty long tonight, but I managed to get on the internet and get those pictures you sent. I loved them, of course, and added them to my little collection. I'm pretty sure I told you before, but I have a special folder on my laptop with all my pictures of you, and nothing else. Every now and them, usually at night, I pull it up as a slide show, and start daydreaming for a little while. It's always nice to have a little 'us' time, even half a world away.

2215 hrs.

Hello once again my love. I just got off of my guard shift watching the trucks, and everyone is already unconscious already. Usually there are a few folks up at this hour, myself included, but today everyone woke up at 0400 so we're all spent. I just looked off the porch at the C-6, and there's a line of Marines a mile long out there.

Well, my birthday went off without a hitch, and the most rewarding part of the day was getting back here alive and in one piece. No one remembered that it was my birthday, and it didn't really bother me because I know how wired everyone was today, and how tired they all are tonight. No big deal. 34 really isn't a big one anyhow.

Tomorrow we're going down Highway 10, to the government center to escort a package up there for some business. Just another trip down the IED highway. Also, on Sunday, apparently there's a big mission going on. We're not sure about the details yet, but the last two times they had big ones like this, we were out for about 18 hours both times. I don't really like those missions, as they keep us outside the wire for far too long, if you ask me. As much as I hate to say it, all this time on the road does seem to pass the time. Tomorrow is Friday already, and that's always a good thing. Every Friday is a holiday in hajji-land, and they usually don't work or do much of anything. It's a little easier on Friday's to pick out the bad ones because most of the time they're the only ones out while everyone else is either with their family or resting. We'll see how it goes.

Well, it's about time for this old man to go to sleep, seeing as how I'm an older man today. Where do the years go? I tell you, when I was a young'n . . . just kidding. I love you my darling. Kiss you later.

30 APR 04 D + 192 0845 hrs.

Good morning my love. To our surprise, we were allowed to sleep in until 0700 this morning. We really did need it though, and for the first time in a while, someone made a decision that made sense. It was good though, because I got up at 0345 to call you. It was so worth it though. I got to talk to you and the kids for about 45 minutes. You and Kevin both sang Happy Birthday, and Abby tried her best as she wrestled with you for the phone. That was so sweet. When Kevin sang 'Happy Birthday Dad', and Abby did her best to follow suit, it did a lot for my spirits. I wasn't' too terribly excited about my birthday this year, but it made me look forward to better times when I get home.

Today, we have a few light taskings before our mission downtown. We have two new soldiers coming in only God knows when, so we have to assemble another set of bunk beds. Nobody really minds either, because we've been so short for so long that even one new Soldier would be a welcome addition. A slight edge off the workload will make a big difference.

Today we've got to get our Decon water truck our here by the barracks, as we now provide water for the battalion to do our laundry with. The laundry service is open again, but no one trusts it after waiting a month to get that one batch of laundry back after the fighting started. Then, we have NCOPD on NCOER's this afternoon with the Battalion Sergeant Major. That should be interesting. I still have that sort of numb feeling about everyday life here. Nothing is really exciting anymore, and all I really care about is getting my guys and me out of here alive. I'll try and call you later on this afternoon. I love you my darling. Kiss you later.

2215 hrs.

Well, tonight's brief was not so unlike the hundreds we've already had. Tomorrow we're going out on Route Mobile, which is Highway 1. The only difference between Highway 10 and Highway 1 is the amount of IED's on any given day. We're going on a leader's recon for a mission that begins Sunday at 1900 hrs., until daylight on Monday morning. If the engineers don't finish it the first night, then we have to do the same thing again for as many nights as it takes to knock down a couple miles of steel medians. It's a long weekend ahead of us, and everyone is starting to get numb to it all. War really is hell. Somehow, I think I forgot that, but every day is a painful reminder in some form or fashion. Oh well, every day is still another day closer to coming home.

I did find out today however that the redeployment order is going to be published on 15 MAY 04. The 1SG is waiting for the order to come out so he can drop his retirement packet. He and I talked tonight awhile, and he really thinks that I should be a Drill Sergeant. He does make a few good points. They're non-deployable, they get incentive pay, and with exception of a few long hours during the cycles, the AIT portion of the deal could be pretty sweet. Also, about 75% of every E-7 promotion list are people who are or have been Drill Sergeants. He does make a good case, and since the Battalion is due to come back to Iraq in 2006, it makes a lot of sense to me. I can't wait to discuss it with you my love.

1 MAY 04 D + 193 1145 hrs.

Hello my love. We just got our briefing on today's mission, and part of tomorrow's as well. It's a scary one this time, not unlike the others, but we'll be out for at least two nights on all nighters.

2 MAY 04 D + 194 0300 hrs.

Hello my love. I just got off the phone with you and the kids a few minutes ago. For the most part, it was a really good call, over an hour. I know that kids react differently when parents are deployed, but Kevin is taking things a bit too far. I couldn't believe how blatantly he was disrespecting you even with me on the phone. I'll have to fix that when I get home. I was so sorry to hear about you being so sick my love. I told you a long time ago that I'd quit smoking before I got home from Iraq, and I will. I would never do anything to knowingly jeopardize your health honey.

I miss you so much my love. We're 2/3 of the way through the tour now, and at least the days still keep on passing by. Over here, we have many enemies. There's always hajji of course, but time is also a big enemy here.

1620 hrs.

The 1SG just came in to notify us that the mortars we heard not 20 minutes ago landed inside the compound. There were 39 casualties from 1-16, Navy Seabees, and Marines. One of the company commanders from 1-16 was sitting in the TOC, and shrapnel shot 65 feet from the point of impact and struck him in the head. When the MEDEVAC bird took off, the medic was breathing for him, and he didn't live long enough to make the flight to Baghdad. Today was a horrible day.

This just drives home the fact that no one likes to realize around here. Going outside the wire only increases the chance for danger, but it's just as easy to die while eating at the chow hall, walking down the street, and even laying in bed.

This certainly doesn't bode well for tonight's mission, to be sure. Everyone's already jacked up about being up all night, and now we're angry. I have checked the men's gear within an inch of their lives, and left nothing to chance. We're supposed to have armor out there with us tonight, which of course helps, but nothing is guaranteed, of course.

I miss you so much my love. I can't tell you how disappointed I am that this happened this afternoon. I wanted so desperately to call you before we left tonight, and now it seems as though I may not even be able to talk to you tomorrow, unless the notifications are made in time. We'll be out all night tonight, and that means that it's daytime in the States, so the chances are good for notifications to be made. I know it probably sounds callous to hope that the families are notified so we can talk again soon, but it's a part of everyday life here, and perhaps it's only a defense mechanism to think this way. It's a real shame, but we all do it.

Well, I must get going now my love. I have to make about five gallons of coffee, and get to chow so I won't be sitting out there on an empty stomach tonight. I love you my darling, and I promise to call as soon as possible after we get back, if the phones are up again. I love you my darling. You're my everything. Kiss you later.

3 MAY 04 D + 195 1500 hrs.

We got in about 0430 this morning from tearing down the guardrails on Route Mobile. We got through three checkpoints last night, about 5 miles or so. We've got about another 25 or so miles to clear. The guard rails are being taken down, as well as the light poles in the medians because hajji likes to plant IED's at the base of the poles and in the medians, hidden by the rails. We were relatively safe last night, due to there being about 30 armored vehicles out with us. We were actually the inner perimeter, and that made me feel a little better.

I miss you so much my love. I wish I could call you right now. Everyone is exhausted and not really ready to go out again all night, but there's no choice. I grabbed some apple pie desserts to take out for the troops tonight, just a little something to get us through the night. We all got a little hungry last night, and then had to stay up until the chow hall opened this morning before we could lie down and get some sleep.

I got a birthday card from my mother today, and I've debated for two hours on whether or not I should write her back. I haven't decided yet, but I think it would have been better off if she'd never sent it at all. I still feel the same way though; I don't want to see her when I get home. The disappointment has been too great for me, and I don't want to set myself up for anything like that again. The only family that's shown loyalty and that I've felt love from besides you my love is Billy and Challas and the kids. I know who's loyal to us and who's not.

4 MAY 04 D + 196 0315 hrs.

Hello my love. We are of course back now from our mission, and I just got cut off on the phone with you. The circuit breaker tripped and something is apparently wrong with the generator that runs the C-6 package. Oh well. At least the barracks has power, and the laptop battery is full so I can write to you. Out here, I've come to deal with the fact that something is always better than nothing. I'm glad that you found the hamster, and Kevin's apology for saying what he said the other night was most welcome. Abby sounded like a wild child while you were in Burger King, and I could only pray to be there with you in person, not just in spirit. I know it has its moments of stress, being at home with the kids on your own, but I'd give anything to be there now, and always.

I have given it a lot more thought since this afternoon, and receiving a birthday card from my mother, but as I stated earlier on the phone with you, she has made her choices, not so unlike the lifelong and continuous series of bad choices she has made with her children, and now she must deal with their consequences. Except she knows nothing about me as a person, really, and to speak of nothing about you either except what she and the rest of the family have chosen to hone in on and bitch about. It's their loss for not knowing you and I the way that they could. The sad thing is that it would have cost them nothing to do it the right way which would have benefited all. Too bad.

You mentioned tonight that under my current situation that I might somehow reconsider my decision to keep the family where they have chosen to locate themselves in our lives, on the outer fringe. You also reaffirmed and pledged your undying support for whatever decision that I may make with regard to this. I of course appreciate this gesture, my love, as I do everything that comes from you, however this will not change. No one is in our shoes right now but us, and although I do not expect others to understand these things, I do however expect that they respect them. As you and I both know, this has not been the case, and that is a luxury that a military family does not have. This is all part of a bigger burden of service, of serving a greater good that you and I and our children will alone have the solemn pride in giving. I cannot begin to assuage the feelings of angst that you and I have acquired through the years my love over many things lost, but can only hope that we can sleep a bit more sound in our senior years, and offer our children a legacy of knowing what is truly important in life. I understand that many of these things come with personal sacrifice; occasionally a sacrifice that seems too hefty a price for its worth at the time, such as a year long tour in the Middle East. With a little hope and a whole lot of effort, we can move mountains. I can only hope that our children have the pride in us that we strive to give them, something to aspire to. When Abby tells her grandchildren one day of her father's time in Iraq and how he was there during the time that Saddam was captured, and teaching her daughter to be as strong as she always knew her mother to be, then our legacy will have come through and have a value all its own.

I know that it seems like I'm babbling, and it being 0340 hrs as well may have something to do with it, but I mean every word of this my darling. I love you so much my love, and God willing I'll call you tomorrow some time. Let's just pray that the phones stay up for that long. I love you my soul mate. Kiss you later.

5 MAY 04 D + 197 0238 hrs.

Hello my love. I just go back from talking to you on the phone, and I was pleased to see that we got to talk for so long tonight. You were picking up the kids and about to head out to Denny's for your weekly dinner out with the kids. I couldn't help but be a little jealous, but I know better than that and I'll eventually be home again.

Tomorrow is a big day for me. I'm getting new armor on my gun truck, and I'm really excited about it. The armor weighs an additional 1600 lbs., and is really going to help keep us safe. I got a new speaker for my radio, and a buddy of mine is trying to get me a fan for inside my truck. It's starting to get really hot. I'm so tired my love, and I should try to get a couple of hours rest now. I love you my darling. Kiss you later.

6 MAY 04 D + 198 0400 hrs.

Good morning my love. I just got off from guarding trucks, and walked over to the C-6 to call you, but it's closed again. Two Marines drowned in the river last night, and although they wanted to keep it hush hush for some reason, it's easy to tell when something goes down because the phones will go down at odd hours. When I came back to the hooch, just a few minutes ago, I decided to write you since we can't talk. I miss you so very much, and was really looking forward to talking with you tonight.

Tonight has been a rough night for my guys. All night long I've heard them wrestling in their sleep, tossing and turning and sounding very upset. As I lay here now, I hear Simmons yelling something that I can't understand. The war has been tough on them all, and although I have such pride in them, I can't help but think that they have lost a certain innocence that they'll never be able to get back. It's like watching our children grow up, and remembering all those little moments that you'll never forget, except everything is compressed into one year. Every time that one of my guys has come back from leave, they greet me with a tight handshake and a hug that is hard to describe. They had all just tasted the sweet taste of freedom, and with a certain reverence in their eyes, it's almost as though they're glad to be back. They've all told me some similar stories of home; that no one could really understand their perspective and the 'understanding' that they did get was more along the lines of sympathy, as well as regret for them having to serve over here.

I love these troops of mine, and for as long as I'm alive they'll always be welcome at my home, my table, and in my life. They are a part of me now, and I consider myself fortunate to have had the pleasure to lead and serve with some of the finest men I've ever known. This is of course not the first time, but again I have been blessed in having the opportunity to walk with heroes. These men truly are that, and no one can ever take that away from them.

With this being an election year, the popularity of this war is rivaling that of Vietnam, Somalia, and the like. I just hope that no one ever forgets that what happened here is a true testament to the spirit of humanity, and in saving it. I feel myself as though I have a sense of closure to some extent, as I sit here and remember the morning that I came home to you sitting in your chair. As I walked in the door after my shift at the fire station, which was extended by a few hours due to the terrorist attacks, I saw you sitting there, tears streaming down your face. You were pregnant with Abigail, and for the next few weeks, it seemed like all we did was watch the news about what had happened, how many people had been removed from the rubble on any given day, and praying for those not found and those left behind. As my soul mate, I could not have survived those waning days of the beginning of the war without you. We were together, and that's all that matters. But that was just the beginning of all this.

Now, having been here going on 8 months, I look back on occasion with a certain pride on you, as my wife, and knowing that I could not have any better support than I do now. I also look forward with many questions in my mind. No one is really sure when the war will end, but we're all praying that it does as soon as possible. We've seen such a terrible cost laid on the alter of freedom, and that cost is in the lives of our brothers and sisters that are also far away from home. And now, many of them will never come home. I only pray that we do. As always, I love you more than life itself my darling. I'll write more tomorrow, God willing. Kiss you later.

6 MAY 04 D + 199 2040 hrs.

Hello my love. Today was a very long day, and I built everything in sight. I built storage racks on the back of our gun trucks, then another shelf for one of the guys. After that I built a desk for Eason because he needs more space, and then another dresser for the new Private. It was about 100 degrees today, and I was sweating bullets. I drank water steadily throughout the day, but I still got a little dehydrated. I'm fine though.

The phones are still down now. It wasn't reported throughout our command when it happened, but two Marines drowned during a 'training accident' two days ago. Also, yesterday morning two Navy Seabees were killed in an IED attack on Highway 10. They are feeling the pains of their first losses, and I can see it in their eyes when we tell them how long we've been here how amazed they seem to be. They're amazed because we've lived this long. Some days though, I'm a little amazed myself.

We got briefed tonight that COL Connor thinks that the insurgents will surge their attacks more frequently and more intensely prior to the 30 JUN 04 date of handing Iraq over to itself again. We've given them so very much; an Iraqi Civil Defense Corps (Army), Police and Fire Academies throughout the country, a freely elected government, and a voting system in place, along with enough financing to keep a consistent bankroll flowing for years. All they have to do now is capitalize on their natural resources like the oil, and of course, the people to not just survive but succeed.

We went over the promotion rosters tonight, and once again I recommended Zhou to go to the E-5 board in July. Hopefully, even with our busy schedule he'll have plenty of time to study and practice mock boards to gain his 'board confidence'. I'm sure he'll do just fine. He's a perfectionist, and is probably harder on himself that I am. Hard to believe, huh? Yupper, sad but true. He's my second in charge, and I wouldn't have it any other way.

After today's day full of building everything under the sun, tomorrow will be quite the switch. We're doing training on our aid and litter team. That's my old truck that the Platoon Sergeant now runs. The truck is set up something like a hastily made ambulance that can fit two full size litters for wounded, along with setting up IV's and a host of other medical capabilities. The medic always rides in that truck, and we're just fine tuning our system now. We've honed our skills over the last eight months so well, that when we're out on the road, I don't even have to tell Eason, Simmons, or Zhou to pick up speed or slow down, rotate their main gun with a change of direction, or how to use the radio. My guys are experts, and I really have all the faith in the world in them, and I know that you'd be pleased that I'm surrounded with some of the finest people walking the earth.

7 MAY 04 D + 200 2100 hrs.

Hello my love. I just got the chance to talk to you for a little bit, but not for long because you were on a field trip with the kids. I would have done anything to be there with you. When I called, you were walking the kids over to the 6th Street Park, wherever that is, and you sounded like you were having a good time. These are the times that I miss home the most, I think. I wonder about how Kevin is doing in school right now, and how Abby is doing at Angel's. I miss everything.

Although everyone is anxiously counting the days, it still feels like Groundhog Day for most of us here. Today was a lot of maintenance on the trucks, and more building furniture for the new people. Some of them aren't even in our platoon, but I just can't say no to the chance to swing a hammer.

I was thinking about something today. I've grown very callous about certain things, and although I've changed a lot since I met you, it seems as though I've had tot revisit some times of my life while out here. Of course those times are previous deployments, but the harshness and bitter feelings I had about some things then were caused by other people, other things. It's almost as if I have to call on those times some days, a lot like 'break glass, only in case of an emergency'. During the time we spend on the road is a good example of this. I have to change into another person when I'm in my gun truck. As soon as I shut that door, it's like I'm not myself anymore, but a cold and heartless machine that will do anything, and I do mean anything to get my people back in one piece. You have to be so aware on the road. Is that just a dead dog on the side of the road, or are there wires coming out of the carcass? The wind is blowing but that cardboard box isn't moving. Is there a remote detonated IED inside it weighing it down? Is that child just waving at my truck, or is he signaling a trigger man? The hyper alertness just never ends. Even down to the slight difference in the color of a small dirt pile can be seen as far our as about 100 to 150 meters by me, my driver, and the gunner too. We are constantly calling things out on the radio and to each other.

We've got it down now, and I have the utmost faith in my guys, but I'm concerned about how things will be when I get home. I don't want to alarm you if we're driving down the road and I suddenly get a little nervous. Also, I'm concerned about my sleep. Since you've known me, I never have slept very well, and of course now am no different, especially out here. Since we have a mission tomorrow, I probably won't sleep well tonight. I go over my guys gear, and then after they've all gone to sleep I check the truck out again. Simmons is an excellent driver, and our truck is always top notch, but I go over it anyway. I got him a cushion seat the other day since we're on the road for so long usually.

I know that you've probably heard it in my calls and letters, even though an NCO should never be this way, but I'm sure you could tell by now that he's my favorite. He and I have been through just about everything together; IED attacks, a huge ambush, hajji guard, vehicle maintenance, and everything under the sun. Usually in these situations, and NCO usually looks to one of his own. At least it usually just works out that way. But in this case, Simmons, a young PFC who's still relatively new to the Army has found a place in my heart. He's dedicated to God his family, and his loyalty to me and the other men is unparalleled. I honestly couldn't ask for a better troop.

8 MAY 04 D + 201 0800 hrs.

Good morning my darling. I'm so glad that I got to talk to you for so long this morning. I had Simmons get me up after his guard shift was over at 0400. You were outside with all the kids, and I don't think that I've missed home so much as I did this morning. Before every mission, every single one, I make sure to listen to our wedding song, and a few others if I have time. I was listening to 'Almost Home' this morning, and it reminded me of the time we went to that diner up in Fairbanks to buy that homeless man some food. I recall how cold it was, and how sad the song is. I remember many a time that you and I cried together over the sadness of the life of the man in the song. I also remember feeling that way some years ago, and how you changed all that for me. I love you so much for that, and I truly do owe you my life if not for that alone. There are so many reasons that I love you my darling, and I really do want to spend the rest of my years showing you how much.

This time away, this war, all of it is tough on the entire family, but it doesn't define us as individuals. It's just a challenge that we'll get through together, whether we're physically together or not. I have to get going now, but I'll call you after we get back.

1400 hrs.

A mortar just landed inside the camp, a big one. I think it must have been at least an 81 mm or 82 mm. There's talk of hajji using chemical munitions on us in the near future, and suddenly everyone is looking to us for answers to questions that we just don't know yet. It's very scary. The mortar landed within 150 meters of our building, and shook the walls as it fell. With mortars, there's virtually no warning at all. Most of the time there's no sound, nothing at all until the explosion. Those are just no fun at all.

9 MAY 04 D + 202 0025 hrs.

Hello my love. I went down to try and call you earlier, but the C-6 was down for maintenance for some reason. The mission went well, and I got lots of pictures today. We detonated about 150 rocket motors that were confiscated about two weeks ago.

They're about 10 feet long, and weigh in at about 75 lbs. apiece. It was a good mission, # 116 for me. When we got back and the phones were down, I laid down for a little while, until about noon or so. Apparently we were done for the day and no one woke me up for anything. I guess my body needed the sleep, because I didn't wake up until about 1730. That's more sleep than I get in an average night. So, now I'm up late of course because I can't sleep. I went and took a shower a little while ago, and I have guard in a half hour, so I figured I'd catch up on my journal a bit. I missed you so very much today. I really wanted to call you after the mission, but I surely will when I first get the chance. SPC Lalicker and I took the containers that grenades come in and made cup holders for our truck tonight, and also made a shotgun mount for the dash on our truck as well. I really don't think that there's much more that we can do to that truck, but I'm sure we'll try and think of something. Just something to pass the time.

I'm so excited. Normally it's nothing big, but I acquired a fan today for my hooch. I have it about three feet off the ground, and everyone thinks I'm crazy for sleeping with it on all night. Oh well, I like it anyway, and the days are getting up to and past 100 degrees just about every day now. Today was about 110. It really sucked, but it's amazing how used to things you can get. I don't want to get too used to it though. I'm pretty sure that I'd rather deal with the cold than the heat any day of the week. The heat just gets really old very quickly. Oh well, I can always look forward to nicer weather an enjoying it with you when I get home. I love you so much my darling.

1400 hrs.

Hello my love. Today is Sunday, and we sort of have a day off. We have most of the day to ourselves, and in about an hour or so we'll clean up the hooch and then go out to finally take our Platoon picture. I've been looking forward to this for a while, but mission and everything else keeps coming up.

I didn't do laundry today, because the contractors are back again, so I'll give it a shot tomorrow. It's a shame that so many of them were killed for working for us, and to be honest, I'm really surprised that they came back. It would save me a lot of time though. We'll see how it works out. I have to get going now. I'm going to rally the troops for our little G.I, party. I love you my darling. Kiss you later.

2300 hrs.

Hey honey. I just got back from 1-5 Field Artillery's C-6 package. I heard through a buddy that theirs was open, and he told me that he thought I might like to call my mom on Mother's day. I explained the deal, and told him that I'd rather call you instead, and by the time I got there, the phone line was already huge, and so I got on the internet instead. You weren't online, but I sent you a few instant messages anyway. I'll try again after my guard shift tonight, and see of ours is up.

Our generator died today. There's no real maintenance schedule to it, so they just spend tons of time fixing it when it goes out. We had no power or A/C for about 10 hours today, enough to really feel the difference. The sand fleas and other critters really don't like the cool air, so when it started to get really hot inside, they started biting again. The air has been on for about an hour now, and I have my fan as well. We cranked the A/C on right away, and a lot of the guys took turns standing in front of my fan. It was really hot today. As usual, it was well over 100, with no relief in sight. I think the only relief we'll see is when we get home.

Well, Happy Mother's Day my love. I certainly wish that I could be with you today, to take you out to brunch or dinner or something. Today is one of my favorite holidays, as it allows us an opportunity to show the mother's in our lives how much they really mean to us. I can only hope and pray that our children see this, especially this year. You've certainly gone above and beyond this year, without much choice in it, and have come through all of this so wonderfully my darling. You always seem to know how to take lemons and make lemonade. I've always loved that about you, and consider it one of your greatest strengths. I certainly hope that our children pick up on this and learn to use this trait to succeed in their own lives.

Well, it's getting late my love, and I have guard in two hours. I'll try to call you after that, and wish you a Happy Mother's Day myself. I love you Helen, more than anything.

10 MAY 04 D + 203 0500 hrs.

Good morning my love. I just got back from calling you, and I'm really glad that I could get through on Mother's Day. We really didn't get to talk for that long this morning, but I suppose that some time is better than none at all. Apparently Kevin is coming into his pre-teen stage, which is of course fun for you I'm sure. I can only imagine.

When I called, you were studying for your Para Professional test. I have absolutely no doubt that you'll do very well on it my love. I have all the faith in the world in you, and I'm sure you'll do just fine.

As I sit here on the porch writing you, I can see across the majority of the camp and it's pretty dark right now. Most of the troops are still sleeping, with exception to the three or four patrols that are on their way out to do route clearance. They go out every single morning to do IED sweeps on Route Mobile and Highway 10. Because they are the first units to see these routes every morning, they are usually the ones who find the IED's first. Some job. After clearing the routes, they radio back to Brigade and let the command know that the routes have been cleared and then and only then convoys are allowed to leave to conduct other business. Other than that, there's little to no other traffic at al this morning. We have to turn our porch lights off at night now to maintain light discipline. We don't want to give hajji any free targets, now do we? Also, any and al formations have been cancelled from this point forward due to the frequent mortar attacks. What a hell of a place we live in. I can't wait to come home.

I'm not exactly sure of what today will bring, so I'm having the guys finish what we started yesterday. We had the G.I. party yesterday afternoon, and in about 40 minutes they got both the front porch and the bay looking great. Today we're bleaching the floors and cleaning weapons. We clean weapons every day, but once a week, I like to go through and have them do a real good cleaning. The dust is just so bad here that a weapon gets dirty just walking to use the phone and back. I want to do the floors because the critters of summer are starting to come out. The flies are horrible. They're absolutely everywhere, and they are relentless. I can't explain in words how bad they really are, and how annoying they can be. We found something that kills them pretty well. It comes in a granule form, and it's blue, similar to rocks that you'd see in an aquarium. They land on it and start eating it, and die almost instantly. They sometimes twitch for a few seconds, which makes me think it attacks their central nervous system. The only drawback is that it stinks . . . bad. It's very pungent, and, like everything else in Iraq, you get used to it after a while.

Well, my love, I must close out for now and make up the rest of my list of stuff to do today. We still have a lot of maintenance stuff to do, and I want to make sure that our vehicles are running as god as they can for when we leave. We use the gun trucks all the time, and our 5-ton's pretty much stay in the motor pool most of the time. When Decon left Ft. Riley, the trucks were apparently in bad shape, and a few of them broke down driving up from Kuwait. I definitely don't want that to happen going home. I don't want anything to get in the way of our coming home. I love you, and I'll write more later on I'm sure. Kiss you later.

11 MAY 04 D + 204 0930 hrs.

Good morning my love. I hope you are getting some good rest right now, as it's after midnight at home right now. I didn't get the chance to call you last night because the phones and internet both went down due to a huge sandstorm. If you can picture this; in the movie 'Scorpion King', where the Rock fought those bad guys in the desert and he rushed towards them with this huge sandstorm following behind him. That's what it was like. I couldn't even go to the port-o-jon without something over my face to help me breathe. The wind pushed the sand through every crack in the wall, and even inside the bay the sand and dust were thick in the air. It really sucked.

Well, the mail is slowly trickling back in again. A couple of boxes came to the platoon yesterday, and I got a really nice letter from some woman in upstate New York named Jude Roberts. At first I thought it was a generic letter to any soldier on some name list given out to people who wanted to do something nice for a deployed soldier. When I opened it up, I was very surprised to find that it was Darrin Numbers' mother. She went on and on about supporting the military and how since neither Darrin nor his brother were deployed that she was adopting me and I had nothing to say about it. I suppose kindness comes from some of the strangest places and when you least expect it. Maybe it's because she's a mother of soldiers, I'm not really sure. It's a nice gesture though, and I'm sure Darrin must have said something to her. She gave me more sincerity in one letter than my own mother has in eight months. Oh well.

12 MAY 04 D + 205 0250 hrs.

I got to talk to you tonight my love, and I was so glad to have made it through. The lines weren't too bad tonight, but the connections certainly were. I think they're still a little rough from the sand storm last night. Either way though, I'm so glad to have been able to hear your voice. I'm not sure what I would've done if I couldn't hear your voice tonight. I tried twice earlier, but with no luck. It gets very frustrating sometimes, and although I get frustrated, I have nowhere to go with it. Usually, I get myself into the mindset that I'll be extra vigilant on our next mission, and somehow I survive. Having my own gun truck and crew gives me something to focus on, and I'm constantly making improvements to the truck, and souping it up as best I can. I have some more work to do to it tomorrow, and that will take the slack out of whatever slow times there may be tomorrow I hope.

Well, I do have a big day tomorrow with more maintenance and stuff, and I should get some sleep now. When I got back to the bay tonight, I couldn't sleep. I just lie here thinking of you, and waiting for the time to go by. I know we have another mission coming up in a day or so, so I'll rest up a little tonight, and try to get ready for it. I love you my darling. Kiss you later.

0825 hrs.

Good morning honey. I have to say, 0700 came up awfully fast this morning. We just got back from breakfast, and the men and I are getting ready to go down to the motor pool for most of the day. We're trying to make leaving here as painless as possible, as far as maintenance goes. In every other way though, there's no heartburn with leaving here, to be sure. I am so tired today. I have to get some rest tonight though, because we have a mission tomorrow. We're going to the V.A. building downtown to provide security for the engineers again. We're putting down more concrete barriers around the building to protect against VBIED's. As the 30 JUN deadline approaches, we're expecting the insurgents to start their crap again. We just saw on the news this morning where an American was beheaded in retaliation of the alleged maltreatment of prisoners at the Baghdad detention facility. Getting charged with maltreatment of POW's here is like handing out speeding tickets at the Indy 500 as far as we're concerned. Then again, the politicians back home as well as the majority of the public have the luxury of forming their own opinions without the benefit of getting engaged by the enemy first hand and knowing what these animals are capable of. I think about these things whenever I think about getting out. I know I of course wouldn't be like that, however, I'm not sure I could handle being around people like that all the time.

13 MAY 04 D + 206 1530 hrs.

Hello my love. Well, after I found out that you'd had a Red Cross message sent my way last night, I didn't get very far. I tried to talk to as many folks as I could to figure out where a message would arrive in the middle of the night. Unfortunately, it didn't come in yet as of now, and I've informed everyone that I need to so when it does come in I should be able to get the wheels in motion. I already told the Squad what was going on and prepared them for my leaving whenever the word comes in. I told them that it would probably be very sudden, and that I wasn't sure how long I would be gone. I told the chain of command that I wouldn't let my wife tote two children halfway across the country under these circumstances by herself. They all had no problem with this, of course, and assured me that they had things 'under control'. They're so funny like that.

I'm very tired. We're getting ready for a mission tonight. We have to go out to Highway 10, clear a building we've only been in once, and then provide perimeter security for the engineers again. All in all it should only take about two hours. The thing is that we leave at 2300 hrs. It's going to be another late night, but it will make tomorrow pass by a bit quicker and that's another day down. Well, I couldn't call you again because a Marine was killed and the phones are down again. The Red Cross will be able to get through still, and that's my saving grace now. We'll see how it goes. I love you my darling. Kiss you later.

1940 hrs.

I just got up from a nap to find that Zhou brought me a sandwich for supper, which is good because I slept clean through supper tonight. We are trying to rest up this afternoon so we're alert tonight. There are only two trailers loaded with barriers, so it shouldn't take more than two or three hours. I was glad to hear that, but we still have to clear that building before we start the security operation. There are supposed to be some Iraqi Police and ICDC guys posted out there to help us out, but they aren't to be trusted and we were briefed to watch them just as hard as the locals that might pass by. I can't stand being around the Iraqi's, because there's not one of them that can be trusted, since many of them have proven that they attend our training for a paycheck and a free issued weapon. It's pretty sad, but it's also very true.

I miss you so much my love. I'm still waiting to be notified that the unit has the Red Cross message, and get things moving about coming home. Even when I took my nap, I tied my radio off to my bed right next to my head so I wouldn't miss it if it came over our net. I never sleep that hard anymore, if at all. I hope it doesn't upset you when I get home, because I'll probably be very tired. I'm not talking about the jet lag from the flight home, but the year of waking up to mortars, emergency trips outside the wire, late night guard shifts, and even the nightmares. This tour is a whole new set of nightmares, and I really hope that it doesn't affect me as much after I get home.

I would go back to see the Doc at Combat Stress, but the Company XO told me just last week that although she has to encourage people to go there if they feel the need, she also doesn't profess publicly, but truly believes that you're a weak individual if you do go and see them. She cried for a month over the deaths of another Company Commander and his guys down in Habbaniyah. After this last bunch died down there in Bravo Company, the XO herself was upset, and after only three days, the Commander told her to 'get over it', and move on. She is the queen of the double standard, and hasn't the first clue about how people really are. She's like a robot, and although that has its time and place, this certainly isn't it. The entire unit has to tiptoe around her emotional state, and rely on her making decisions that could be pretty serious, even if she isn't in the right frame of mind to make them. I can't believe that I'm here with this unit. I used to think that I could change the Army one soldier at a time, and that may be true to a degree. But when the leadership is questionable, then it makes it just that much harder for people at my level to enforce things. They see the senior leadership getting away with stuff that would never be tolerated from them, and they start to question things in their own head. This is very dangerous, especially in this environment. All I can hope for is to get everyone home in one piece and start living my life again. I believe that what I've done here is important, but I'm not the only one, and there will be many more after me as well.

2020 hrs.

Speak of the devil. The 1SG just came by the hooch, and I asked him if they'd received my Red Cross message yet, and he told me 'no'. I can't believe that it's taking this long. I can't help but wonder where the delay is, and I'd do anything to fix it right now. I want you to know that if there was anything that I could possibly do, and then I would. You have to know this. I love you so much my love and I can't wait to get home to you again, be it sooner or later. Preferably sooner. I don't want to come back to this place again. I don't think it really matters if it's Iraq or not, anywhere where we'll be apart for another year. I don't have to tell you how much this pains us both, and what an emotional roller coaster it is. I'm missing out on so much with you and the kids. I still know how important this is in a global sense, but no one ever said that the sacrifices in the Army came easy. I love you my darling, more than anything else in the whole world. I'll either write in here again, or preferably call if the phones are up. They probably won't be up before we go on our mission tonight, but they might be up in the morning. We'll see. Well, I have to start getting my stuff ready for tonight. I love you sweetheart. Kiss you later.

14 MAY 04 D + 207 1415 hrs.

Hello my love. Well, I just got up for the day about an hour or so ago. We got in around 0430 this morning, and everyone was totally exhausted. Still, we were only an hour from the chow hall opening for the breakfast meal, and only two hours from my 1-hour guard shift. Still, I felt like my stomach was touching my backbone, and Simmons and Dorelus and I decided to drive over and get something to eat anyway. We sat there like zombies slowly eating our meal, which was nice because it cured the hunger. While out on Highway 10 last night, Simmons and I, along with the other three troopers with us talked at length throughout the night about coming home, and what we'd do when we get there. I miss you so much my love. Today is an okay day because we were out all night and slept most of the day. Tomorrow is Battalion Organizational Day, so the events will help us in passing another day with a little speed I hope. We had to be up in the early afternoon today to check out the trucks, so now that we're done, I told the guys to relax for the rest of the afternoon.

2350 hrs.

Hello honey. Well, I've been organizing my stuff for most of tonight, ever since I got the Red Cross message, and filled out my leave paperwork. I will take the squad to Battalion Organizational Day tomorrow, and hope for a flight out sometime tomorrow night, or first thing Sunday morning. The flights are always shady, due to the enemy activity on any particular day. They've been mortaring us during the daylight hours lately, and they seem to be getting pretty bold in a lot of ways.

I think I'm still in a bit of shock. It seems so hard to believe that I'm coming home, even for a little while. The circumstances under which I'm coming home are of course not the greatest; however I'll take anything I can get right now. It's not a complete happiness either, knowing that in a short couple of weeks that I'll have to come back to this place, but the up side to that is that it won't be for long and we'll all be home. I'll be able to bring all my men home, God willing, in one piece. Then we'll all be home again, and the happiness will be more complete. I do have my apprehensions about coming home, although at the moment I can't think of a single one. I just don't want you to be disappointed with me in any way. I know that I'm more tired than I've ever been, just plain worn out from all the missions, and I know that I look drained all the time. Hopefully I can recharge and bounce back as soon as possible. I think I'll still get worn out at home, if not from you, then from the kids. That's the good kind though, and I can certainly live with that.

I have to get up at 0400 for my guard shift, and then wake everyone else up for Organizational Day at 0530. So, I'm off to sleep, and hopefully I'll talk to you more tomorrow. I love you my darling, and I can't wait to be with you again soon.

15 MAY 04 D + 208 1000 hrs.

Hello my love. I'm making a pit stop in the bay, and taking a break from Organizational Day. It started off well enough, and although there are games and a lot of entertainment, my heart just isn't in it today. I found out that an E-7 from 1-5 got out on a flight last night for his emergency leave for a terminally ill father-in-law. The system never ceases to amaze me. In all honesty though, I think that Brigade had already coordinated his flight, and didn't receive my paperwork from battalion in enough time to add me to the manifest. Eventually, I'll be home. The good part is that my actual leave doesn't start until the day that I land at the first port of entry into the United States. That's very good for us, so I won't burn any leave time in transit. The other good part is that not only will I lose a lot of leave, but leaving the theater of operations and coming back in especially; usually there's a delay. Our last batch of guys to go on leave came back in time; however, they had to stay in BIAP for almost a whole month. Flights coming back are really hard to come by, and units can't just put together a convoy to go to Baghdad for that reason alone. They have to be on a logistics run or something like that as well. This actually helps us, because I should be good and relaxed by the time I actually get back to Ar Ramadi, and recharged enough to hit it hard and come home only a couple of months after that. Good deal. I love you so much my love. I so can't wait to see you again. I miss everything about you, and I miss you more than I could ever say or show you. I just can't wait to be home for good and be a part of 'our' lives again. Kiss you later honey.

16 MAY 04 D + 209 0915 hrs.

Hello my love. I am sitting here ever so patiently and trying not to throw up. I've been waiting for my flight out since last night, and being that it was cancelled due to weather last night, I can only hope that it will be rescheduled for today. When I spoke with you this morning, you sounded about as bitter as I feel right now. All I know is that I just want to get out of here more than anything in the world right now. I also realize that I have to be as patient as I can be, even though neither you nor I want to be. Although I'll only be on actual leave for just two weeks, in reality, I probably won't be back here in Ar Ramadi for at least a month. It takes a while to get somebody back to the camp after a leave, and I just thank God for the hiccups that come up in the logistical part of all of this. I can't wait to see you all again, my love. I know for sure that I'm repeating myself at this point, but I don't care. I'd do anything to get home, and I really am looking forward to getting there. I really do miss everything about you and home so very much my love. Well, I'm going to go and check in on the flight schedule again to see if anything is coming in today. I love you.

2230 hrs.

Hey honey. Well, I slept a lot today, amidst the packing of last minute things, and counting ammo and stuff like that. I grabbed Abigail a stuffed camel from the PX, and now I have something for everyone when I get home. I love you so much honey. I'm leaving in a few short hours on a convoy to TQ Air Base, and then hop a plane to either Baghdad or Kuwait from there, so I'm told. I don't believe anything anymore unless I can see it myself. Everyone's a little cynical, but this tour has really done it for me with the Army, as far as trust goes. One last mission, # 118 before I get out of Iraq . . . . I can't wait. I actually still can't believe that I'll be home in a few days. It's amazing to me still that I actually get to leave, even under the circumstances.

I was talking to each of my guys individually earlier in the night. It's funny that how when they went on leave, I felt like a Dad with a child leaving home, except leaving home here means going through an area where people are trying to kill you all the time. When I talked to them earlier, they came to me, one by one, and wished me a safe trip, sent well wishes for you, and told me to talk to my mother and don't be too rough on the kids. Zhou and Simmons in particular were borderline emotional about my leaving tonight, especially Zhou. He's really come a long way. I couldn't do this job without him. I told him that I have the utmost faith in him to handle anything that may come up while I'm gone, and Simmons will back him totally if the younger guys get out of line. I doubt they will because they know that I'm coming back. Well, it's about time for me to rest up a little bit before I have to go hook up with the convoy. Never soon enough, but I'll kiss you soon my love.

18 MAY 04 D + 211 0230 hrs. Mid air between Amsterdam & Detroit

Hello my love. Well, it's really been an exhausting couple of days, although worth every minute of it. Leaving Kuwait was somewhat of a fiasco in that they spelled my name wrong on the plane ticket, and had to correct it before we left. I finally got my ticket about 5 minutes before they closed the gate. Then, when we got to Amsterdam, there was a 1 ½ hour layover, most of which was spent going through international customs. I swear those folks want a blood sample and your first born. Even after a couple of years now, international airport security is still no joke. I'm actually glad to see it like that though, because it makes it a lot harder for terrorists to get through to the States that way. It almost makes me feel a tad better about being gone for so long, and the deep seeded reasons why.

6 JUN 04 D + 228 0010 hrs. Mid air between Minneapolis, MN and Amsterdam

Hello my darling. I deeply apologize for not being able to call in Minneapolis; however it took me a while to find my way around there. There have been many changes since I was there last. Security was a pain in the ass all around. Apparently, I have been pre-selected as the guy to get searched at every destination. Well, due to the fact that I'm on orders and going back to Iraq, the company that dies the searches and security checkpoints (TSA) charges the airline $5,000 every single time I get searched. U.S. military are exempt and therefore costing TSA money in the way of doing extra work every single time they screw up like this. Anyway, it really didn't help anything on my end, but I have a four hour layover in Amsterdam, where I plan on calling you as soon as I get to my gate.

I miss you so very much my love. I really can't believe that this is happening, and although I'm still in a little bit of shock, I'm going to try so very hard to keep my head in the game. Compared to now, when I first left was a little easier . . . easier to focus, easier to not stress over time, easier in a lot of ways. The only thing that is never easy is hearing your voice, and not being able to hold you, touch you, and see you in person. That's hell on me.

Well, there's only about four hours left on this flight, so I think I'll catch some sleep. I already took my boots off, and I'll call you as soon as I can in Amsterdam my love. Kiss you later.

7 JUN 04 D + 229 0330 hrs. Camp Wolverine, Kuwait

My love, I cannot begin to tell you all the feelings that are going through my head right now. I am beginning to remember the layout of Camp Wolf, here in Kuwait, and that only tells me that I've spent enough time here to know. I just talked to some guys from 1-5, and we'll probably leave here sometime tomorrow to go to Baghdad, and then try to swing a ride from there. I am very tired. I have a bad case of jet lag, and all I want to do is sleep right now, but I have to report to the manifest tent in about an hour and a half. If I lay down right now, I know I won't get up. Oh well, I guess we're all right back into the mix here.

I can still remember every single moment of my leave, and I cherish every one. I miss you and the children terribly already and there are moments that I think that it may just be too much to bear. I know of course, that we'll all make it through this just fine in the long run, but after being home for a couple weeks, I think I am changed forever. I miss being at the lake, all of us. That catfish was a great moment, and I'm so glad that the entire family was there for that. I know you and I were confused with crossed fishing lines, Kevin was excited, and to be honest, I think it scared the hell out of Abby at first. It was just too funny, and it's a wonder that the fish was ever even landed at all in that cluster. Sitting next to you on the rocks, Kevin stalking fish all along the shoreline, and Abby's first fish. I'll never forget that day on that beautiful lake together.

I'm getting very drowsy now, and I think I'm going to go and look for a phone to call you on before I go to my manifest call at 0500. It'll help me stay awake, and make me feel a whole lot better too. I love you my darling.

8 JUN 04 D + 250 0250 hrs. Camp Wolverine, Kuwait

Hello my love. Well, here I lay in my cot, once again unable to sleep. Fortunately, I got to talk to you a couple of times today. We get cut off with the Ft Riley morale line after 30 minutes, but at least I can call you right back, and the phones are reliable here. I really miss you.

Well, of course the travel plans changed today. If they had gone as planned I'm not sure what I would have done. Anyway, it looks like we'll be flying out of here sometime tomorrow night and heading to Baghdad. And then a convoy will come and pick us up sometime on Friday. It's all subject to change of course, but then again I expect it too.

As I lay here I was thinking about writing a story or article for the Army Times or Start & Stripes; something about Americana, or what in our own lives is America to us. I also wanted to add n there something about our history as well. We'll see how it goes.

10 JUN 04 D + 252 1945 hrs. Camp Stryker, IRAQ (BIAP)

Hello my love. Today was an interesting enough day. I have not been very motivated lately, since our return to Iraq, and since all we're doing around here is waiting for transportation back to Ar Ramadi, there's no real reason to be. For some reason, the Commander here, the 1st Brigade liaison, has taken a liking to me, and puts me in charge of just about everything. This always seems to happen to me no matter where I go.

There's a civilian security group here called Triple Canopy. Triple canopy is a term used in the Airborne and Special Operations communities. It means that an individual has three tabs on his shoulder, an Airborne tab, Special Forces Tab, and a Ranger tab as well. These civilians are all proven operators that were at one time in the military, most likely Special Ops. Yesterday, one of these guys gets an intelligence tip that there will be a possible mortar attack on the camp sometime in the next few days. This was yesterday afternoon, and I was appointed the NCOIC of the perimeter and all security forces. Rey DeLeon and Dwayne Beckles were assigned to the inside of the building to account for all the soldiers in this detachment, around 80 or so.

Both Ray and Dwayne wanted me to thank you for saving our asses today. We were over at the internet tent, emailing our wives and sending pictures home when we realized what time it was. We decided to go to chow after using the internet, and they finished before me and waited outside, talking to some old Iraqi man while they waited for me. I decided to email you all five of the pictures that I had taken over the last couple days, so it took a lot longer than theirs did. After I finally got done, we walked out of the internet tent and towards the chow hall. We got about 100 meters through this huge field, when I heard three big hollow thud sounds in the distance. Rey and Dwayne haven't been here before, and I told them that that didn't sound too good. No sooner than I got those words out of my mouth, three rockets impacted our area, two of them within 100 meters of our location. They were, of course, very loud, and the invisible shockwave was a harsh reminder of explosions past for me. We immediately ran into our building and got everyone to get their gear on and accounted for everyone. It was over in about 45 minutes or so, and then the Triple Canopy guys told me that there was an IED along the access road to our building. They were right, and it only took the Air Force EOD folks 43 minutes to show up. It was a long day, and very stressful at times. Well honey, I'll try and call later on my love. Kiss you later.

11 JUN 04 D + 253 1200 hrs.

Hello my love. I have to tell you that it was very nice seeing you a few hours ago. Even though the hajji internet doesn't have any webcams, it was very nice to see you on ours at home. I love you so much my love. It was very nice to finally get in touch with you. I miss you so very much honey.

Well, the convoy from Manhattan came in this morning, and we are not due to leave until this afternoon. We are scheduled to leave here sometime after 1600 hrs. and go to St. Mere Eglise, an old 82nd camp now run by the Marines. We'll have to stay there until midnight, and then leave to J.C. as we are supposed to travel during the hours of darkness only now. It would be nice to get stuck at St. Mere, also known as MEK, because it's so nice there. That's the place that had web cams when you and I flashed each other the first time over the internet. It's a very nice camp to get stuck on. The facilities are first rate, and everything down to the chow is better than we're used to. Hopefully, we'll have the chance to get on a web cam again, and you could see me for a change.

I am missing you more and more with each passing minute honey. This second time around is no joke, and I haven't even been back to J.C., and back to work yet. I am dreading going to the motor pool in this dreaded heat, and spending so much time in the sun. Anyway, I am going to try and catch a nap before my 1600 briefing. I'd like to get up and get in touch with you before we leave, so I'd better get some rest now before we're up all night on the road. I love you my darling. Kiss you later.

12 JUN 04 D + 254 1500 hrs.

I was so glad to be able to talk to you for so long on the computer this morning honey. I do feel a bit selfish in seeing you were asleep and got up to talk to me. I certainly do appreciate it, and I was feeling a bit needy this morning. I sometimes wonder how you feel when I'm feeling needy like that. I hope that it doesn't bother you. I do know you, and although I'm sure that it doesn't bother you, but rather comfort you in that I am needing you and I'm sure it makes you feel good to some degree; over here somehow the distance plays tricks on me and makes me question that somehow. I know that this sounds like babbling, but the distance between us and this intense heat are absolutely making me crazy.

Well honey our convoy should be here in about 9 hours or so, and although I am looking forward to getting back with the men, I dread possibly going out on a mission merely hours after returning. We'll see. I'm going to go and lie down some more and see if I can get some rest in case I do end up going out to Anaconda. I love you honey, and as promised I will cal you before we depart BIAP. I love you honey. Kiss you later.

2030 hrs.

Hello honey. I'm just sitting here during what I hope are my last few hours here at BIAP. I was talking to the Triple Canopy guys outside for a while, and swapping stories of our adventures here. I talked to this one guy who was in 5th Special Forces Group at Ft. Campbell and got out just two months ago. As an E-6 making all sorts of specialty pays, he was making about $65,000 to $70,000 a year. Now he's making $240,000 a year here. He's single though, and already paying on a huge house which will be paid off in the next year. Unbelievable. I know the money sounds nice, but the time away from home sure wouldn't be worth it to me. There was a time when I would have jumped all over that sort of thing, but not any more. Money can't buy what I have, and there's no amount that would be worth it to me to be away from you and the kids for another year.

I really don't know why, but today I'm having one of those really needy days. I think it's because I know that I'm going back up north, into the storm again. And with the 30 June deadline fast approaching, I predict that there will be a bloodbath throughout Iraq. The transitional government isn't anywhere near ready to take over its own country again. Oh well, I'm sure we'll see what happens soon enough. There's so much going on inside my head right now. I'm sitting in Baghdad, Iraq with no weapon or SAPI plates for my vest, I'm dehydrated, overheated, tired, on edge, and already ready to go home. I love you my darling. I'll write more later on, probably after I get to J.C. again. I promised you that I'd call before we took off, so I'll be heading over there in a little while. I love you honey. Kiss you later.

14 JUN 04 D + 256 2030 hrs.

Hello my darling. Well, today is the first complete day with the entire platoon gone on mission. I didn't do very much today; just a little prep for the upcoming range. I am to brief the Battalion Command Sergeant Major about the range in three days, and the platoon should return that same night. I was blessed to be able to talk to you again early this morning, and I will try again tonight. I miss you so much honey. At the risk of repeating myself, I have to tell you that leaving the second time was much worse. We are blessed in that you have the church and newfound friends back home; I wish I had something, anything similar out here . . . but I do not. I don't mean to sound so depressing, as I know that I love the love in my heart for you and the children, and my prayers of a safe return trip home. Somehow, though, the loneliness doesn't stop coming. It is a constant companion that I can never seem to evade.

I spent the better part of today cleaning my weapon, and adding some new equipment to it that I got from some Marines. I acquired a set of rails so that I might add my laser and flashlight to it without being so bulky. It really does help a lot, and doesn't look too redneck. Not that that's a bad thing, but everything has its time and place.

It's been a very long and lonely day. Everywhere I went, everyone asked about you and your family to see if you were alright, about the emergency leave and all. There is an attitude here that I see in just about everyone I see, that the end is coming and there's a light at the end of the tunnel as far as coming home. I simply cannot wait my love. I feel as though I have been on the verge of breaking down al day today. Several times I retreated to the hooch, only to find it lonely and empty, just wishing I could hold you. I have our music, and, sad as it may seem, some of it seems a little sad to me now when I listen to it and can't be near you . . . dancing with you. I know also that it's not the music that saddens me, but not being with you. This only tells me one thing, of the inner scars that I will bear from this tour will carry forever in some small way. I do feel that way my love. I feel as though there's a giant scar across my heart, and that it's the only thing keeping my heart together and from dying. I'm sorry my love, but at times like these I realize over and over again that there's no love like ours, as it should be. I may make jokes about Abby being a nun, or Kevin always mentioning that he likes the qualities in women that he sees in you. But I seriously hope and pray that our children find the kind of love that we have one day. They will know a happiness that they cannot even imagine. You are the root of all thing great in all of our lives my love, and we all truly do owe the possibility of all our happiness to God of course, but also to you. I love you my darling.

It is getting difficult for me to even write to you this evening, so I shall go for now. Kiss you later my love.

17 JUN 04 D + 259 0600 hrs.

Good morning my love. I just got back from talking to you just a short while ago, and woke the guys up for PT. No one is very motivated this morning, as two of my buddies were injured earlier this morning coming back from LSA Anaconda. They were near Baghdad when a daisy chained IED with four bombs with gas cans set on top of them went off. One guy, SSG K. got shrapnel in his leg and throat while SPC Moody got his finger shredded to the point of barely hanging onto his hand. The word is that they probably won't be coming back. It was a rough morning. The best part of it was that I got to talk to you, my love. I will write more later on my love. I have to get to PT now, and I still have a lot of work to do today in preparing for the range in two days. Kiss you later.

0800 hrs.

Hello my love. I really can't stop thinking about you today. Not that that's not the norm for me, but after this morning's attack, I really don't take anything for granted. I just really can't wait to come home to you for good honey. It was great to hear your voice this morning. It was a welcome reminder of reality in this uncivilized hole we're in. Things are very unsure here right now. No one knows if the guys who got hurt will return to us, but the general consensus is that they will be sent home. If so, then I'm happy for them and their families, even under the circumstances. I find myself almost wishing that something like that would happen to me, as bad as that sounds.

I love you so very much my love. Please don't ever forget that. I'll never give you a reason to forget that either. Well, once again, I must get going to start my work for the day. I love you honey. Kiss you later.

18 JUN 04 D + 260 0005 hrs.

Hello honey. Well, here I sit on guard again. I am not yet fully awake, and the stale night air is hot, sticking to my skin before I even realize it. Well, I think that I am legitimately depressed now. I have gone to bed between 2000 and 2100 hrs every night, also napping through the day at every opportunity. I dream of you a lot, and it appears that sleep seems to bring me closer to you, even in the smallest way. I will of course call you after my shift is over in an hour or so, but as much as I look forward to that, I look forward to seeing you even more. It may seem twisted, I know, but I always wake up exhausted, not wanting to get up at all.

As I sit here on our front porch, I am sweating profusely, as it's 88 degrees right now. Yesterday peaked out at 117 degrees and the next couple of days don't look any better. The heat is one thing that I certainly could have done without. I am fighting to stay hydrated, as it wears me down during the day and I spend as much time inside as possible in the air conditioning. The only drawback to that is getting cabin fever. Oh well, something's got to give here.

We were attacked yesterday in broad daylight. We got mortared again, although they didn't say for sure, they may have been more rockets. They landed near the 1-16 area, and of course, that's close enough for me. Of course, everything stopped for a little while, and then resumed about a half hour later. The big guns from 1-5 started going off and I was glad to see that we're once again allowed to fire back. That's always good news. I forgot how much the sounds of incoming fire really rattle me, and, when they came crashing down I was writing at the time. I jolted and found my pen all over the page. It felt as though my soul jumped right out of me. Did I mention that I really can't stand that feeling? Well, I really do. I certainly won't miss it later on either.

There is a lot of air cover this evening my love, and the choppers are flying low all over the place. I'm going to try and find out what's going on. I certainly hope that they're not MEDEVAC birds, because that will mean that the C-6 will be down again. The best news that I heard when I got back though, was that the Marines got their own phone and internet package. Thank God for small miracles. I love you my darling, and I'll kiss you later.

0730 hrs.

Good morning my love. I had dreams of you not once, but twice last night. It wasn't anything sexual, but simple things like our day in Manhattan and hanging around the house. I miss everything about you, and although I'm not sure where all these dreams are coming from lately, I just hope that they can carry me through the rest of this tour until I get home to you for real. Sometimes, when I think about it, I think that I may just be losing my mind with all these dreams and all. But then I figured out that I really don't much care even if that is the case, because anything that brings me closer, or at least makes me feel closer to you can't be something bad.

I truly do think about you every moment of the day. Our two weeks together has had many effects on me. Nothing else matter to me except you my love, you and the children. I love loving you.

I really miss you my love. I have to be patient about a great many things, among these having to wait to be with you. I also have to be patient about this damned rifle range. I want very badly to just get it done, but I have to teach a class on pre-marksmanship instruction this afternoon, and then we'll get up about 0430 tomorrow to pack up and head out until about noon. It's going to be hot tomorrow too. I just hate the thought of my guys and I standing out in the sun for seven hours wearing all of our gear. Oh well, at least it will pass another day waiting to come home to you my love.

I'll try and get some rest tonight, but I'm sure that I'll crash pretty hard tomorrow afternoon. I have a great deal of difficulty sleeping here since I came back. I have dreams about you every time I close my eyes, and I think that I have this deep seeded fear that a small piece of Abigail's heart will be broken forever because I left again. I'm just hoping that her anger is quelled by the time I get home. My baby's birthday is in five days, and it's really ironic. I can almost remember exactly what I was doing last year on her birthday, while I was in BNCOC. This lifestyle is just unreal sometimes. I always thought that I was a man of my own convictions, and I am. But what I also thought was that if I believed in something, I also had to take an active role in living out those convictions as well. This may be true sometimes; however I now know that this is certainly not true. I can still be a patriot, and have my convictions and not do what I'm doing now every day for the rest of my life.

I love you so much my darling. My darling Helen, I will always love you till the day I die. You truly are the best thing that ever happened to me, and you are truly the best part of me. Well, I have to sign off for now, and I'm sure I'll write more later on. I love you my darling.

19 JUN 04 D + 261 1630 hrs.

Hello my love. I'm going down to the motor pool later on with Zhou to do our laundry in the electric washing machine that they think no one knows they have. We have to wait until dark, but it gets our stuff cleaner and it's a lot faster than hand washing. I should have known my guys would find a way to work smarter, and not harder, even while I was gone.

Have I told you how much I miss you today? Well, let me pull my head out of my ass and tell you now. I do, I really do my love. I think I would have done just about anything to hold you today. The entire day was hot, hard, and mean, and really took a toll on me. I am physically and mentally exhausted, and it would be so rejuvenating for me to hold you right now. It's almost as if you energize me, and I am dearly missing that.

It's about Saturday morning at home right now, and I can't even imagine what you and the kids have planned for the day. I certainly hope that you enjoy your day. At least this week, I know you'll enjoy your Saturday more than I did mine. I am always grateful for that though. I haven't checked my email today, haven't had the chance yet, but I will later on tonight. I'll probably do the usual; check the stuff you sent first, then look at jobs, and then delete anything from Emily, and maybe see the occasional email from Pastor B.J. He seems very nice, but I respect his calling, especially at his young age. I really hope to develop something of a relationship with him over the coming months, as he's apparently now our pastor. I told him the other day that I'm glad to see that you're diving right in, even though it's no surprise to me due to your awesome personality honey. I can't wait to do the same. The team's just not complete without us being together. Well, I'm going to go and change, and get my laundry ready for washing'. I love you honey. Kiss you later.

2230 hrs.

Hello again my love. I just got back from the C-6 tent, and, although the phone line was way too long tonight, I was able to get on the internet. I left you a few messages but no luck talking with you. I do so look forward to that my love, even the conversations on instant messenger. Not only do I really miss our talks, but it's the only intelligent conversation I ever get to have. Talking with you makes me feel so good my love, and makes me feel a part of things at home. I'll probably wake up incredibly early again tomorrow morning, which is only in a few short hours, and try to call you again. I love you my darling. Kiss you later.

20 JUN 04 D + 262 1015 hrs.

Hello honey. I just got back from talking to you for about a half hour, and it really lifted my day. I'm sorry that I vented so much online prior to our phone call; I just have no outlet here. I can't really vent here at all, because the Soldiers are under me, and Nick feels the same way already. It sounds like you have everything covered with Abby's birthday. I know we always worry about making ends meet and making things happen, but I'm not sure why. I have more faith in you than anyone in the whole world my love. I think sometimes that we're hurt by the ones we love, our families, because they underestimate us and it leaves a bad taste in our mouth. Maybe one day they'll come around, and maybe they won't. Either way my love, I love you just the same, more than anything. I'll keep it short for now, and write more later on. I love you.

21 JUN 04 D + 263 1900 hrs.

Hello my love. Well, today was a lot better than yesterday. I still want to come home more than anything, and I still want to find a great job and move to somewhere where we can establish some roots. I really miss you and the kids a lot today. I should have called you at 0300 this morning while I had the chance. I got up to go to the bathroom and I was exhausted. Unfortunately, I went back to sleep.

This morning, four Marine snipers took off from the Combat Outpost, about a mile and a half from here, and went off to go and establish an OP (Observation Post). Usually, they go do this to observe some bad guys or something like that to gain some intelligence if possible. Well, I went to go and find out why the C-6 package was closed a little earlier, and those guys are the reason. Two hours after they left, their relief went to the OP to relieve them and found all four of them dead, execution style, with a single shot either in the back of their heads or in the face. That really got me rattled. They weren't even two miles from us when they were killed. The thing about it that sucks is not just that they were killed, but that reports have it that the enemy just walked up on them and caught them off guard. The reputation of the Marines has really taken a dive in my book. When they first arrived, I was even to the point of being on the same sheet of music with them as far as being on the same team. But since they got here, they've just screwed up so many things, created so many stupid rules, and not listened enough to those who preceded them that their reputation goes down another notch every time one of them gets killed. This is not because some Marine got caught off guard, but because most of the time their leadership allowed it to happen, passively or not. They just take too damn much for granted. I've faced the fact that I can't change it, and everyone I talk to just wants to get out of here so we don't get killed due to one of their stupid mistakes.

We also got briefed on the Anaconda mission today, at least just a FRAGO. We'll leave the night of the 25th, or early morning on the 26th and stay for three or four days. I haven't heard it officially yet, but I think this is the last logistics run for the battalion before we start packing up to go home. After the last run, where SSG K, and SPC Moody go shot up pretty bad coming back from there, no one wants to even talk about it. Everyone knows we're going, but everyone is just a tad bit on edge. We're supposed to return to Camp J.C. on the 29th, the day before the official turnover to the Iraqi's. It seems the closer we get to that day, the more violence spills over into the streets of Ramadi. This truly is the worst place on earth.

22 JUN 04 D + 264 0630 hrs.

Good morning my love. Although I couldn't call you last night, I did dream of you again. This is becoming a regular thing, nightly in fact. You know how I don't usually sleep too well, but lately, it's not that I'm sleeping well, just deeper and more soundly. I am dreaming a lot more than I ever have before, and I think this is leading me to want to sleep more often so I can see you more often. I'm really not sure what it is, but it works for me right now. Normally it's not about sex or anything like that, but last night it was. And damn were we good. Thank you, by the way.

Well, today we have a lot of work to do. We have to acquire our conex inserts. These are really big cardboard inserts, like boxes, that we use to pack our stuff in. Also, there's a big rush to get all the tires in the battalion fixed as soon as possible. We'll be working a lot outside over the next month or so, but for good cause. I honestly don't think that anyone will bitch about the workload coming up due to the fact that it's what will get us home. I know I surely won't.

I'm so glad that you've found some good company in the church. I can't tell you how much that pleases me that you not only have decent company, but what a warm welcome you and the children have received there. It's almost a relief to me that there's finally a church that we can 'tolerate', as it were. After that one up in Fairbanks, I didn't think we'd ever be open minded enough to attend another one. Anyway, I truly am glad about this though, and I can't wait to get back home and be there with the entire family.

From the porch, I can see Dusty Sinkes and his platoon getting ready to head out on yet another mission. I always pray for them as Charlie Company goes out often. They were already out for about four hours last night, getting back in around 2300 or so, and now they're at it again. There is a fair share of dirt bags here, but there are also some great folks. I am trying now more than ever to see the good in people, even the ones who don't rate so high in my book. I'm trying very hard to not be judgmental. Even surrounded by the Army's 'zero tolerance' mentality, somehow I have tried very hard to just be a person at times, and be more opening minded. I attribute this to you, my love. I probably never would have done this without you; having met you, had the chance to love you, be loved by you, and be a better man because of being with you. I love you so very much.

Well, I have a very busy day today, and I should get started making my list of things that I need to get done soon here. I will cal you as soon as the C-6 comes back up again, and write more later on. I love you more than anything my darling Helen. Kiss you later.

0800 hrs.

Hello honey. I just finished my list of stuff to do this week. Unfortunately, it's long and not too easy to do, but the men still seem motivated to some degree. All I seem to be able to think about lately is you, and coming home to you. I know this must sound repetitive right about now, but I feel like this feeling just won't leave me. That's good in a way, but at the same time, I feel like I've lost a little of my edge since coming back here. It's more than my head just not being in the game . . . just something different that I just can't put my finger on. Speaking of coming over here a second time, I'm listening to my music right now, the Black Crowes "Twice As Hard' to be exact. How ironic, because it was 'twice as hard as the first time I said goodbye'.

I think that our music has kept me sane, at least to some degree, during the tour. I know that I probably also mentioned this before as well, but it's funny how in touch with you I feel when I listen to our music. I still keep our date every night at 2200 out on the porch. Maybe it's the music that keeps me dreaming of you, or taking the time intentionally every day to spend some with you, even 10,000 miles away. 'Tonight girl, it's only you and me.' . . . . every night honey.

It's just amazing how close the music brings me to you, my love. Every song, it seems, has a story, or a memory, or some sentimental attachment to it. I hold it very near to my heart, and I cling to it like I would my very last breath. And it's not just those moments or memories in particular that I cling to, but those that have yet to live together. I miss you so much my love that some days I feel like my heart will dry up in this dusty desert. I just want to survive long enough to get all my men and I home to you and our families.

Well, the men should be back any minute from chow, and as usual I have my coffee. I'll brief them on what's going on, and then we'll start our day. I'm also starting night rehearsals for my gun truck so everyone is more than ready to drive, gun, and dismount while wearing their night vision goggles. More on that later on.

1800 hrs.

Hey honey. Today was steady, but not overly busy. I got a lot done with my trucks today, and finished playing catch up with my counseling's from when I was on leave. I've had to send troops out in ones and twos all day long to help with different missions, but at least the hard part of the day is over now. It's not right, but Rafael and the LT are across camp right now, taking down some old concertina wire, and they've been there for hours. The bay is so nice and quiet right now, in part because the generator just went out again. It starts to overheat in the afternoons, with the sun beating down on it as well as the heat from the unit itself. Usually it doesn't last too long, and is more than an inconvenience than anything. Today was 116 degrees, not nearly as hot as the other day. Sunday it was up to 120. The heat really can be unbearable at times, but it is a means to an end in some strange way. I look at it as if I can get through the majority of the hot weather, then I can come home. I keep telling myself that.

2200 hrs.

Hello love of my life. Well, it was short and sweet, but I finally got to talk to you again just now. The C-6 just reopened, and I can see by that that the Marines are getting better at their notification process. I still can't believe the level of complacency they have. It's ironic; the maximum punishment that the military allows under the UCMJ for failure to perform as a sentry is death. Unfortunately, they paid the ultimate price for their own complacency. As if that wasn't the worst part, the hajji's that killed them made off with their comms, two sniper rifles, ammo, and all their gear. Now hajji can get a shot off at 900 meters without anyone having a clue where it came from. To be honest, that does spook me a little, being that where I sit in the truck gets hit 9.5 out of 10 times. I know that this isn't confidence inspiring, and I'm not sure it really even bothers me anymore. I just want to do my job and come home. I love you so much honey, and hearing your voice tonight brought me back to reality just a tad. I love you my darling. Kiss you later.

24 JUN 04 D + 266 1300 hrs.

Hello my love. Well, thank God I got through last night. My worst fear was that I wouldn't get to talk to you and the kids for a while, especially for Abby's birthday. I'm glad that her birthday party went so well, and you're absolutely the best mother in the world my love . . . one of the endless reasons that I love you. I can't imagine how happy Abby must have been with her presents and cake, and all that company. And then to follow it up with church with the whole family, it must have been something.

Although the most important thing is that Abby had a good birthday, I can't help but feel the emptiness of not being there. I can only hope that with all the excitement of the day that Abby didn't miss me much. It just feels like another piece of me, chipping away at me a little at a time. Okay, enough feeling sorry for myself for one day.

This morning, we were supposed to go out with the Dog element again, to baby-sit the engineers digging a trench around the perimeter of J.C. It's wide enough and deep enough to where a vehicle, any vehicle, could not successfully negotiate it, and make it through the wire with a suicide VBIED. I hate being in a place where things like this are normal.

2030 hrs.

Hello my love. Ar Ramadi is burning tonight. This morning, some insurgents walked into a police station downtown, a place where I've been many times, and told the IP's that they were going to blow up the building. The IP's naturally retreated by evacuating the building, prisoners and all, and the insurgents came back later on with three VBIED's which of course leveled the building. In the meantime, the IP's never notified anyone of the potential threat, so when it happened, they finally called Brigade. After being on standby for about five hours, Brigade decided that the Iraqi's would have to deal with this one themselves. They just sat there and took it, and took it for granted that we would come to the rescue after the fact.

Another good reason for staying out of this one is the intelligence that we've received recently. The intelligence stated that the insurgents intent was to do something like this to draw out a QRF unit, be fortified and in position before we got there, and just commence an all out slaughter. We knew this going in, and everyone was really on edge. I loaded extra ammo in some extra magazines that I 'acquired', and prayed most of the morning. I got my heavy machine gunners another thousand rounds each, and just to be sure, packed extra stuff in my overnight bag including lots of batteries for my night vision stuff. Thankfully though, we declined the invitation to go out and 'play' today.

Today was really nerve-wracking, and I'm glad, at least for now, that the immediate stress is over. We were told the obvious today, that it would get worse before it got better. Anyone can see this. After the VBIED's today, there have been fires and isolated incidents of small arms engagements all over town since the weekend, and all through today. It's ironic, that we're in relative peace here on our camp, and we can see the columns of smoke all over town around us. It's like some ominous scene from a war movie all around us, except the sounds and smells I live with every day will haunt me for a long time, to be sure. The reminder of what I have at home is with me every single moment of every day. It's still fresh in my mind, and I think that's what makes feel like I'm riding the razor's edge now. Before I went home on leave, I was accustomed to this every day, and memories of home had faded to a certain extent. I suppose that that may have helped me deal with the here and now of Iraq. Don't get me wrong, I'm absolutely glad to have had the opportunity to go home and see you and the kids for a couple of weeks my love. It's just that now, I think about you and the kids all the time, and I think that over the years I've been wore down as far as how much I can take.

I must have gone over every possible scenario that I could possibly think of today, regarding going down to the ghetto in Ramadi, where we were supposed to be going. I know that neighborhood pretty well, and it's just not good. There are too many high-rise buildings around the area, too many alleys and corners everywhere. Hajji would have definitely had the advantage, and I honestly believe that if we'd one out there today that it would have been a disaster where we would have filled a lot of body bags.

I have to say though, that the guys were all very brave in the face of danger, and all were motivated to go with me, and the platoon. It was obvious that no one wanted to go, but everyone was motivated, even during the five hour wait prior to getting cancelled. Most of the guys played cards, smoked, drank water and soda, and did some of their little pre-mission rituals. I truly believe that everyone was ready to die today, if that makes any sense. Not that anyone wanted to, of course, but we all knew that the deck was stacked against us from the beginning.

2230 hrs.

Hello honey. Well, we got to talk online for a short while. You're helping Dave and Brandy move, and are very mobile today. I'm not upset, but I couldn't get a hold of you after I called the Settlemire's, our house, and your cell twice each. I know that it sounds like I'm bitching, but I'm really not. I just needed to hear your voice today. I can't wait for the day I get home and don't have to worry about this kind of thing anymore. I love you so much my love.

Tomorrow should be filled with maintenance. We have to put a ring mount on one of my cargo trucks so we can mount a machine gun on top. This makes the gunner very vulnerable, and I'm not really sure why the command made the decision to do this. I've been around the block more than once, but I suppose I still don't understand a lot of things that go on around here.

25 JUN 04 D + 267 0700 hrs.

Good morning my love. I just got back from talking with you. It was a good conversation, however I do need to be a bit more patient. As a husband I have no apprehensions about us, and as a father I'm glad that our children have so many people in their lives right now. Sometimes I get a little paranoid that it may be just a bit too easy for me to be replaced, seeing that I'm not around that much. There's guys like Dave, which is more of a negative influence than anything, but then there's guys like B.J., and Richard the therapist. Don't get me wrong, I'm glad that we've finally found a therapist that is open minded and sees al the wonderful qualities that make up Kevin, but it seems to me that he may be a little bit over complementary. And what's with the whole 'princess' thing with Abigail. Oh hell no. There's not a damn thing I can do about this right now, so I'm not going to focus on it so much. But when I get home, this crap better have stopped. I'm sure he's okay, but the fact is that I've never met him, and he's a successful therapist, and . . . I don't know . . . . bottom line, he can just kiss my ass for now. Okay, I'm done.

I miss you so very much my love. I wish so badly that I could be there right now. Kevin sounded great on the phone tonight, and Abby was just adorable when you asked her who you were talking to. I miss all the little things at home.

Last night, you told me of the reunion briefings coming in July and August. I could hear the excitement in your voice honey, and I confess, it made me a little excited too. There's not much t be excited about over here, except waking up breathing again the next day. Like my other tours, this has once again taught me, reminded me I should say, that sometimes that's all we can hope for.

0800 hrs.

Well, today's plan has just gone to shit. I just got back from the Doc for Simmons. He has walking pneumonia, and is down for the day. Zhou is gunning for the LT all day, and my only other soldier, Clark, is on guard until 0900. I can't see getting very much done today, except for the very basic stuff. My ring mount for the 5-ton is going to have to wait. Oh well, some days that's just how it goes. I love you my darling. Kiss you later.

26 JUN 04 D + 268 1300 hrs.

Hey honey. Well, I got to talk to you this morning, and that started my day off better than it could have. I was tossing and turning al night, coughing like I had razor blades in my throat. Simmons started this all off the other day when he started coughing, and it turned out that he has walking pneumonia. Yesterday and this morning both Nick and I turned up the same way. We both are going to the doc today and will probably have a chance to rest tonight and tomorrow. We really worked the soldiers hard today, but not the hardest that they ever have. It's good though.

The LT wants to 'take all the NCO's to dinner' tonight. This is supposed to be some sort of pow wow with us for one reason or another. He had one with the Soldiers the other night, and I'll say one thing: my guys are totally loyal. It wasn't over for even ten minutes and both Nick and I knew every word spoken in that meeting.

It's a funny thing about leaders and their troops in this environment, they're tighter than most folks can imagine and the only forbidden thing is disloyalty in any form. My guys hold true to this and I am forever appreciative. Lately the LT has been turning into a 'yes' man with the company and levels higher as well. He really doesn't fight for us for anything, and every tasking that comes down the line he says yes to, even if it interferes with one or more that we already have going. We understand this, and our guys perform every task without question. He explained that we have to shoulder a heavier load within HHC than the other line companies. This means that all the QRF missions, the mayor's cell, the construction and earthmover engineer assets, the work order section, and anything else that they can think up comes from HHC. This we know, but we can't understand why every time a Marine or a Seabee, or even another Battalion asks us for something that the answer has to be yes very single time. Sometimes, you can honestly say 'no', because the workload is too much. To some people, being a politician is too important than having the admiration of your soldiers. That is sad.

When we spoke this morning, you mentioned that Emily sent you a message that because neither Gary nor I got through on the phone on Father's Day, that 'her boys tried to make up for it, but there was still pain there.' I really think that she doesn't really understand the living conditions over here. Nor does she understand that when the phones are down, then so is the internet, and not just here on J.C., but all of western Iraq. Any unit falling under the 1st Marine Division (or 1MARDIV) is subject to this if anyone should die or become critically injured in our area of operations. I suppose that our families will never truly understand us, but I'm finally okay with that my love. As long as I have your love, I can get through anything. I love you so much honey.

Well, I have to get going now my love. I have to get ready for a mock board this afternoon, and make sure Zhou does well. I'm also going to check my email. I love you my darling. Kiss you later.

2215 hrs.

Hey honey. I know we got cut off today online, because the NCO at the C-6 desk had low power on his computer and although it was ten minutes prior to shutdown time, he cut off the main switch for all the computers. It was annoying, and he was dead wrong, but at the same time I think that it shows a piece of the big picture here. People are starting to get a short temper. It's been that way for some time, but I got somewhat refreshed on leave, and since it took me out of this mentality for a short while I had to get back into things here to see it again. My guys are like that as well, although they do their best.

The LT had his sensing session with us tonight, and although I wasn't open minded at first, I did eventually open up and all of the Squad Leaders did some talking. He briefed us on the results of his session with the soldiers the other night, and he shared some things with us, among them that the soldiers were getting burned out. He also brought up certain things that Nick and Dorelus and I do that the soldiers don't appreciate. We also told him that some of those things wouldn't change because although the soldiers are getting burned out, some of the things we do with and for them, although annoying to them, shouldn't change in staying true to them as NCO's. I probably will let up a little, but not too much, because I too am feeling the strain of our entire situation. You can see it in this journal, and I'm quite sue you can hear it in my words that the tour is taking its toll on me. I have never been so serious about getting out in my entire life. I told the LT that tonight, and it felt good to actually say it out loud, to other leaders, and mean it. This is a first for me. I don't want to mention it to anyone higher than the LT because in this unit, there is an unspoken prejudice experienced if they know you want to leave the Army. It's a funny thing too. I think they take you wanting to leave for your own reasons as a personal thing, and then take it out on you professionally. I've never seen anything like it.

27 JUN 04 D + 269 2130 hrs.

Hello my love. Well, I got to talk to you a little earlier, while you were in church, but the satellite had trouble and we were cut off yet again. I really do get tired of that. I am still feeling really sick, and there's not much I can do about it. I suppose I'll just let it run its course and hope it goes by quickly.

So, I've been thinking about the bar lately, and where we're going to live when I leave the Army. I just want to avoid the stigmatism that I 'used to be in the Army', and get over that insecurity soon because sometime, God willing, in the next year, we'll be looking at that. There seem to be so many things to think about; where to live, what type of job to get, what kind of schools for the kids are in the area? I just wish it were all just a tad bit easier. I'm sure that it will be when I get home, because it feels like such a burden when I'm here alone thinking about all these things. I have so many ideas about Smokejumper's, however I realize that my first priority should be to find a location and a job first. It's almost like I'm eating dessert before the main meal. I've been thinking about this stuff nonstop for three days now, and I just get excited when I think about it all.

I tried to call Challas & Billy this afternoon. I really wanted to talk to them, and Stephanie as well. When we talked last night, you mentioned that Chance was screwing up lately, about wanting to go out with friends, and leave Stephanie and Taylor at home. I wasn't going to get on him, just find out what the deal was, and maybe talk to him a little. We'll see how it goes. I'm very tired now, and I'm going to try and get some rest. I got a short nap today, but I think that my body is just worn out. Anyhow, I'll try to call you in the morning my love. Kiss you later.

28 JUN 04 D + 270 2045 hrs.

Hello my love. Today was a steady day, but not too busy. I got to talk to you this morning for about 40 minutes. I was really glad for that. I got the added bonus of catching you in the bath tub when I called. To most people it wouldn't be much over the phone, but I have an imagination, and even over the phone I'll take what I can get when we're ten thousand miles apart.

Well, you've probably heard the news by now on your end, but we pulled a surprise on the enemy today. Intel suggests that the enemy is planning a massive wave of attacks to create chaos within the entire country over the turnover on 30 JUN. In order to give hajji a disillusioned sense of timing, we handed over formal sovereignty to the new Iraqi government today at noon. Things are pretty tense right now, and we now have a curfew of 2100 hrs. at least for a while. The threat is heightened for now, but hopefully enough Iraqi Police and ICDC guys will stand up for their own country and start to rebuild on their own. I really have my doubts though.

We have another mission early tomorrow morning, pulling 'Dog watch' again. The good news is that we should be done by 0800 hrs. and then off to the motor pool to change even more tires. My squad has to change five out of six of our trailer tires, which doesn't surprise me at all. It should be yet another hot day in the desert. Today it only went up to 117 degrees. It's late right now, and it's still 100 outside. I can't wait to leave this third world hole.

I worked on a lot of the planning for the bar today, as I was on light indoor duty today all day. I got a little bit of cabin fever towards the end of the day, but I really needed the rest. I had a slight temperature this morning when I followed up with the Doc, and my congestion hadn't really changed at all, so I got to stay inside today. I got more water in me than I ever though I could. I think that I really needed this today, although I'd rather not have been sick at all. That's just the way it goes. I've given it a lot of thought about where I'd like to talk to you about us settling down. I'm still not sure about anything yet, but I think about the family of course. And then I think about the people whom I know you wouldn't mind being near, and there's really only one choice there. So I think I'm going to job search as much as I can in Nevada, to be near Billy & Challas, and Stephanie and the kids. I really think that would be the best for our kids too, since we chose them as the benefactor of our children in the worst case scenario. We'll see what happens though.

Well, I'm off to try and call you one last time for the night my love. I'll check my email and see if any good jobs came up. I love you my darling. Kiss you later.

29 JUN 04 D + 271 0745 hrs.

Good morning my love. I got an early start this morning, and got to talk to you before I took off on our morning mission. I was glad for that, and even more so in seeing that you were having girls night with Brandy and Angel. I really am glad to see that you're having the girls over as well as so much interaction with the church.

I'm in the bay watching weapons right now, and I just got back from the port-o-jon . . . not feeling too well this morning. It's amazing how fast you can get dehydrated out here. I'll just push the fluids again today and try and pick myself up again.

Today should be a very long day. The LT wants everyone to be at the motor pool all day long working on trailer tires. We may as well, because it has to get done before we leave anyway. It's just that so much time in the sun makes me really irritated. I think a lot of it nowadays is the fact that I know I want to get out and have already started making plans for that. Nothing special showed up in my email last night in the line of jobs, but I'll keep looking. I'm going to go now and try to call you before we get down to the motor pool all day. I love you my darling. Kiss you later.

30 JUN 04 D + 272 0700 hrs.

Good morning beautiful. I just got back from grading a PT test. Clark failed the setups, but other than that, everyone else did fairly well. I got up at 0430 this morning, and although that's really early, I'm not very tired right now. I'm sure that I'll feel it later on. I suppose it's another day of breaking down tires at the motor pool. I think that we're going to have some classes today as well. There's really nothing to e excited about here lately. The threat is heightened nowadays, and when we went outside the wire yesterday, both times I was more nervous than I ever have been. I'm starting to get very numb with everything going on here; the length of the tour, the people, the ongoing mission, and not seeing you and the kids. I know it sounds like I'm bitching, and I suppose I am. I don't care though. I just want to make it out of here alive, and get on with my life.

Yesterday, an American POW that the insurgents have been holding for over a month now, was beheaded on Al Jazeera, the Islamic media network. This was of course in response to the handing over of Iraq, confirming their sovereignty. And although it's sad that another American had to lose his life over here, the reason that they gave for killing him did something else besides kill another American. I believe, and I may be alone on this one, that killing him for that reason not only made him a martyr, but also allowed him to die for Iraq's freedom and sovereignty . . . basically for their cause and country. I don't think the insurgents see it that way, but it's a logical reasoning. I pray for his family.

2130 hrs.

Hey my love. I finally feel tonight like I made a little bit of progress because I finally got a chance to talk to you about the job I applied for and a little bit about the bar and our future. It was nice to have some feedback and interaction with you honey, as I miss that on a daily basis more than anything. I'm beginning to seriously tire of everyone around me very quickly.

I just feel so alive sometimes these days my love and it's all because of you. For the first time in my life I have more than hope that we can make it on the outside. I'm sure that as resourceful and creative as we both are we can always figure something out. We always do. I think that we can really make something out of this family bar and grill idea of ours. I really do hope that that one dream comes true. I love you honey. Good night my love. Kiss you later.

1 JUL 04 D + 273 2215 hrs.

Hey honey. Well, today wasn't very hard to deal with on camp. I wanted to call you after we finished our mission, but another Marine got killed today and of course the C-6 is closed. They've had a lot of practice in the past months, so we're all hoping they're on point with the notification process and get it open again as fast as possible.

Today's focus was on 'Super Sapper', a Battalion-wide competition that tests the agility, skills, and determination of combat engineers. We just provided gunship security towards the outer edge of camp. Of course, the engineers had to ruck march out there, about two miles or so. That's not really that far for a ruck march, but with all that gear on, plus a ruck, and in 120 degree heat, it really was a test. Our purpose was only to provide gun ships, however my squad loaded heavy on water in anticipation of the contestants. Sure enough, when they got to us, they were all but exhausted. A couple of buddies were on the teams, and they certainly appreciated the water. We iced it down in our coolers, which was a really nice touch.

Other than the incomprehensible pain of not being able to contact you today, today wasn't too bad. While we were out on mission, Clark, my gunner was playing with a wart on his hand. Apparently, he has a hard time seeing his own blood . . . a real hard time. When he saw it, he barely got out a 'Sergeant Breland . . . ', and went unconscious. He was in the gun hatch, and his body immediately went limp and he fell over backwards. A million thoughts raced through my head, the first one being that the Marines killed last week had two long range sniper rifles stolen by hajji, and my first reaction was to get on top of the gun truck and look for holes. I couldn't find any which was a relief, but at the same time I still didn't know what was the matter with him. I leaned him up on my chest a little, and I could hear him breathing. I think that's when I started breathing again myself. He was going to be okay, and I surmised that he must have just passed out. I was force hydrating the men all day, knowing how hot it is. I thought he must have locked his knees while resting against the rear side of the gun hatch. Nope, that wasn't it either. When I got him conscious enough to tell me what the deal was, I almost had to laugh. By now, the medic was over at our vehicle, and the engineers had helped pull him clear of the truck, which is no easy task when he's standing up in a gun hatch and slumps over backwards. He was pale, as if he'd seen a ghost, but was going to be okay. I rode in the gun hatch on the way back and got an instant education about life in the gun hatch. I wouldn't recommend smiling when riding up there, especially in a desert environment.

Also, we were briefed today that sometime in the last 24 hours, hajji got one of his wishes granted. Apparently some soldier near Fallujah wasn't paying attention, and got kidnapped by some insurgents. The announcement was made this afternoon around here, and everyone fears the worst about his fate. I can only pray for his safe return, but deep down I know that he probably isn't ever going to make it home.

This brings up another good point about how much politics and policy have changed this war from when it first started. I don't see the kid from Ohio a few months ago, or the kid from today getting a whole lot of publicity over this deal. Yet when Jessica Lynch was taken as a POW, the whole damn world was on its knees, begging to get her back. I would like to think that there's a SPECOPS team or something out there planning an operation to somehow go out and get this kid. I can't even fathom what his family must be going through right now. I can only imagine that it's their worst nightmare come true.

Well my love, today did have a positive note too. DECON only got two slots for our trucks to get transported back on the back of giant trailers. The good news is that two out of three of my squads trucks will be the two from the platoon to go. That's really good news for us as we've had trouble with these twenty year old trucks since the day they got here. The squad was of course excited to hear this, as this means talking about this kind of stuff gives us another indication that we're starting to wind things down here. That's always a good sign.

Well, it's time for me to say good night once again my love. I hope you're having sweet dreams tonight my love. Kiss you later.

2 JUL 04 D + 274 1000 hrs.

Good morning my love. I'm sorry to report that today is a really bad day for me. I am starting to visibly see my own depression. I am isolating myself further and further form my peers, and occasionally my soldiers as well. I am becoming very introverted, and my frustration is growing by the day.

We have another mission today. We're taking the Firefighters over to Champion for a video teleconference or something like that. I'm taking some music and my chair so I can write a little while I'm there. Anything to keep me busy.

1930 hrs.

Hello honey. I can't tell you the disappointment that I feel right now, since we got back from Champion and our C-6 is still down. I even went down and talked to commo to verify if we actually should be open or not. They said no, to my dismay.

Our battalion never seems to track the little things, the things that everyone deems as so important. I'm whining, I know. I jus want to talk to you so badly my love. I was so excited to have you both on the phone, and then on the webcam as well, and then crushed when I had to disconnect so quickly and get back to the trucks.

The depression that I spoke of earlier is really getting to me. I just went to take a shower, and it's my first in three days. The shower units and water are actually plentiful this week, and should be from now on, but I've had no motivation to go there, even when it's hot as hell. The last thing that I like to do before I turn in for the night, and can actually try and lie down without you is call you. Hearing your voice my love, has some sort of soothing effect, some kind of healing power for me, and I actually feel physically weakened without it. I know I sound pitiful, but I am truly needy for you. I always used to worry that you would eventually resent me for being this way, but I have come to love the fact, among many other things over the last years, that you've embraced this about me; and I you my darling. Our neediness for each other is one of our most endearing and adorable qualities. As a matter of fact, I think that when people look at us, they probably can't help but see that in us. A lot of folks probably don't understand us when they see us, o course because they themselves aren't, but perhaps wish they were. Even our friends openly admire our great marriage and relationship, yet don't do anything about their own. Is it me or is that totally ironic? I'm not sure, but I have always loved the way people react to you and I as a couple. It's not so much how we are, but how we are together. I love you so much my darling, and I am missing you something terrible today.

Well, I have already had my day go better than the last couple, since I got to talk to you today. It's more than I had the last couple of days. I do so miss you honey. I am going to try and get some rest now, since we're cleaning out our conex tomorrow morning, trying to prep it for our impending redeployment. It doesn't really mean anything as far as our timeline goes, but it is a physical symbol of progress towards everyone's ultimate goal. Good night my love. I pray that you have sweet dreams tonight. Kiss you later my love.

3 JUL 04 D + 275 1230 hrs.

Hey honey. The C-6 is open once again, and I got to talk to you online for a while this morning. That was nice, as I felt horrible about yesterday and having to cut you off in order to leave Champion to come back to J.C. again.

With Nick gone, that will leave me with no one to talk to around here. The last months of this tour are going to be unbearable, as they already are without you my love. Now I'll have absolutely no help whatsoever in any area. The only thing I can count on is you, on the rare occasion that I do get to talk to you, and my weapon. I really do detest living like this, and I pray every day that we do not get extended. I really don't think that I could take much more than this. This tour already has a burden which I don't think I'll recover from anytime soon. I only pray that one day I do.

INDEPENDENCE DAY D + 276 0800 hrs.

Good morning my love. I just got off the phone with you a little while ago, and although we got cut off, I know I can call you again soon. I want to call you before you go to bed anyway. It sounded like you and the kids were having a good time watching fireworks. God, I wish I could have been there. The kids sounded really excited, and I wish I could have seen their faces.

They're having a barbecue and a softball tournament here today. I still can't seem to relax enough here to leave my weapon 300 meters away from me and go play some game. We had another mortar attack this morning, before I called you. It's getting so routine that it barely phases me anymore. I've always said that it's truly amazing what you can get used to, but at this point, all that seems to matter is that everyone is okay after the attack and just go on with our day. I really do hate living like this, but one day it'll be better, and I'll be home.

Thanks so much for the pictures you sent last night. They really were great, and it's always a morale booster to get pictures from you honey. Any time that I get to see you in any form or fashion; it always makes me feel better.

Hey honey, we just got back from holding a mock board for the soldiers going to the promotion board this week. I'm taking Zhou, and he smoked it today. He did really well, and the bio that I helped him write really knocked the board off their feet. In the middle of the board, though, we got hit with mortars again, and 1-16 took wounded, however no one was killed thank God.

This afternoon serves as yet another reminder that we're never really supposed to relax too much. It reaffirms my beliefs that I can't really breathe easy until I get home. I really can't stand living like this. On the brighter side of things, at least we had our own fireworks today. The only difference is that this kind will kill you.

1745 hrs.

Hello honey. I am feeling a bit frustrated today. After the two mortar attacks, and the consistent heat, I fear that I am just wearing thin . . . my patience, and some days even my hope for ever leaving this place. Whenever the mortars and rocket attacks come, I always seem to hear the thud in the distance, and I just wait for it to come, and pray that it's not coming for my men and me. We've been blessed thus far, and I pray for all of our continued safety. As a matter of fact, I'm praying for a lot of things lately, and I just hope that God sees his way to granting these prayers.

2200 hrs.

Good evening my love. Let me say first that I do apologize for my odd words and seeming lack of faith lately. I'm sure this is a test, and if it is, I'm sure that I'm failing miserably. I would never take for granted one of God's tests for me; however, my basic need of you is overwhelming at times. Never in my life have I had such a need my love, and that, rest assured, will never go away. Every day I feel like I'm suffocating without you honey, and it's not the fear or concern of not breathing that bothers me, it's just the time apart from you.

Well, we all lived through another day. The Command worked hard to have a nice meal for us today. At dinner, they served lobster tail, steak, shrimp, and vegetables. It was very nice, but I started feeling rough in the middle of the meal. I had a stomach ache, but it didn't come from eating too much or not enough. I think it was a physical manifestation of my feelings of late. I can't stand the thought of missing another holiday with you and the kids. Our anniversary is just going to put me through hell, I know. I can't even bear the thought of it my darling. After all, our anniversary is supposed to celebrate us, and unfortunately that isn't possible this year.

5 JUL 04 D + 277 0700 hrs.

Hello my love. I just got back from talking to you on the phone, and I'm glad to hear that the barbecue went well, and there was such a good turnout for the 4th of July picnic with the church folks as well. I'm glad to see that you and Pam and Brandy are hanging out too. I hope it breaks up the time apart and gives you something to do.

I came back to the hooch just now and found Zhou asleep with two study guides in his bed with him. He's been studying so hard for the board tomorrow, and he's a little nervous, just as everyone is before their board. Our Command Sergeant Major is pretty tough, and it's kind of a shock when you go to his promotion board because he really lightens up a lot. But I'll be in there with him, and thankfully he takes comfort in that.

Well, we're on our own schedule now that the last company PT test is over, and CTT and NBC training is as well. We got some info from the Brigade Commander last night about his new command philosophy since the turnover. Basically, the mission for the platoon is still the same, and although it takes Brigade approval for us to leave the camp now, even to Champion, our missions should decrease dramatically. I have 130 missions now, and I could honestly use the slower pace. I'm sure you'll be glad to hear it too honey. I haven't left anything here that I ever need to come back for, so hopefully everything will go as planned when I get home, and after the stop-loss is lifted, we can get out and move on with our lives without any more combat tours.

When you told me that Kevin didn't want to go fishing with Dave and Sawyer because he wanted to wait and go with me, I didn't know what to say. The right thing to do as a father is for me to tell him that it's okay if he goes with his friends, which I did. But Kevin is Kevin, and he didn't budge on that one. I'm so proud to be his Dad.

I'm so proud of all of our kids. I think the mixture of their stubborn nature, (where they got that I'll never know) and the way we are raising them is a good combination. I believe that not only will they grow up with good morals and in a loving home, but that mix is a good reason that they're so loyal as well.

1700 hrs.

Hello honey. I just got back from making a water run with Zhou. We had to go and get 1200 gallons of water, which completely fills up one of our TPU trucks for a mission tomorrow. We're doing a practice run for operating a wash rack. That's a good sign. We were also told that we couldn't order any more parts unless it was for a deadline fault on a vehicle. Another good sign. The bad news is that my pump on my TPU took a dump today and we have to order a new one very quickly, due to the fact that it's a DECON vehicle, and there still is a chemical threat that we have to be prepared to contend with. I hope and pray that it doesn't come to that.

The temperature topped out at 121 degrees today, one of the hottest days since we've been here. I don't think that I drank this much water even when I was in Somalia. I just can't ever seem to get enough. It's good for me, so I really can't complain.

We just got a mission handed down to us from Brigade this afternoon. They want us to help build two tent cities for the incoming troops, the 2nd Infantry Division . . . . our replacements. That's definitely a good sign, and I can't wait to see them roll into Camp J.C. and start asking questions. That will definitely be a good day. It'll be another day closer to you honey; something tangible that I can actually see and hear . . . something that will show us that the end is really near.

2230 hrs.

Hello my love. Well, I just got off the phone with you, cut off actually, and that really frustrated me a lot. I am wound up pretty tight these days, and I went off earlier in our first conversation of the night. I'm sorry about that, so sorry that I don't even have the words. You deserve better than that. I didn't mean to get upset at what you asked me, however I've always been self conscious about how I look, and I took it way too personally. If you're still concerned about how you look to you, and you still want to do something about it when I get home, then we will . . . . we both will. I promise. Whatever it takes my love. I just want you to be happy, and whatever it takes to make that happen, then so be it.

Of course, it didn't help that Mike called earlier, just before my second call, and started bitching at you about stuff. I can hardly believe that he didn't realize that he wasn't divorced yet, after almost two years. I really do find that hard to believe. And then to bitch about a court order that he's known about for quite some time, I guess I'll never understand. Apparently, he's coming to Kansas for Kevin's birthday, and it's already causing some problems. I'm sorry that once again you have to endure this crap with him. I do understand that it's about Kevin, however he has no right to infringe on our home, nor our family's routine and the way we do things. I'm glad to see that this time he at least is providing his own transportation. His lack of understanding about the whole divorce deal concerns me a little, more so as to his mental state. That's very interesting to see that he's so far from reality.

Well, today was a little exhausting, and I'm really tired right now. Things always look worse at night, and I'm sure this will all look a little better in the morning. I love you my darling. Kiss you later.

6 JUL 04 D + 278 0715 hrs.

Good morning my love. I was right, everything looks better today. Plus, it's another day closer to seeing you. When I called, you were on your way back home from the video store where you bought Peter Pan. Oh, the cleverness of you.

Well, today is Zhou's big day at the promotion board. He woke up and couldn't find his I.D. tags, and as usual is stressing horribly over the ordeal. I have the utmost confidence though. After all, I trained him. I'm not meaning to sound cocky about it, but I do know how to prepare a troop for the board. His inspection arms drill is tight with his weapon, his bio is just top notch, and all he needs to do is just relax a little bit and he'll do just fine.

When I checked my email this morning, I didn't see anything about the job I applied for, but that's okay. At least I know that there are jobs out there where we want to eventually settle, and that alone is very exciting to me. I really do look forward to the day that I sign out on leave for the last time, and drive off towards our future. I just know it's going to be great honey. I even look forward to the little things, like the 'road trip' it will take us to get there. Kevin is a great traveling companion, and Abby is older now, so the trip should be all that much more interesting. And then there's seeing family again. I really do miss them all, even the dysfunctional parts. But, as in most cases, that's what makes a family a family.

7 JUL 04 D + 279 0545 hrs.

Good morning honey. I just got back from talking to you and making sure that the guys going on mission were up and ready to go. They're all good to go now, just a local babysitting mission here on post with some hajji's building a tent city in preparation for our replacements coming in. All in all it's a good deal, and I don't think they really mind getting up extra early for that reason.

Yesterday afternoon there was another rocket attack on camp. This one actually hit a barracks building, and although it tore it up pretty bad, no one was killed. Thank God for small miracles. Over the course of time, they've been bound to get lucky, just with the sheer number of rockets and mortars they've fired at us. We often joke about it that if they had a place to zero their weapons and sight them in properly, they'd almost be dangerous.

Well, the convoy that left for Baghdad last night hasn't returned yet. They went out to pick up the people coming back from leave, including Eason. I'm anxious to get him back in one piece; also, I'm a man short. When I only have four guys to work with, that takes me down to 75%. With the platoon being as small as it is, a single man being gone is really felt with all the missions and the heavy workload we have.

This week, we are running an M-16 range, pulling our share of maintenance, pulling extra guard duty due to the hajji's installing our window frames and glass, and then doing a Battalion wide cache mission on Saturday. It's certainly not over yet, but everyone can sense that the end is coming. It's just not quite within our reach yet. Today is a new day, and we'll see how it goes.

0815 hrs.

Hello my love. I am alone once again, here in the hooch. Everyone that's left should be returning from breakfast soon, and getting to work for the day. I'm listening to our music, and, I think I prefer to listen to it myself nowadays. It gives me a little bit of 'us' time. I am missing you more and more with each phone call and email. I got some pictures from you this morning that Kevin took. I surely do appreciate that. Abby sounded like she wasn't willing to listen to anyone this morning, and Kevin told me that he was 'slacking off' lately. I'm glad to see that he can be brutally honest, even when it wasn't provoked in any way. He just brought it up all by himself. I'm guessing that he thought you and I had already talked about it, and even if that was the case, I'm glad he was the one that brought it up. It shows me that he's maturing, and that's always a good thing. He's growing up so fast it seems, and I hate that I'm missing so much of it.

2200 hrs.

Hello my love. After trying for at least half an hour to get through to you, I finally did, and it was such a relief for me. I'm sorry, however, that I was in such a foul mood. I can't believe that I mistook something you said for sympathy for hajji. I had just left a conversation with one of my soldiers under those same circumstances before I came down to call you. I suppose I need some more time between dealing with troops and stuff and going down to call you. I love you so much honey, and I don't want this place to make me into something that I'm not and drive you away from me.

The troops have told me that they often hear me talking in my sleep, even crying once. It hasn't seemed to phase their opinion of me, as most of them have been through the same things as I, and are very understanding of it all.

8 JUL 04 D + 280 1200 hrs.

Hey honey. We just got back from the Hurricane Point mission a little while ago. That makes over 130 missions for me. It was relatively smooth, with no shooting of course. I just can't get comfortable going downtown . . . . ever. Anyhow, we came back and did our recon for the rifle range tomorrow, and that went pretty smooth too. All I have left for today is brief the troops on what their individual assignments at the range are and then we're done for the day.

2230 hrs.

Hello my love. Well, I finally got through to you tonight. I've tried all afternoon, but the phones were acting up again, and I could dial all the way through, and then get disconnected before ringing. Everyone is in bed right now, resting up before the range tomorrow. Range days are always long ones, about seven or so hours in all our gear. After that though, we should be able to rest up some. And then Saturday morning, I have a PT test. I don't anticipate doing too well, but as long as I pass, that's all I'm really concerned with. I'm still getting over Bronchitis, and it's generally a pain in the ass throughout my day.

I'm going to try and get some rest myself now my love. I'm very tired, and I need to be alert tomorrow for the range. I love and miss you my darling. Kiss you later.

9 JUL 04 D + 281 0345 hrs.

Good morning my love. My day just started out right, because I got to talk to you just now. You were at an FRG meeting, and told me that SSG K, SPC Moody, and SPC Howard were all alright. They've all come home wounded in the past month, and there has been much concern over their well being and recovery. The incident that wounded K and Moody was a crucial one. After that, virtually no one wanted to go out on the road anymore, and lots of soldiers told their supervisors that they 'weren't going out anymore, no matter what'.

You told me of how Kevin got some pizza on one of my t-shirt's, and how he's into wearing my stuff nowadays. And apparently Abby likes to go 'bye bye' with Brandy a lot too now. That's a little scary for me now, because every time I leave to come here, the images from home that I last remember stick with me, and the last image I have of her still is having to peel her off me, and always wanting to be held. I simply cannot imagine it any other way. I'm sure that she'll break my heart a million more times growing up, and I should probably get used to it.

Well, I have to get dressed and get ready for the range my love. All is well for now, and it was a pretty quiet night. No rockets or mortars to be heard. I like it when it's quiet. I love you my darling, and I'm sure I'll write more later on. Kiss you later.

10 JUL 04 D + 282 2300 hrs.

Hello my love. Well, everything that could happen this week certainly happened. We hosted a range, and I didn't get yelled at this time. It was very smooth and that was of course a good thing. Salah, the Battalion's interpreter was arrested for espionage, and of course there was more than our fair share of maintenance.

I got to talk to you earlier in the day. It was 0400 at home, and although I was feeling bad for waking you up, I felt this desperation about hearing your voice. I was elated to hear you halfway awake when I called, even though I thought it weird that you were even close to being up at that hour. Then Abby must have heard you, and woke up asking for some Coke. Her voice, other than the whining, is so sweet when she wakes up in the middle of the night.

I am missing you a lot today honey. When I finished talking to you tonight, I did my laundry, which is drying at this moment. I thought about what we'd be doing on a Saturday night, and I'm pretty sure that laundry isn't it. I was thinking about our talk on the phone tonight, and I miss you in so many ways honey. I don't think I have words for them all.

11 JUL 04 D + 283 0900 hrs.

It's midnight at home right now, and I can only hope that you're getting some decent sleep. Kevin is at Sawyer's overnight, and Abby was being a witch earlier. The 'terrible two's' are bad enough with both parents present, much less with one gone for a year of that time. You really are my strength my love. Your strength, desire to do the right thing, and awesome abilities as a parent, wife, partner, best friend . . . everything that you are, are something to be proud of. I am so proud to be your husband. I simply couldn't be any more proud. You really are the best part of me, and for that I am eternally grateful. I'm grateful to God, to you, and to our children. You humble me, my love, and have given me reason after reason to come back to God after many years in my life when I wasn't as close to God as I should have. You've helped me grow in many ways, and realize that all the good things in my life are due to Him. I could never express just how much I love you. You are God's greatest gift to me.

Well, today is Sunday, the day of rest. Unfortunately, in the Muslim world, it's their version of Tuesday, as they have a different schedule than we do. The troops get to rest today, and catch up on things like laundry and letters home. I enjoy Sunday mornings, early morning in particular. Last night I did my laundry, and since it was 102 degrees at 2130 in a pitch dark sky, I hung it out to dry then. I also took a shower last night, so this morning, I really had nothing to do but make coffee and enjoy a little 'Ron time'. Just like home in a way, as I walk out of the bay onto our front porch, I look at the troops lying there sleeping, glad for them to have the opportunity to rest. They work very hard, and they deserve the time to rest.

1400 hrs.

Hey honey. It's amazing how this down time every Sunday or so really gets me down. It's almost like it's in my head that there's nothing else to do but go out on missions, nothing worthwhile anyway. And then again, the thought looms that I may not ever leave this place. I've seen and heard the atrocities that are a part of every day life here, and just hope and pray that I never personally live them. I am by no means complacent, but at the same time it's a fine line of keeping my edge and paranoia. I've got so many missions outside the wire now, and I could care less if we ever have another single one. I see my buddies getting all torn up out here, and getting sent home wounded. I just wonder how their lives have changed, how they deal with their families. I wonder how much of a dominant thought in their daily lives it is, the things that happened to them.

I've been dreaming a lot lately about the ambush we had. Except in my dream, I'm calling Nick on the radio telling him that I'm coming to him because he's called in that he has two wounded and his vehicle is disabled. The only difference is that in the dream I don't make I to him in time, and when I finally get past the smoke, his vehicle comes into sight and he's laying there dead. His gunner is slumped over the gun, still sitting in the hatch, and his driver is leaning over the wheel, dead. It's very disturbing to me, and although we did live through that ambush, I can't help but think that the possibility of it happening again while we're here is very real to me. We're supposed to go to LSA Anaconda again on 17 AUG, and I have to admit that I really am concerned. I've acquired all the toys and tools that I need to do my job, but I just want to be ready. I really think that I may have lost some of my sharper side since I came back from the emergency leave. I am trying so hard to maintain, but it's a challenge every day just to stay afloat.

12 JUL 04 D + 284 1500 hrs.

Hello my love. Today was another long day in the sun, however we made a lot of progress on our trucks, getting them beefed up for the trip down to Kuwait, whenever that may be. We also have another mission this afternoon. We're going out to CP 279. It's about five or six kilometers out of Trooper Gate, along Highway Mobile (Highway

1). It's another babysitting mission, taking the engineers out to drop some concrete barriers to fortify an OP that 1-16 occupies on a daily basis. It should be a short mission; we're only dropping eight barriers. I don't think I've ever been out where we've dropped less than fifty or so.

Everyone is a little edgy, but nowadays that's how we all are when we go out. I talked to the Chaplain about it this morning at the motor pool. I explained to him that I do not doubt my faith at all, but I do have my concerns about each trip outside the wire, and even making it through this tour at all. He reassured me that I was indeed not questioning my faith, but it was a natural reaction to the potential threat. He said that God put that instinctive nature in us to survive, and when it kicks in, which out here is quite a bit, that it's nothing to worry about.

2300 hrs.

Hello honey. I jus got back from talking with you a little while ago, after we got back from our mission. Everything went well, and although I should be really used to it by now, but somehow I am really hyper alert whenever I go out. I think that's what the Chaplain was talking about earlier today. The trip went off without incident, and we were all glad to get back to our 'home' in the barracks.

You also mentioned tonight about Mike's visit this weekend, and how he was upset about only being able to spend an hour there, setting up Kevin's computer, and then going back to the guest house or wherever he's staying. I'm glad he's pitching in for Kevin's school clothes this year. That's certainly a welcome change, and one that we haven't seen before. I hope that you're not too concerned about this visit. I am certainly not, and although it's easy for me to say that from over here, it wasn't always that way. The last visit Kevin had from his father, I was very anxious for it to be over. I just hope and pray that Kevin can share his feelings with his father openly and honestly. He's a lot stronger than he used to be. I'm very proud of him, and I hope it stays that way.

14 JUL 04 D + 286 2115 hrs.

Hello my love. It's been a very busy few days. We've been up as early as 0400 for four days now. We've been hot on maintenance, and now we're spraying down (Decon) a building so the Marines can use it. Apparently, it's all part of the job. Anyhow, we have to go out in the morning and finish up the building, and then go back to the motor pool to finish up our trucks. Hopefully, barring any disaster, they'll be in good shape for now, and be roadworthy for the long trip down to Kuwait. I've heard that it's three or four days to get there by road. That's a lot of driving, and I don't want any problems with the trucks.

We were in the middle of our Decon Operation at Ogden gate when we got the call to go to REDCON 1, all gun trucks ready and dressed to go immediately. Rarely does it happen that way where we get no notice at all. Every QRF in Brigade was simultaneously activated because Devil 6 was out in town, and not only did his vehicle hit an IED, but then took RPG and small arms fire right afterwards. We're so close to going home now; I'd hate for anyone else to get hurt or killed.

Tomorrow looks a little bit lighter than the last week or so. I'm glad too my love, I'm so tired right now, I can barely stay awake to type. I will close out now honey, and dream of you. I love you so much my darling. Kiss you later.

15 JUL 04 D + 287 2200 hrs.

Hey honey. I just got off the phone with you for about a minute or so. You were about to start taking your Para-professional test. I feel bad for not knowing that, because I want you to be in the right frame of mind for it, and not worrying about when we'll talk next.

I got two cards from you in the mail today, as well as the one you sent for the platoon. They really thought it was nice, as did I. Those cards meant the world to me my love. It's just another extension of you honey, and I love it of course. I miss you so much honey, and can't wait to hold you again.

Tomorrow we escort the Battalion Commander to Camp Manhattan. We're taking Highway 10 again, of course, because the Commander likes to save time. It's 26 minutes of driving through hell, as opposed to the two hour drive through the open desert. I'll never understand why we still do this. Anyway, the Commander already had his 'big' meeting, and we'll know tomorrow if he has anything decent to put out to us about when we're going home. I dearly hope so. Anyway, still nothing to tell you about yet, but I'm sure that it will come in time. I love you my darling. Kiss you later.

16 JUL 04 D + 288 0645 hrs.

Good morning my love. Well, I'm finally awake and not as tired as I was this morning or when I tried to write last night. Today is somewhat normal, as everyone is off to breakfast and I'm here alone with my coffee. I like this time of day a lot, because it gives me a few minutes to myself, and some time to reflect on everything around me.

We have rehearsals for today's mission in a half hour or so, and everyone is a little nervous about it. We have to go through the same neighborhood that Devil 6 did when he got hit with two IED's the other day, followed by small arms fire and RPG's. The good news is that they took 21 enemy KIA's and 19 enemy WIA's as well. I only hope that we do so well today. Of course, the good news for us is that at least there are 21 insurgents that won't be around to mess with us today. That's probably not as funny to most folks as it is to me right now, but oh well.

I'm sure that everything will be okay though, and we'll all get there just fine. I'm looking forward to seeing Mo and Matt as I've not seen them in a while. The last time

I saw Matt was on my way back in through Baghdad coming back from leave. And Mo, the last time I saw him was about three weeks ago when he came through here on routine business for the company, doing an escort mission. They've taken a lot of hard hits our in Habbaniyah since we all got here, and not unlike the rest of us; they're tired and ready to go home too.

Well, I'm going to cut it short for now, my love. If all goes well, I'll call you from right here at J.C. this afternoon or tonight, barring we don't stay over night at Camp Manhattan. LTC Brinkley is going out to deliver the redeployment information to Bravo Company. Since it's Top Secret, it cannot even be sent out over a secure internet line, so it must be delivered in person. I'm really glad for that. Hopefully it's good news for all of us; and there's nothing like good news in person. We shall see. Kiss you later my love.

17 JUL 04 D + 289 0520 hrs.

Good morning honey. I just got done talking to you for a few minutes, and then I called Billy on their cell. He's doing the moving with Ian and Chance, while the girls are at the new place. I got cut off twice so I decided to call them back in about an hour or so to talk to Challas and Stephanie. Billy told me it was really hot and humid in Vegas now. I almost had to laugh, but it was great to talk to him again.

As I sit here on the porch writing you, Little Birds from the 160th are all over the sky this morning. Makes me wonder what's going on in town. It was a pretty quiet night last night, and thank God, after the IED strike that happened yesterday afternoon. When we went to leave for Habbaniyah, my truck wouldn't start, so Simmons and I stayed behind. We were bummed out at the time, but then came to realize that everything happens for a reason. When our guys came back, they weren't 10 minutes from getting back here when an IED went off and SPC Lalicker took a piece of shrapnel across his cheek, and our platoon sergeant got the compression blast on his side of the truck, and his ear started bleeding. Chalk up two more casualties for DECON. That brings us up to five now for the tour. And thank God that no one has been seriously wounded to the point of having to go home or being killed. We've been very fortunate in that way so far.

Yesterday was very depressing for me. Simmons and I had pretty much the whole day to do what we wanted, since we were stuck here. We did some work, but not much though, and took our time doing that even. We took the opportunity to relax a little, and have some personal time. It was a well needed break from the pace we've been keeping lately. He's my hardest working guy, and I really couldn't succeed without him; or any of the guys for that matter. I may be their Squad Leader, but they've all taken care of me as much as I've ever taken care of them.

Today should be a pretty light day. We do have a little bit of work to do, but Simmons and I took care of most of it yesterday, so unless we get a last minute mission, we should get the whole Squad some down time. And then tomorrow is

Sunday, so today ties in really well. We tried to plan it like that yesterday with the head start we got on maintenance, but you just never know around here.

The day before yesterday we spun up for a mission last minute. We were at the gat doing an actual DECON mission, and right in the middle of it we went to REDCON 1. We had trucks and hoses everywhere, and had to jump through our tails to get it put up and get all of our gun trucks on line and ready to go. The Battalion Commander commended us for doing so well, and getting our stuff together so fast. We even beat Cold Steel to the punch, and they were all around the Company area at the time. Our guys really are great. Anyway, we were standing by for a firefight that was going on downtown between the Marines and some insurgents. Apparently, they finally got it under control, because we were told to stand down about 30 minutes later. That was a good thing.

Before every mission, I take a minute and give my guys a good look, because I just never know if I'm going to see them again, and I don't think I could bear it if something happened to any one of them. I look down the line at the four gun trucks, and it just makes me so damn proud to be there with them at that very moment. Don't get me wrong, I'd rather be home with you and the children any day of the week, but if I have to be here, then there's no one I'd rather be going outside the wire with.

0700 hrs.

Hey honey. I just got off the phone with Challas and Stephanie, and I was glad to actually get through to them, but I still got cut off anyhow. At least I got through for a little while. The satellite has been acting funny this morning, so I couldn't call you back just yet, but I will just as soon as I get the chance again today. I'll check on it later on to see if they're up again. I hate to keep getting cut off, but I still consider myself lucky to have gotten through at all at this point.

I want to do some more job hunting today if I can, so I think tonight I'll go put my laundry in the washer, and then go jump on the internet for about an hour, and then go hang my laundry up to dry, and then do another load of laundry after that. It's better than doing it on Sunday morning. I'll still probably get up again early on Sunday, but at least I won't have to do any laundry. I still don't like doing it, but after the Decon mission earlier this week, my stuff is just absolutely nasty.

Well, I have to get the men up now and get them fed and put them to work for the day. I'll call again the minute I have the chance my love. I love you more than anything honey. Kiss you later.

2300 hrs.

Hello my love. Well, the C-6 is still down, and that is very disheartening for me tonight. We were told about an hour ago that we'd be going out tomorrow morning to the same spot that Devil 6 got into a firefight the other day, as well as our guys getting hit with an IED. The neighborhood is a common hot spot, and is a known anti-coalition neighborhood. Everyone is just a tad nervous tonight, but as usual, I'll pray and count the blessings in my life.

My love, I would love nothing more than to hear your voice right now. Since that isn't possible, as it so often happens here, I'll try to use this as an opportunity to quietly reflect on you and I, and our children. My love for you knows no bounds my darling. You are the best part of me. Please don't ever think of these as idol words without meaning. You and our children have given me my meaning. You are my life, and, since the moment I met you the reason I get up in the morning. You truly are my everything honey.

I must rest now honey. Tomorrow, we're going into a really hot location, and you will be with me, as I am always with you. I love you my darling. Kiss you later.

18 JUL 04 D + 290 1000 hrs.

Hey honey. We just got back from the Recon mission downtown. It looked solemn enough early in the morning. It was very quiet on Highway 10, as we waited for the Commanders to do their assessment of the building that was the focus of the mission. We're going back out tonight to drop barriers around the entire building to protect it from potential VBIED's. The building is the Ministry of Agriculture, and, seeing how the entire Al Anbar Province is primarily an agriculture asset to all of Iraq, the building is pretty important to the local economy and the nation itself. Not that it's a particular priority of mine. The downside is that the mission is probably going to be an all nighter again. We'll see how it goes.

1915 hrs.

Hello my love. Well, our test of intestinal fortitude continues I suppose. The internet and phones are still down, and it has been impossible for me to call you or anything today at all. I've spent most of the day wishing that I could call you. I was lying in bed most of the afternoon, going over the plan for the night. We're not leaving until about 2100 hrs. and not coming back until all the barriers are dropped around the agricultural building.

I really don't like the spot we're going to tonight. The anti-coalition we're going into tonight has fired on the building we're working on tonight about every other day since we've been here. The ministry has taken a lot of abuse since the Marines started using it for an OP on top of their building. Instead of distracting the anti-coalition attention by moving to another building, perhaps one that isn't so essential in the area, they make that building a magnet by staying there. That's also the building that the Marine sniper teams were killed at when they fell asleep while on guard.

I must go now my love. I should get my last minute checks in before we start lining up our trucks. We're taking out six gun trucks, three armored vehicles, and about a platoon's worth of dismounted Marines since it's their area. I'm hoping that it's enough to ward off any attack that the hajji's might be planning, and keep tonight as quiet as possible. I love you my darling. I promise I'll call you as soon as possible after they come up again. I love you more than anything my darling. I will be praying for you and our children tonight as always. Kiss you later my love.

19 JUL 04 D + 291 0630 hrs.

Morning honey. I just finished my second load of laundry, and hung it on the line to dry. Of course I was glad to talk to you this morning after we got back. The C-6 was down most of the weekend, and it came up about ten minutes after we left on our second mission yesterday, which lasted all night long. We got back in about 0300, and everyone was exhausted once again. I had no choice but to do laundry though, after the gas station Decon at Ogden Gate and all the time down in the motor pool. But, it's finally done, and I realize that I'm probably babbling due to being up for 24 hours now. I just wanted to start writing you today, since we're off until 1300. We'll start mission recovery then, and probably get back down to the motor pool again. It's a vicious cycle here, and it will only end when we get on the plane to come home. I love you my darling. I'm going to bed now, because I'm falling asleep at the keyboard. Kiss you later my love.

1300 hrs.

Good afternoon my love. By now hopefully you and the children are sleeping peacefully, as you are halfway around the world in a better place than I. I hate the thought that we are apart, but if we are, it comforts me in some small way that I am up and working hard with the men while you sleep. Sleep safe my love.

I actually got five whole hours of sleep last night. My recent entries in this journal from yesterday must have sounded weird, as I was totally out of my mind yesterday. I hadn't been up that long in a while now, and it really kicked my butt. I'm still young, but some days I feel so damned old. This place just wears on you like that I guess. One thing is for sure and for certain though. Some of the things that bothered me in the past probably never will again. This tour has taught me a lot about myself, and how much I can take. It's not so much the point of taking so much over here, but what it prepares me for during the rest of my life. The things that I have seen and heard, been apart of, and prepared my men for have developed things about me that hopefully I will never need again. God willing.

Death has always been a silent companion. And as far as that goes, I have to say that I have dealt with it better now than in my prior tours. I think, however, that only now do I see and hear about it so much that a part of me is simply numb to it. Death, here, translates into me not being able to contact my family for a few days. I realize that this is selfish, in that some of the deaths have been very foolish and very unfortunate. However, death is still death, and nothing can change that once it's happened.

2300 hrs.

Hey honey. I got to talk to you online for a little bit, until the satellite went out again anyway. It was great to see you and Abby on the web cam. It feels like forever since I've laid eyes on you my love. You are so beautiful, and I don't think I'll ever be able to get over that. I'm amazed every day at not only how beautiful you are, but what a beautiful person you are, what a beautiful soul you have. I am the luckiest man in the entire world.

It's almost actually starting to feel like we're getting closer now. Today we got some wood to block and brace our boxes that will go inside our conex, and we're still scheduled to run the carwash for the Battalion when the time comes.

There are a few drawbacks to the coming weeks though. Everyone is getting really short tempered lately, and I suspect that that won't stop anytime soon. This is typical for a unit that is redeploying, at least in my experience. It'll probably be worse in Kuwait, once we get there. Kuwait is hotter than Iraq, and, with al the vehicles being inspected and washed and re-inspected again, even that will only pass some of the time. Once we get there, we were told that we will work 24/7 until it's done, and then we can relax. Even with that being the case, we should have a few days of down time before we fly, and that will be the most heart wrenching of all. It will probably be worse than downtime on a Sunday here, but at least we won't be in Iraq anymore. We shall see. Well, it's off to bed for me now my love. I'll write more soon. Kiss you later.

20 JUL 04 D + 292 1830 hrs.

Hey honey. I just got finished emailing you some pictures from our mission the other day. It always makes me feel good to at least shoot you an email or call you because it makes me feel like I can reach out and touch you sometimes. There must be about a dozen or so times a day that I'd give anything to touch you my darling. You *are* my everything my love, and I miss you so much it hurts. I think I'm going back over there shortly to try and call you. I really miss you today honey.

Tomorrow is Kevin's birthday, thus the reason for Mike's visit. I wish so badly that I could be there for him tomorrow. It's just another huge day in my life that I have to miss this year, and I just have to suck it up just like every other major day this past year. It never gets any easier to deal with, and after this year is over, I want to get away from everything that can make this happen again. I love you so much honey, and God willing, I don't ever want to have to spend another moment that I don't have to away from you my love. Kiss you later.

2130 hrs.

Hello honey. Well, about ten minutes after I got off the phone with you, we got mortared. Luckily, hajji isn't a very good shot with a mortar tube, nor lucky enough to hit anything tonight. Tonight, they didn't even hit anything on the camp, but just a tad off camp outside of Trooper Gate. Another opportunity to count my blessings. I love you so much my darling.

When we spoke earlier, you were on your way out the door to meet Kevin and Mike at WalMart to get his school clothes. I guess Mike messed up with Kevin's shoes already, so you needed to supervise. It's only fair, since you know what Kevin likes and dislikes, and his father probably doesn't have a clue. Plus, you can make sure he gets what Kevin needs, as opposed to what he wants, and it will be appropriate for school.

I'm hoping to let the guys sleep until 0700 tomorrow morning, since they busted their tails today and got every single one of our trucks out of the motor pool. I told them that that was my goal for the day, and they even got the mechanics to work past noon, which is normally the time they get off due to the heat of the day. All of my NBC equipment is now up and running well, and I'm excited. The Battalion likes to use it for everything but what it was intended for. Because it has pumps and hoses, they got the bright idea for us to run a carwash for the entire Battalion before we leave Ramadi. It's a good idea, but at the same time it's rough on our equipment. Hopefully soon, this will all end. Oh well. For now my love, I have to get going if I'm to get any sleep tonight. I am praying for you, love of my life. Kiss you later.

21 JUL 04 D + 293 0745

Good morning my love. I just got off the phone with you a little while ago, and it was a bit upsetting. Apparently Mike thinks that because I'm not there, or for whatever reason, he can be rude or not civil to you for even as little as 48 hours. It's really starting to irritate me, and although I'm not there now, he's really pushing his luck. From this point on, he is no longer welcome in our home, and in lieu of a two hour warming up period for Kevin in our home, he has now lost that privilege, and the warm up period will be at an alternate location. I think that we should do it in a public place, and in the Summer time have it somewhere like a park or something like that. If Kevin's father should choose to visit during the winter months, then maybe somewhere like a McDonald's would be more appropriate. All I know is that Mike is trying to take advantage of your emotional state while I'm gone, as well as my absence. No more.

I just got back from going over to Combat Stress. I think that this depressive state that I've been in for a while now is really taking its toll. And as I promised you before, if I felt overwhelmed for whatever reason, I'd go talk to these folks. When I got there today I was informed that the former Combat Stress unit that was here took all of their records with them, including mine. There are four visits down the drain. After seeing mental health in Alaska for two months before we PCS'd, and then again at Ft Riley for a couple of weeks after getting there and then deploying two weeks after that; it's getting a little disappointing. It just feels like I'm not making a whole lot of progress. We shall see.

2330 hrs.

I just got back from the phones. They just opened back up right after we go back. We were on a mission tonight, and I'm so glad that I got to talk to Kevin on his birthday. I was praying that we'd get back from the mission in time to call him on his big day. I ended up calling just in time before Mike took him to the pool before he leaves town. He sounded really happy to hear from me, and was also sad to get off the phone because his father was waiting. He just makes me so proud.

This mission came up so suddenly today. One minute we were talking about going to chow, and the next we were checking weapons, and counting grenades and flares. The Marines got hit downtown pretty heavy, and after the Devil PSD went out there, then we went out there and had some more in reserves standing by just in case. There were so many explosions, so much gunfire, and RPG's buzzing around like fireflies. It was downtown Ramadi, in the marketplace; quite possibly the worst place in the world. I'm just glad it's over, and no one had to fire a shot from our end. Some guys from Assassin and Cold Steel got engaged, but it didn't last very long and everyone came home alive tonight. It was a good day.

23 JUL 04 D + 295 0700 hrs.

Hello honey. It was so great to be able to talk to you yesterday, both online and on the phone as well. Yesterday was a very stressful day for me, and although part of it I'm sure, was just the tension of still being here, the sound of your voice still calms me and makes me feel better.

Our last mission on Kevin's birthday was a big one, and everyone was a little shaken from it. We went to downtown Ramadi on Highway 10 and staged there in a defensive position for about three to four hours. The enemy was trying to flank the Marines, who already had a whole Battalion out there. Once they took casualties though, we were called in, along with two mechanized platoons of engineers in tracked vehicles as well as two other dismount squads on standby. The whole city was on fire. Smoke plumes poured from every corner of Ramadi, and the explosions and gunfire were everywhere. I remember making the turn onto Highway 10 and the picture in my head just said 'war zone'. It was probably exactly what you might imagine the scenery to look like, and it was very ugly. I did wind up getting some pictures that day, but nothing could capture the stench of the city, with trash everywhere and pools on not so clean water festering in the gutters everywhere. It almost made me gag.

At the risk of sounding like we're getting complacent here, Nick and I both talked about it out there on the street and both agreed that we're too short for this crap. Although we've certainly done our time, our time is by no means over yet. We've been told that we may turn over our PSD vehicles in two or three weeks. Although I love the Steel Horse, I'll certainly turn her over in a hot minute when I get the green light.

As the Unit Movement representative for DECON, I attended another meeting last night and got some more information in preparation for our departure. I honestly cannot wait for that day. I can't believe that the next time I get on a plane will be to leave this place for good. I almost can't even imagine that. I know that my life is not here, at least not permanently, however I suppose that I will miss a few things from here. The evening sunset on the west side of our building is absolutely awesome, but I know that I have bigger and better sunsets to look forward to with you out on Milford Lake, to be sure.

These days, I often think about how many things still have to look forward t in my life with you. I just feel like I've just got to get out of here, and of course I have to in order to start enjoying things with you. It feels like I'm on a treadmill going uphill, and I just can't run fast enough.

0945 hrs.

Today is maintenance day, and although we had every intention of completing our weekly session in the motor pool, the LT came over the net and announced that the whole platoon was to report up to the bay immediately. We are on REDCON 3.5, which means that we have to hang out in the barracks and watch movies or whatever until we're called. We're not quite at the 30-minute recall point yet, but we know that something's stirring up out in Ramadi.

Apparently, last night three VBIED's were prepared, and left Fallujah heading this way with the intent of blowing up a police station. Now, although I still have compassion for all mankind and all that stuff, I think that if the Iraqi's know this, then they should beef up their own security. We've trained thousands of IP's and ICDC guys up to now, as we still are. I think it's time for them to take control of their own country now that they have their sovereignty already. We really are getting too short for this kind of thing. The Devil PSD, along with tons of armor have already pushed forward, thus our being on standby here. We'll see how the day goes, but for now we'll relax while we have the chance.

2100 hrs.

Good evening my love. I can't tell you when I enjoyed a whole 'family' phone call like tonight. Maybe it's been the constant level of minor depression over the course of this last year, and the many life-altering events over that same time, but tonight I almost had the feeling of being home. Abby was blowing raspberries on your stomach, and I haven't heard you laugh like that in a long time my darling. It was absolutely a great moment to be a part of, and it was truly the highlight of my day.

We're going out tomorrow again, this time to do another escort for EOD. I really do like these types of missions more than nay other. Usually we're out in the middle of the desert, and, although still in the Red Zone, we're not in a much danger as usual, and we actually get to have a little fun by blowing some stuff up. It's actually a little bit therapeutic as I see it. I'm going to try and videotape the mission, at least part of it. I just want to give you and the kids a little piece of my world as best I can. I love you so much my love.

25 JUL 04 D + 297 1200 hrs.

Hello honey. Today is Sunday, and after working for thirteen straight days, we have a little down time. Everyone is either finishing up their laundry, sleeping, or watching movies. I've already done all of the above, and am now bored out of my mind. I even washed my sweaty old hats, formed and shaped them, and set them out in the sun to dry. I cleaned up my hooch, and took my newer uniforms down to commo to get sewn. One of them is my 'going home' uniform. I want to look as nice as possible for you when I get off the plane. I'm going to iron it, fold it just perfect, and then air seal it in plastic to be packed neatly in my carry on bag. I know it sounds kind of anal, but these are the things that I have to think about when I have down time. I suppose it's better than being out on mission. I just feel like I haven't been clean in a year. These conditions aren't really conducive to being clean, and I want to be.

26 JUL 04 D + 298 1130 hrs.

I am missing you as always and today we started to clean out our trailers, and break them down to their simplest form. Anything that is extra or attached is being removed, cleaned, and then packed. We are starting to see some tangible results of our work. It's funny, that no matter how much we worked to help the Iraqi's, how many roads, berms, buildings, and all the other missions and miscellaneous work we did during the last ten months; in one afternoon with a few hours working on some trailers we can see and feel a world of difference in that.

27 JUL 04 D + 299 0720 hrs.

Today DECON became a construction crew. We are going back out to Ogden Gate to the building that we washed down a couple of weeks ago. Now we have to spackle the walls, paint them, and I have to build frames and doors, and board up the windows as well. I actually like the project itself, however, we only have until Friday to complete this project, and word has it that Battalion knew about this one for three weeks already. Once again, it's not very confidence inspiring, however, I'm sure that we'll pull something out of a hat and it will come out just fine. The good part is that I get to play with tools this week, and SPC Lalicker has a cement/masonry background. That will certainly help since we are using some brand of hajji mortar mix for the walls. It's not like there's a Home Depot anywhere around here, and what we have is what we have. I'm sure that it'll work our just fine. There's nothing I love more out here than the chance do something that I actually like, especially involving building something, and a strict deadline that's completely out of my control . . . yeah, I just love that.

Yesterday we disbanded 3rd Squad, as Dorelus wasn't doing such a hot job due to him wanting to get out and simply not being a leader. It's a shame, but I still feel like I did everything I could for him when he was in my Squad. I now have SPC Taylor back in my Squad. Both Taylor and Zhou will both be promoted on 1 SEP 04, and then I'll have two E-5 Team Leaders in my Squad, and that will make my job a lot easier.

28 JUL 04 D + 300 0010 hrs.

Hello my love. I got back a little while ago from talking to you. You were laying out at the pool, while Kevin played with some kids and Abby was at the CDC. You told me of all your plans this week with both old friends and new, and I can't tell you how happy I am about that. I'm very excited about your week, as it will not only pass some more time, but give you a bunch of positive things to do as well. I don't mean pass the time like you're doing nothing but pining over me and need to find things to do, but everything I do over here is another thing to do to pass the time here. It's very difficult for me to think in any other terms. Anyway, it sounds like you've got everything under control, and all seems well. I'm so proud of you my love.

You also told me of Gary's visit, and how well that went. I'm really pleased that you had such a good time while he was there. I'm also glad that he got to spend some time with the kids too. I'm glad the two of you had a quality visit, and that we all have so much in common as well. I think having a daughter really cooled his heels a lot, and I'm glad for that, especially since he's going to Bragg this week. He's going to need all the help that he can get. God only knows that he should be gone a lot, but I'll be praying for him.

0720 hrs.

Good morning honey. I woke up really early this morning, having a really good dream about you. You came into the hooch and laid down with me, and I could swear that it was real. That's what woke me up, and we were talking. Anyway, after that I woke up for real and went down to call you. Our talk was brief this morning, but a good one nonetheless. I got to talk to the kids quite a bit today, as they were both very talkative. Kevin didn't want to get off the phone again, which of course made me feel really good. Abby was singing in the background, and when she got on the phone, I had one of those moments that are growing more regular for me. Her sentences are getting longer, and she's talking very well now. It never seems to amaze me how fast they grow up . . . then they do.

Today we're off on the second day of our big construction project. We're mortaring the walls and doorways today, and if I feel up to it, I might start hanging doors and window filling. We're just boarding up the windows, and two out of the six doors, but it's still as much wood to cut wither way. We spent from 0700 until 1730 yesterday cutting wood and attaching hinges and doorknobs that we 'found'. It's amazing what you can find out here if you really look hard enough. I'm taking pictures of the whole operation phase by phase so we have a record of our accomplishments out here. Our platoon is very versatile, and most folks out here seem to forget that on a regular basis. Plus, the building we're working on is just outside the wire, and we have to do the whole thing in full battle rattle. We're going to sweat today, no doubt . . . just like every other day. It's okay though because we know we're good, and that goes a long way with the troops.

Well, I have to get going now my love. It's off to the construction site for the day. I'll try not to let my ass crack show out of the back of my pants. I'll try and video some of it.

2045 hrs.

Hello my love. We never made it out this afternoon to finish up our mortar work and carpentry stuff. Just as we were getting ready to roll out to the gate again, we received heavy incoming fire from a big rocket attack. There were at least six or seven that landed over in 1-16's area, and then another by our mayor cell, about 150 meters from us, and two more by the Navy and Marine compounds. It was a big day for rockets, but miraculously, no one was hurt or killed, thank God. Simmons was out on CSA duty today (escort), and one of the rockets impacted just the other side of a 1 ½ foot barrier he was parked next to. He said it scared the hell out of him, and I surely don't blame him. Once again, I came really close to losing one of my own. I thank God that he was okay, because I don't think I could bear it to lose him or any of my guys. We're too close to going home for this.

Simultaneously, Combat Outpost and Hurricane Point were also attacked. Normally, the insurgents don't coordinate this well, at least not while just attacking the Coalition. Today was different though, because instead of just attacking us, this mass coordinated effort was nothing more than a diversion. We didn't realize it until later when the intelligence came in telling us what actually happened. If any Americans were killed or wounded today, that would have been just a bonus for the insurgents.

The real purpose of the diversion was for the insurgents to pull off a kidnapping, which they did. They entered the home of the Governor of Ar Ramadi, and snatched four of his five children. Somehow, his wife and the fifth child escaped the attempt, and were held at the Combat Outpost under the care of Coalition forces there until they could be safely moved to a more secure location. So now, somewhere in Ar Ramadi, if they haven't been moved elsewhere, no one really knows if those children are alive or dead.

As a husband and father, I can only imagine how I'd feel if it was me; and I find myself feeling sympathy for the family. It is evident by today's activities that the Governor of Ar Ramadi has true and honest intentions toward the rebuilding of Iraq. This is a tragedy of course, but also signals a shift in the insurgents' activities in our area. This incident was Iraqi versus Iraqi, something that we haven't seen on this scale or at this level thus far. It'll be interesting to see how things pan out, at least in our area. This is life in the Sunni Triangle, and it never seems to make any sense. We're dealing with international terrorists though, and no sense can ever be made of this.

Today's incident was a personal one to me, whether it should be or not. I am praying for that family, especially the children who are not with their parents and sibling tonight. I can only imagine the fear and confusion that they must feel, provided they're still alive. I suppose I can only hope that God will see this through for them that they may be saved from any additional horrors of this war. I would not wish this on anyone, especially a child . . . even an Iraqi child.

I love you my darling. I have to get some rest now, because the command cut short my project timeline by 24 hours, and we now have to finish the mortar work, hanging doors, and painting all tomorrow, as we're going out into Ramadi again Friday night. I'll be praying about that too. I love you my darling. Kiss you later.

29 JUL 04 D + 301 1515 hrs.

Hello honey. Well, this afternoon brings with it yet another potential threat, and another afternoon of fruitless efforts. We only worked this morning until noon, due to intelligence suggesting that at 1300 there would be another attack.

We finished most of the mortar work, and I got to hang all but one door and one window. We can actually start painting and finish it up. It looks really good, and all the troops did a great job. Everyone worked really hard, and despite my anal nature during a project of this kind, they all tolerated my ways and exceeded my expectations. Even the ones who are normally lazy did a great job. All in all it went very well, and if I could get a solid day without hajji interfering, I could actually get this thing done. I don't know why I'm so attached to this project. Maybe it's just something that I like to do, and I just want to see it through.

I really enjoyed talking to you this morning my love. I know you were probably tired, or at least you sounded like it. Abby has a cold, and is apparently in a less than happy mood. She was whining and crying a lot, and for some reason I found that heart wrenching and just wanted to pick her up at that exact moment and tell her that everything would be okay. I miss sharing the load of parenting with you too honey. I know I do. I love hearing you on the phone and seeing you in person though. I absolutely adore how great of a parent that you are, and I think it makes me love you more, if that's possible.

I got a box and a very nice letter from Chaplain Melvin today. He's Darrin's boss, and the Family Life Chaplain at Wainwright who ran the program that took us to Chena Hot Springs that weekend. He wrote of Linda being home with the girls in Montana, and of him King Salmon fishing last week in the Chena River. It was a very nice gesture, and it was great to hear a friendly voice in the form of a really nice letter. Both he and Linda were always so supportive of our goings on, no matter what they seemed to be; everything from our wedding, to Abby, to the trip to the Hot Springs, and working with Darrin.

31 JUL 04 D + 302 1600 hrs.

Hello my love. I just woke up after a really long nap after I got off from the C-6 tent this morning. It was actually nice to check my email and do some writing without time limits. I had a few busy times, but I got to talk to Kevin for a long while. He seems to be very upset with all this business with Mike, Cathy, Dave & Brandy. He told me that he didn't want me to call him 'buddy' because it reminded him of his father, with whom he was very upset right now. Understandably so.

I'm still very tired right now. I haven't stayed up all night in a while, and I'm still feeling it. At least I got to talk to you this morning though. Your social schedule this week is very busy, and I really am glad to see that you're staying busy. Not that you're just staying busy, but that you're out with friends as well. You mentioned that you and two other girls went for a walk last night with twelve kids . . . good grief. After that, I don't think that hajji would have a chance against you honey.

2320 hrs.

Hey honey. I went down to use the internet earlier, and wound up talking to Kevin for a little while. You were out picking up pizza for the kids, and I remember thinking how on top of things you are. I'm so proud to be your husband, and even though the routine must be very old by now, you are still finding things to do with and for the children. I can only imagine how tough this year must be for you, and although it wasn't our choice to have me come here, I still think, of course, that you've dealt with everything beautifully. That's more than I can say for me. Some days I feel so weak, and just when I think I can't take another minute without you, I hear a song, or get to talk to you, or something involving you makes me press on and I'm able to deal with everything for a while longer.

I'm going back down in a while to try and call you again. By then, it will be after midnight here, and I can honestly say that we're going home next month. I truly can't wait for that day to come. I almost can't even imagine it, even with having been there on leave. Coming back here has had an odd effect on me. Any depression that I felt before coming home has only been magnified since coming back. We're still getting sent out on missions, and we're not sure when the end of that will come. We were all talking about it just today, how we've all heard the stories about some guys have been so short, some only a matter of a single day, and then get killed in a rocket attack or something like that. I think that this may be everyone's worst fear right about now. I know that it's mine.

I pray. I pray as often as I can talk to God. And when I do, I always pray for you and the children, and my men. I'm trying to not allow fear to creep into my daily thoughts, but a lot of the time it's unavoidable. It's not that I'm not giving this over to God, or at least I don't think so anyhow. But the closer we get to going home, the more concerned I am. Our time passing here doesn't change the level of danger in this place. As a matter of fact, the insurgents are actually picking up the level of their activities. I know that I've told you all this before my love, but the area we're in is one of the worst places that we could be in this country. I'd venture to say that it's truly one of the worst places in the world.

And when it comes time for us to leave this place, the job overall will certainly not be anywhere close to being done. By that time, we'll just have done our part, that's all. I just wish that I could see some tangible results from all of this. I've never seen an entire nation so unappreciative, and not just that, but so willing to waste the lives of those trying so desperately to help them. The irony never ceases to amaze me honey. I'm so glad that our children won't ever have to live like this, and, God willing, see half the things that I've had to. The only consolation that I can ever hope for is that our children and grand-children will have a much better and safer world than when we first came into it. I suppose that that's all we could ever hope for any of our children, but that's a parents wish.

1 AUG 04 D + 303 0730 hrs.

Well, today was already a good day for me my love. I got up early and got to talk to you for almost a half an hour. Then, I came back to make a pot of coffee, and went back over to call Taylor for her birthday. Billy, Challas, and the whole gang are at

Chucky Cheese for her birthday party, and everyone sounded like they were having a great time. I really miss them all, and I really do appreciate how supportive they've all been throughout this tour.

Challas answered the phone, and automatically went into her 'How's our hero?' stuff. Everyone there in Vegas has got to be tired of hearing it by now, but it is quite flattering. I read the post cards from Vegas to the guys, and they all say that it sounds like we've got some sort of fan club. They just don't know.

We're trying to make sure that everyone gets plenty of rest today. We have yet another mission tomorrow morning, leaving the camp around 0400 or so. It's a movement to contact mission. Movement to Contact pretty much means exactly what is says; you move around an area, and just keep going until you make contact with the enemy. So, somehow, one way or another, tomorrow there should be a fight. A movement to contact is different in this environment too. In an open desert or in a jungle it's a lot different than in an urban environment. The area we're going to is on Highway 10, and we'll be searching the slums going from door to door. We're not really looking forward to this one, for one because we're getting so short over here. Also, this is some more infantry type stuff, and although we've done it before, every soldier doesn't always do their normal job, and is subject to be called on to do anything. This is just a nasty mission.

Today I' going to try and take it easy and I borrowed 'The Hulk' from a buddy. I'm just trying to keep up with at least some of the movies that I've missed out on since I've been here. I told you the other day that I saw Spiderman last week, but it was a cheap hajji copy, and it probably would have been better if I'd seen it with you. I know it would have. Anyhow, today is a day to catch up on sleep, and then sleep some more in reserve for the morning. I'll probably spend the entire afternoon going over my gear, as my vest has grown quite heavy over the past year. There's always something else that I seem to need out on the road; some other toy or piece of equipment that seems to come in real handy. Oh well, that's the price of being prepared I suppose. I'll write more later my love.

2 AUG 04 D + 304 2130 hrs.

Hello my love. I am writing to you tonight with a heavy heart. I have prayed about tonight, and although I know that everything is in God's hands, I am still concerned. It's a natural thing, I know, but tonight's mission is different from the others. We've been attacked with rockets and mortars the last two Wednesday's in a row. In anticipation of that, the entire Brigade, plus a battalion of Marines are going down Highway 10 to the Farouk neighborhood, a known anti-coalition stronghold out in Ramadi. We're staging at a nearby camp, and when the Marines start the raid around 0500, then elements from 1st BCT will move in to secure the neighborhood and create a 'funnel' of sorts, in case the High Value Targets attempt to escape. If, or

I should say when that happens, that's where we come in, and we'll be on Highway 10, watching all the alleyways and rooftops for RPG's and small arms. Basically, we're going out to pick a fight, which should disrupt, if not deter the flow of weapons and insurgents into Ramadi. Insurgents and foreign fighters are flowing in from Fallujah, Baghdad, and as far away as Iran and Syria. Ramadi is white hot right now, and I just want to get out of here alive. We were told today that it's getting so bad that when we eventually leave this place, we'll probably have to fight our way to the border. This place is always so full of good news.

I have to get up in about two hours or so my love. You are my everything, and I love you with everything I am. You're the best thing that ever happened to me, and you always will be. Nothing, not even our children have given me what you have. I love you so much honey. I'm sure that everything will be just fine, and I'll call you when it's over. Kiss you later my darling.

5 AUG 04 D + 307 0515 hrs.

Hello my love. I just got back from the best shower in a long time. We were out about eight hours or so, and when we got back, the phones were flooded, so I shot you a quick message so you knew that we were back, and then hit the showers. I'm very tired. It seems as though that's all I know how to feel lately. I hope that will end when I get back home. Anyway, I'll write more tomorrow. Kiss you later honey.

12 AUG 04 D + 314 0700 hrs.

Good morning my love. I just realized that I lost a week's worth of entries in my journal because I copied the wrong one from my memory stick to the laptop. All things considered, I suppose it's a small thing in comparison.

I apologize for having to get off the phone rather quickly this morning. I started calling around 0400 our time and I couldn't get through. I called the boys and got to talk to all of them, which was of course great. They seemed to be doing well, but I couldn't help but feel the void, a certain distance between us through not only miles, but time as well. I can't wait to visit them when I arrive back in the States. It always seems as though when I do see them it's a repair job more so than a visit. Maybe it's just me, but I just hope the boys enjoy the visit, and I anxiously await your first visit with all the boys.

I only hope that you're not too worried right now. I'm sure, (God willing, that no one was hurt this morning) that I'll be able to call you back sometime today. While we were on the phone this morning, we had another rocket attack. As a matter of fact, they pounded us for about an hour this time, the longest attack since we've been here. It's almost funny, but not really, how you just cringe, and hope that the next one inbound doesn't have your name on it. We rarely mention this here, as it's unspoken but known by everyone. One landed in our motor pool, and several by the gates, and two landed within ten feet of our building. There is no rhyme or reason for the pattern of the attacks, just randomly launched ordinance inside the wire. There were also several rounds that impacted outside the wire too, and, sadly, I can only hope that some of them misfired and took out those that would do us harm.

I'm sure the hajji's that work on post will be looking for a damage assessment throughout their travels on post today. I'll be spending most of my time in the motor pool today changing tires on our trailers that must make the long trip back to Kuwait in a month and a half or so.

We've had a series of attacks lately, too many to mention, as they all have but one intention; to kill us. The reality of knowing that us being killed is a daily possibility is rather unsettling. I've spoken to you and all of our children today which is a rare occurrence. This brings me great joy, however, it somehow feels tarnished when things like this morning happen. I feel blessed to have moments like those this morning on the phone. I truly do. But there is a definite damper on our days when things like this happen. Sadly, by supper time, most of this morning's activities will not be forgotten, however hardly mentioned at all. Some of our people even slept through the first attack. It's ironic when this gets to be our 'normal'.

I will close for now my love, as I have to get to work here shortly. I love and miss you so very much. I hope to be able to call you soon, and tell you this in person, so to speak.

2255 hrs.

Hello honey. It's getting late, and I just got back from taking my first shower in three days, as well as doing laundry. All I seem to be able to think about is going home. It dominates my every thought, and it seems that everything I do is leading up to that, just not fast enough for me. My patience is very short these days, and I fear that it's starting to show.

While I was up at our little 'laundromat', Murph stopped me. I'd heard the other day that he was getting really stressed out, and although I was in a hurry to get things done, I actually looked for the opportunity to hear him out. They were right. He's a young E-5, and he's been basically running the TOC for almost a year. He goes in at about 0600 and stays most nights past 2200. He rarely gets a lunch, and really needs to be home. I tried my best to reassure him that things would be okay, and inquired if anyone would be waiting for him when we got off the plane. He told me that he wasn't sure if his parents were coming, and it was more than noticeable that this bothered him. I felt as though the little things that have been bothering me lately suddenly didn't matter. I know that I have my whole family waiting even now for me, and I instantly was made aware once again of my own blessings. Poor guy. We ended the night with a 'see ya later bro', and a hug. I wasn't aware until that moment that he was as bad off as he is. Murph is a big guy, and when he hugged me, I could feel him trembling. He mentioned that he never has any way to vent, and I recall thinking that I should mention this to the Chaplain. I'll have to get on it first thing in the morning. I really hope he pulls through this, for just the short amount of time that we have left here.

13 AUG 04 D + 315 2200 hrs.

Hello my love. I'm not superstitious or anything like that, but today is Friday the 13th. Normally that doesn't even concern me; however today was a rough day by all accounts. We talked about it a little while ago, and we seem to be straight on this morning, although there are some reservations about the whole homecoming deal all together on both our parts. This is normal, and completely understandable, and I'm sure whatever comes up, we'll deal with everything together.

After lunch, we went back down to the motor pool to finish our trailer tires, and after making a simple mistake, Zhou blew up at me. I couldn't believe it, and for the first time ever, I told him to 'at ease'. It almost hurt me to go to that level with him. He was quiet the rest of the day, and told me earlier this evening that he wanted to go to Combat Stress tomorrow morning. He's very self critical, and although a lot of people are, Zhou takes everything very personally. I have been thus far unable to convince him that this isn't always good. I wish that I could though. He's getting promoted on the 1st, and I just don't want him to get swallowed up in the Army, or people to take advantage of him

16 AUG 04 D + 318 2200 hrs.

Well, it's been a few days since I wrote anything in here. That's because our schedule has been nonstop, and there's finally a little bit of a break in the hectic schedule. Today we washed our trailers out, in hopes that they will go out on transport trucks and we won't have to tote them along when we drive south. Good deal.

Today I woke up very early again, and to the same nightmare that I've been having for quite some time. I just can't keep going like this, because I'm literally exhausted all the time, and I'm starting to feel the effects of being so tired all the time. I hope they stop sometime before I get home. I don't want to show up after all this time looking like crap for you honey. I know what you'd say to that, but I'm still concerned with it.

We were just about finished with the trailers today, when the LT came up and told us that Dorelus and Clemens would both be leaving this week. Three of our trucks, two of them mine, will be taking off on big tractor trailers at the end of the week. This is of course good for us because it means that not only two of our guys get to leave Iraq a little early, but that's also fewer vehicles on the road so close to the end of the tour.

17 AUG 04 D + 319 0630 hrs.

Good morning honey. I just got back from talking to you just a little while ago. One of your girlfriends answered the phone because you were mowing the grass. Although out of breath, it was good to hear your voice. I missed calling you last night because the satellite was giving us trouble again. I was exhausted too. I'm still getting up around 0230 to 0300 or so every morning. Insomnia is becoming a close companion of mine, and as much as I hate to say it, I'm almost used to it now. I look forward to the coming month in leaving this place, and more relaxed times in Kuwait. I don't think we'll be totally relaxed in Kuwait, as the wash rack to hose down vehicles is open 24 hours a day, however, at least no one will be shooting at us . . . hopefully. I almost can't even imagine being somewhere where everyone doesn't want to kill us. I've said it before, and I'll always live by this; and that's that everything truly changed after 9-11. It really is a different world we live in now.

1900 hrs.

Hello my love. Tonight, we are all in bed early. The Platoon is down for tonight at 1900, because we'll get up about 0200 in preparation for another Brigade-wide mission. Tonight we're doing another cordon search mission. We're going from house to house in an area the size of Junction City, Kansas tonight. With elements from the entire Brigade and a battalion of Marines with us, it should take no more than eight or nine hours. Even with a lot of people, that's still quite a feat.

This area that we're going to tonight hasn't been thoroughly manipulated by the Coalition in almost two months. It's primarily a Marine area, however, apparently we're not trusting their abilities publicly now. It's a shame too, because they're leaving here within a couple of weeks of us, and they still haven't learned yet. They're not losing troops in the numbers they once did, but they don't shoulder near the same responsibilities as the Army does. The local Division size element in the area is of the Marine persuasion; however they just don't play the part. Everyone misses the 82nd and not only their support, but their way of handling business. The Marines only handle from Ramadi to somewhere the other side of TQ, near Habbaniyah. The 82nd had everything from here to Baghdad. Basically, when they were here, we handled Midwestern Iraq to Central Iraq.

Anyhow, between briefings and stuff, I didn't get the chance to get to the phones today, but I pray I'll have the chance after we return, sometime around noon tomorrow. It's going to be a very long night, especially if we end up doing more than security for the Command Group. We're equipped with mine detectors, and TCP kits as well, but no matter what we do, noon tomorrow won't get here any faster. We stocked up on Reese's cups and Red Bull energy drinks today. We shall see. I'm already lying down, so I suppose I should try and get some sleep. I will dream of you.

19 AUG 04 D + 321 2130 hrs.

Hello honey. Today we repacked our conex again, and started washing our vehicles. These are also good signs, but again, it all really starts when our replacements get here. We had a briefing tonight from the Battalion Commander where we were briefed on a tentative timeline for our redeployment, as well as received our 'war coins'. Nick and I were at the very end of the line, which had every NCO in the Battalion in it. I wound up being the very last NCO in line, and I never would have thought what happened next would have happened at all. The Commander slapped the Brigade coin in my hand with the words, 'Here, let me give you another one of these.' He actually remembered that I was the first soldier in 1st BCT to receive the Brigade war coin. This was only about a half an hour ago, but I remember thinking that I was impressed by his memory. We shook hands, and I then moved to CSM Bush, where I got the Battalion war coin, which, incidentally, was designed by a DECON soldier. All in all a good night. When we got out of our briefing, we all came back to the hooch where the soldiers were anxiously awaiting our return to see if we had any more info. We had a little, but not much. Either way, it was nice to be back and back with our guys after over an hour. It's funny how after this much time with each other, we still look forward to seeing each other so soon after.

It's been a very long day today, and I'm going to try and get some rest tonight. I do want to talk to you though, so I'll try early in the morning. I love you my darling. Kiss you later.

22 AUG 04 D + 324 0200 hrs.

Happy Birthday my love. I just got off the phone with you a little while ago, and I was just delighted to hear that the girls had all pulled together and surprised you for your birthday. Actually, at home right now, it's the day before your birthday, but Bev, Desire, and Ali silly stringed you when they showed up and you sounded so very happy honey. That's all I truly wanted for you today, and I'm glad that you got it. I wish so badly that I could be with you now, but I emailed you a little message that I wrote for you for your birthday.

Although I cannot physically see you on your birthday this year, I'm sure that you're just as radiant as ever my love. With each day, you are more beautiful than the day before. And year after year, I am amazed at how beautiful you are. Oh my God you're so pretty I can hardly stand it. I love you my darling.

We have a mission tomorrow night, and we'll be out all night long again with the entire Brigade. We're going out in search of weapons caches in our sector. We're also taking out some of the 2nd Infantry Division people that are here to show them how it's done. The last time we went out, we scored big, and took in hundreds of automatic weapons, rocket propellant, and 400 lbs. of explosives. We've been pretty lucky so far, so we'll pray for another successful mission with no injuries. I'll dream of you tonight my love.

0600 hrs.

Good morning once again my love. I got to talk to you for a little while longer this morning. I didn't sleep well, but that didn't stop the fireworks. While walking back to the hooch, I decided to walk over to the trucks to check on them, as we periodically do. I heard a faint whistle in the air, and the last thing I remember is saying to myself, 'Please God'. It was another rocket attack, and although they were as close as they'd ever been, for some reason I just froze in my steps. The first inbound round was about 30 feet over my head when it came whizzing by, and impacted about 100 meters from me. I remember looking over my shoulder, following the sound as best I could. At the same time, the second round impacted the row of containers next to the PX, sending one up in flames. Our X-Ray (TOC) called the fire department, and they made it over there in decent time to put the fire out. That was a really hairy one this morning. This only all happened about twenty minutes or so ago. My heart is still pounding as I sit here. I took a few pictures, and although they didn't come out too good, the images of that conex on fire are permanently engrained in my memory. Maybe it's just pride, but in my glory days, my boys and I would have made better response time. The National Guard guys didn't do too badly though. I didn't realize it at the time, but I must have dove for the deck sometime shortly thereafter, or as I was following the sound over my shoulder, because I had to dust myself off and I felt something on my arm. I had two small scratches where I guess my arm grated over the rocks as I went down. What a great way to start the day.

1950 hrs.

Hello honey. Well, unfortunately you didn't get to sleep in to late today. When I called just a little while ago, you were getting ready for church, and for some reason or another, Kevin was being a little hellion. After I had to call back because he hung up on me after picking up the phone without answering it, I finally got him on the phone. Things didn't pick up from there. He was rude, and then refused to answer any question I asked him, so I told him to give the phone back to you. I was really mad when that happened, but I have to focus because tonight we're pulling another all nighter. We're hitting another area that the Brigade overall hasn't been through in some time. This is due to the fact that it's a Marine controlled area, but once again, we have to go in there and do their job for them.

After the mission, I'm sure that we'll recover our gear and vehicles, and then rest up for a while. After that, I'm not even sure what we're doing because all of our vehicles are cleaned up with the help of our wash rack, and our conex is packed up.

We were told that anytime after the 20th of this month we should expect to see some more of 2nd I. D. show up. I've heard rumors of anywhere from the 26th to the 30th as well.

23 AUG 04 D + 325 2330 hrs.

Hello my love. After we got back from mission this afternoon, I got to talk to you twice between then and now. I also sent you some pictures and an email just a few minutes ago. I felt so great after the last time we talked this evening. I came back to the hooch, and listened to some music, and started singing aloud with the tunes out on the porch. Everyone asked me why I was in such a good mood, and I just had to tell them that it was you my love. Only my Helen could put me in such a good mood. I was thinking of you having good times at home with your girls, and maybe I'd get Kevin and Abby to help me bolt my new steps to the truck, and wash it. I remember it being so funny how Abby wanted so badly to help wash the van when I was home that she'd wash the same spot over and over even though we'd rinsed it four or five times. Kevin is turning into a pre-teen, and although it may prove to be challenging at times, I welcome it, so long as no one is shooting at me. Abby seems as though she's wanting to be just like her mommy in every way. I just absolutely love that about her, as it's of course a credit to you, her mother; the ultimate example of a woman. I love you my darling.

Well, I'll close this out for now, as it's getting late. I feel so fortunate to have talked to you so much today my love. I miss you so much, and I can't wait to hold you again.

25 AUG 04 D + 327 0440 hrs.

Good morning my love. Well, I've been up for a long time now. I woke up at 0130 and went down to call you. We were lucky this morning, as we got to talk for over an hour and a half. The kids were being rambunctious as usual, and although I miss everything about them, even those times, I can't wait to get home to take some of the burden off of you. I know it really has to be tough.

Well, yesterday was interesting enough. We now have a small hajji village here on post where a lot of the contractors live. They are allowed to live here, for fear of being killed if they live off the camp, as has happened to so many of our other contractors. Apparently they're starting to take a lot of things for granted. Their little village is located near the Contractor Staging Area, or old Escort area and the burn pit, on the outskirts of the camp. Yesterday afternoon, I sent four soldiers out to take some bulk trash out to the burn pit as we often do. Upon arriving there, the two trucks were immediately mobbed by about 70 hajji's trying to steal trash or dumpster dive. They also had trucks outside the wire, so they could throw their treasures from the trash over the wire to be distributed through the town to other folks as well. After not being able to maneuver the vehicles without mowing over a bunch of local nationals, Zhou made the call for one of the men to fire a warning shot into the berm next to most of the locals. They of course scattered at this point, and the incident was reported to higher, and statements were filled out. The Commander thought that our guys were wrong, but then again she wasn't even there. This sounds all too familiar with her. I told Zhou that under those same circumstances, I don't think that I would have acted any different. Then again, she probably would have sent me to combat stress again. Oh well, the incident went off without any injuries, and I told the guys that I think they did a great job.

2040 hrs.

Hello my love. Today was a very busy day, as several changes affected our day and altered our plans of relaxing for most of the day. As a matter of fact, we just got done putting our bay together again about a half hour ago. Nick and 1st Squad are back upstairs with us again, and the Platoon Sergeant moved in with the LT, a move that the LT has been actively avoiding for about a week anyhow. He even went crying to the commander about it, so the 1SG busted him out over the company radio net yesterday and told him to quit whining about it. The LT thinks that as a new First Lieutenant, he doesn't have to live with any of us lowly enlisted people. Oh well, he got punked out and it only confirmed to the entire company what we've known all along. The downside to that is that DECON appears like the leadership isn't on the same page, which they obviously aren't.

There are pros and cons to this move. As I've mentioned before, there's been an obvious separation in the platoon since they moved downstairs, but I'm hoping that this will be a decent arrangement for at least the last two weeks or so before we leave. I've actually always preferred it this way because since we're such a separate entity from the rest of the Battalion, it's just naturally better like this. With the Platoon Sergeant gone now, this is actually what we've always wanted. Having been a Platoon Sergeant myself, I would have done it this way. Not only does rank have its privileges, but in this close environment it also allows somewhat of a distance from the Soldiers. I think that he may have actually had more respect, among other things during this tour had he done it that way. Too late now, but many lessons have been learned as well.

Anyway, back to the reason that the whole platoon is back together again. Our new First Sergeant and I ran into each other today. He's an old school combat engineer. We butted heads a few times in Kosovo, where I worked directly for the Task Force Commander, but was still attached to his Engineer Battalion, under him in particular. He's a really fair guy, and a no bullshit kind of straight shooter. He's not one to really ever go outside the chain of command, even when going down the chain. So when he mentioned something to me on the porch today, and I inquired what it was about, he told me that he had a meeting with all the Platoon Sergeants and that we'd all find out soon enough. Of course, he told me anyway. This move for the Platoon was supposed to happen no later than Friday, but it got bumped up to today by close of business. So, basically we had to finish before we did anything else. So we got our war stock of MRE's, water, and extra cots for our trip to Kuwait, and stacked them up outside, and got the move completed. This is because our replacements are coming in the afternoon the day after tomorrow. Everyone is very excited, and of course we can't wait until they do, and we can start doing our right seat/left seat rides with them.

There's also a rumor that our Platoon may be leaving before everyone else, because our replacements don't have a DECON Platoon, so there's no replacement for us. The only down side to that that I can see is that we may have to train up a PSD. If that's the case though, I really won't mind. I wouldn't want someone that's getting here as a cherry to go through some of the same stuff that we have. Things really got moving for us after the ambush at the end of March, and after going out so many times ill equipped, and then receiving the apologies from both the Battalion and Brigade Commanders, we really started perfecting the art of the gun ship escort. There are countless little things, too many to mention really, that have helped us get to where we are today. And the gun ship teams are so tight, the kind of tight that only comes with being in combat together. Like I've said before, I don't even have to tell Simmons what to do, because he's already inside my head, and acts as a reflex to my thoughts. The same with my gunners, rotating on instinct and gut reaction. I'm so proud of my boys, and I'll always be forever grateful for their loyal and dedicated service. I'll always be more grateful though, that that very same service that helped us all get home, and me to you my love. I've never had to fight so hard and be so patient and strong in my life; but you of course are the only thing in this life worth it honey.

This tour has taught me so many things. I've had to learn to exercise patience, not be such a control freak, control a temper here and there, and learn to absolutely respect a people who's sole purpose in life was to take mine. I have respect for so many things now; some the same as before, and some deeper than before. I've grown a lot personally here, away from my home. I think that I've become a lot closer to God during this time as well. I have had to be more patient, trusting, loving toward my fellow man and a host of other things than I ever have before. And all of it was a result of trusting in God, and realizing that we're all not really in control of much in our lives. If we just trust absolutely in God during the toughest times in our lives, then we can truly feel a sense of freedom that some people wait their entire lives for and never get to see.

26 AUG 04 D + 328 2315 hrs.

Hello my love. Today was interesting enough. I was on our balcony, watching trucks so that the Soldiers could go eat before our customs inspection, and the all too familiar sound of incoming rockets screeched through the air. I had heard the sound, but there was no visible or audible explosion. I didn't dismiss it right away as just hearing something, but I just couldn't understand it. I found out later on that the rockets had indeed landed, one tearing through the roof of Alpha Company's barracks. It was a 107 mm rocket, and although it had penetrated the roof of the building, it landed in the middle of the bay, in between bunk beds, and there was no detonation. Apparently the round had been bent at the tip upon impact, and thus been disabled. God was watching out for those men today. There's no other reason that any of them should have lived. God bless them. I got some pictures of the barracks from Matt De Vries, the guy whose mother in law we mat at the t-shirt place in Manhattan when I went home. Matt's a hell of a guy, but even this evening he was still visibly shaken by the whole ordeal. I really can't blame him. We're all shaky nowadays, and things like this surely don't help.

We broke a land speed record in getting our conex done and sealed by the inspectors. We were completely done in two hours, and got to move on relatively smoothly with the rest of our day. It certainly was a big relief to get that conex done.

Later on in the afternoon, the temperature rose pretty quickly, and topped out at 142 degrees. It was horrible to even simply walk outside. I have to say that it was just miserable. After we got tasked out for about four more missions in the late afternoon and I was in a pretty foul mood. When I called you, the call ended badly, and you and I were both upset. I should have known better than to have called when I was already upset. I ended up calling back a couple of hours later and talking it out with you. I see that we both have our own concerns about the reunion, and there's nothing wrong with that, and that we have to recognize each other's situation. With the tunnel of time narrowing before I come home, I also know that there are certain apprehensions on both our parts, and that's something that we're also going to have to recognize.

27 AUG 04 D + 329 0625 hrs.

Good morning my love. Well, we're up early again to head over to Champion, hopefully for our last time. It's always been a good run, nice and easy without incident. The only thing we'll have to worry about here is a rocket attack, because they fire those at us at any time of day, and they also know that something important is at Champion, they just don't know what. We're of course hoping that the day goes off without a hitch, but hope sometimes doesn't go very far out here.

We're expecting about 200 soldiers in today from the 44th Engineers. A buddy of mine went out on a convoy last night to escort them here, and he was talking about bringing them straight down Highway 10 so it only takes them 26 minutes to get here as opposed to the two hour southern route. I told him that I didn't think it was wise to take an unnecessary risk like that so close to the end of our tour. He replied that they have to start going down Highway 10 sooner or later, and they may as well start now. Everyone's getting pretty callous around here. Then again, our replacements have been messing around in Kuwait for over a month now, and we've been still sitting here going on mission after mission and still taking casualties.

Either way it goes, they'll soon be here, and the Platoon is still very excited about seeing fresh faces and new equipment roll in here. I'm sure it'll do a lot for morale; mine included, to see all of that. Unfortunately, the C-6, DFAC, and PX are going to be very crowded, and for a short time life will be frustrating here, just like when the Marines came. Overall though, it's a small price to pay for going home, and I'm sure we'll just take it in stride just like everything else that has come our way. After all, what other choice do we have?

28 AUG 04 D + 330 1800 hrs.

Hello my love. I hope your day is going well. Ours is going okay. We were supposed to ship out four of our nine trailers on semi trucks called HET's, but today they loaded up the rest of ours, so all nine are gone now. They also loaded one of our five ton trucks as well. That convoy will leave early tomorrow morning, and that's a few less things that we have to worry about.

This afternoon, things slowed down a lot, and everyone is sitting around watching a movie right now. A couple of the guys ran out to get to go plates for everyone, and now they're watching 'Old School'. It looks pretty funny so far. I think this is the first time in a long while that I've got to see this much of a movie at the same time. It's actually nice to have literally almost nothing to do. They took our equipment out as they offloaded the stuff from the guys from Korea. Although there are a lot of people here now, there's still no sign of our replacements. The Infantry Battalion is here, as are a few others replacing some other smaller slice units here. They're saying that they should all be here in their entirety no later than Monday at the latest. With a ten day schedule of right seat/left seat time; as long as they get here by the first of September, we'll still be on schedule. Everyone is excited, but a little impatient at the same time.

I got to take another nap today. I slept for about three hours. This probably means that I'll be up pretty late, but that's no concern to me. I want to be up late to call you anyway. There is a noticeable difference around here already. The lines for everything are longer, but it's a means to an end. I love and miss you so much honey. I can't even tell you. It's all going to be over here soon, and with each moment we get closer and closer to going home . . . home to you. I can't wait my love.

30 AUG 04 D + 332 1100 hrs.

Hello my darling. Today hasn't been very eventful so far. We're only at half strength today, because some vehicles broke down on the advanced convoys preparing the way for the rest of us going down to Kuwait. Our Platoon Sergeant and Nick took their gun ships out last night and spent the night in Baghdad. They should be back some time this afternoon. The spare time gave me an opportunity to take care of some things and get a little ahead of the game before the other gun trucks get back from their mission. I felt kind of awkward last night, as Rafael took Zhou and Eason with him. It just feels weird with them out on mission without me. I'm sure everything will be fine and they'll be back safe and sound tonight.

Another replacement company came in last night, and they're all griping about how nasty and 'without' the camp really is. I told one Squad Leader that if his guys thought they were doing without so much, then they could eat MRE's three times a day, don't use any of the port-o-jons and burn shit in barrels with diesel fuel every night, pretend there is no PX, and don't use the phones or internet; and then they'll have an accurate picture of what life was like when we got here. I understand that this is all new to them, but hopefully they'll come to appreciate what they have and be glad that there's not more that they don't have. When we got here, we really had no choice to be appreciative of every little thing because there simply was nothing here. Oh well, this is their baby now, and they can surely have it. There's nothing here that I ever need to come back here for. I'll write more later on honey.

OUR ANNIVERSARY D + 333 2230 hrs.

Hello my love. Today is our anniversary, and I am missing you terribly today. At least I got to call you for a little while. When we were talking, you were ordering your lunch at Subway, and this afternoon I took a nap. All in all, it's not a bad anniversary, but by far not the best either. Actually, this year makes last year's anniversary at the guest house look like a pleasure trip.

Anyhow, I take comfort in the fact that in our own small way we can still celebrate the anniversary of the biggest day of my life. I love you so very much my darling. KYL!

1 SEP 04 D + 334 1445 hrs.

Hello my love. Well, today is the first day of September, and the excitement is in the air all over the place here. It looks like we're going to ride this one out until the very end though. We turn over the Steel Horse and the other gun trucks Sunday evening, and I have to say that I am having a little separation anxiety. That truck has saved my ass on more than one occasion, and we did build it from the ground up. I'm sure I'll have no trouble with it when I get on that plane. Most of the decent memories that I have from this place do involve that truck, and of course the crew of the Steel Horse. I bought some OIF coins from the PX, one for each member of my Squad. I've said it before, as I'm sure you know that I will again; I've led them out here, but they've taken care of me as much if not more than I ever did them. Once again I've been blessed with the opportunity to walk with heroes.

I can hardly imagine them in the rear. Most of the things that we do, prep for, the way we act; all these things will hardly ever happen in the rear. I am thankful for this; however, I think it's going to be like learning everyone all over again. We'll lose a couple to getting out or going to another duty station. I suppose that my separation anxiety is deeper than I'm willing to admit, because I remember getting over here and Dorelus was my second in charge, and Zhou and Taylor were just Squad members. Now Dorelus is a SGT, and Zhou and Taylor both will pin their stripes this evening. It seems as though they were all just kids when I met them. Combat time has a way of aging you beyond simple years. It burns a certain wisdom into your mind and soul forever.

I have thought long and hard about the moment that I first see you again. Being a soldier as long as I have, I have come to appreciate the invaluable and indescribable feeling that only a homecoming from war can bring. However, I have never had that feeling with you my love, and as overwhelming as your love for me, and mine for you can be at times, I feel like this is a foreign thing to me. I'm not just building it up in my own mind, but the anticipation is just phenomenal to me. I am entranced between the ecstatic feeling of being with you again, seeing our beautiful children, and knowing also that I may not have to come back here . . . the place that tried so many times to take me from you.

It would seem that any one of us would hate this place without question, but that's not really the case with me. Of course I'd rather be home with you and the children than here any day of the week. I have to look back, to when you were pregnant with Abigail, to truly appreciate the value of these times and the pride I have in my family for your patience and the sacrifices that you've endured over the last couple years.

2000 hrs.

Hello my love. Well, the fruits of our hard labor paid off yet again this evening. Taylor and Zhou were both promoted to E-5, and I couldn't be prouder. I pinned them both, along with the Battalion Commander, and in an instant they went from 'one of them' to 'one of us'. It was very nice.

2100 hrs.

I just got back from talking with you, and while we were talking, you got a phone call from Irwin Army Hospital telling you that you'd been referred to a surgeon because you have some gall stones. I know you're concerned about this, as am I, but I'll be praying for you over this in particular. I'm so sorry that I can't be there to comfort you right now my love. I'd give just about anything to be home with you anyway, but this just makes it worse for the both of us. I feel shattered inside right now my love, and I pray that there's more that I could do. I love you my darling. I'll call every day that I can until we find out what the deal really is all about. For now though, I must rest due to having missions three out of the next four days. I love you my darling.

3 SEP 04 D + 336 0730 hrs.

Good morning my love. I woke up a little while ago, and made a pot of coffee to have a little 'Ron time'. My bed now sits adjacent to the open window across the bay. The sun rises with the sun shining on the far wall. It's nice being able to sleep in a little, even though I never really sleep in that late.

I went out on the porch to check on my guys earlier while they were on guard, and I watched as about 300 new Marines marched in a huge line going off to chow. Everything is crowded now because our camp was only designed to accommodate about one third of the troops it currently has. It's very frustrating nowadays, even with the thought of going home, because we just thought it was crowded before, and now the phone lines and line into the PX are at least an hour long each. The chow hall is overwhelmed, and most of us don't even go anymore. It's simply not worth walking a half mile in 130 degree plus heat just to wait almost an hour to get a meal that you're not really interested in anyway. I don't mean to sound like I'm bitching about everything, but the frustration level around here is on the rise, and the new unit really doesn't help at all.

Our first mission out yesterday morning was to take the new HHC Commander and 1SG out to one of our commonly visited checkpoints, and show them how we developed the force protection around one of the Iraqi police stations. Well, on the way out there, the inbound Commander and 1SG both fell asleep, so of course there was no way they could see the route out there, much less remember how to get there. The trip was just about a complete waste of time. It's bad enough that the IP's are crooked cops anyway, and we risked our lives just going out there. The point is that the whole mission was for them, and them falling asleep was a big slap in the face to every one of us out there. After we got back, our Company Commander was fuming, and was yelling something fierce when she reported back to Battalion. Anything newsworthy spreads like wildfire around here, so their reputation is shit right now. Overall, they just don't seem very motivated about the mission, and to be honest, they have big shoes to fill when it comes to following in our footsteps. They're taking over completely in 48 hours, this Sunday evening, and they haven't even formed a PSD yet. I really hope for their sake that they start taking things seriously soon; otherwise they just might wind up like the Marines in their complacency.

I'm sure it'll be easier to detach from this place when we leave, but for now I'm concerned because no one here wants it to ever be said that we didn't have a smooth handoff with the new folks. We'll see how it goes.

2100 hrs.

Hello my darling. I'm just lying here, watching yet another movie. I think I've seen every movie the whole platoon has, at least twice each, and it's just to pass the time. I am missing you so very much today. We got spun up for a mission earlier, to get an ACE vehicle that had broken down outside the wire. We weren't looking forward to it, because an ACE vehicle is the same size as a tank, but different in that it's used as a haul asset by the maintenance team. It's absolutely huge, and it can only be hauled with another ACE. We wound up standing down and just ended up sweating a whole lot for nothing. Thank God for small miracles.

Well, when tomorrow morning comes, we can say that we only have exactly one week left. It seems hard to believe that we've been here this long, or that we're actually leaving. I am very depressed these days, my love. I am not only missing you and the children, but over here it seems as though we still have mission after mission, with no true end in sight. With the complacency of the replacements, no one in the platoon believes that Sunday will be the end for us. There's always another 'hey you' mission, and we're helping out just about all the other platoons as they're not finished packing yet.

At the very least, I did get a really good nap in today. I slept solid for about three hours or so, and wasn't interrupted even so much as once. My mattress wasn't too bad, and the guys kept the noise down for a change. If they didn't, I sure didn't hear it. I was pretty tired though. The C-6 was down for most of last night and throughout today, but is open again now. The generator went out and it wasn't a priority to fix until later on. I'm going to try and call you later on tonight. The sound of your voice does wonders for me honey, but I fear that even that will take time for me to get used to again and slip out of this war mentality that I've been in for so long. I just hope that it doesn't take too long.

We're going to Habbaniyah this Sunday, and taking our Battalion Commander and the new Commander up there to show him around. Of course we're taking Highway 10, because our command wouldn't have it any other way. He really prefers to save time on these runs. We're all calling it the 'death run'. We'll probably travel at close to 60 mph most of the way, except when going through the market place. The village of Khalidiyah, which is about two miles out of Habbaniyah, is the worst place. We've been hit there every single time we've gone through there with an IED. It's because of this that no one is looking forward to the trip. I suppose I can only equate it to a woman's period. You know it's coming, and it may hurt badly or it may not. You're not sure exactly when it's coming, but you know it is, and it's usually a bit of a surprise when it does. The only difference is that this little trip can get us killed. I just want to get through this last one. After we return from this one, we just clean out the trucks and sign them over. We'll just pray for a safe return.

4 SEP 04 D + 337 2200 hrs.

Hello my love. We're all just sitting around talking about the mission tomorrow. I think that because it's our last mission as a PSD, and we're taking Highway 10, that everyone is just a tad nervous. We're pulling out all the stops. I've got more ammo than I've ever had; I stocked up on extra grenades today as well, and washed the windows myself.

I'll be short a gunner tomorrow, as Clark got injured today hooking up a trailer to a 5-ton trailer. He broke the tip of his middle finger, and his flesh was split down the middle to the first knuckle. It looked really bad, but the Doc said he'd be alright. He's slightly out of commission though, but at least it wasn't his firing hand.

Dorelus and Clemens finally left tonight. They're mounting up on the HET's that are carrying our 5 tons that were loaded today. We got three trucks loaded yesterday, and two more today, leaving four more to go. At the rate we're going, we won't have to drive down to Kuwait at all. If this is the case, the whole platoon will fly, probably out of TQ. We're all very excited about this. No one is looking forward to a two-day drive, half of it being still in Iraq. It really is looking up though. If we get more loaded tomorrow, then I have to send Taylor, Eason, and Clark out with those HET's. I'm a little uncomfortable with sending my people out without me. I know that it's in God's hands, and whether anything happens along the route or not; is irrelevant whether I'm there or not. But the three of them, especially Clark and Eason are like kids to me, and I know that they'll be scared to some degree. I suppose that I just don't want them to have to go through a long journey like that without me. I suppose I'll have to let go with our kids a little at least someday, although I dread the day.

5 SEP 04 D + 338 2230 hrs.

Hello my darling. I certainly hope that you're having a great day. I have a lot of weight off of my shoulders today, as we had our last PSD mission this morning. It was bittersweet handing over the Steel Horse to our replacement unit, however at least our truck, the Steel Horse, is going to a guy who used to be in our unit back at Fort Riley. Bennie Washington is a little cocky, but used to talk a lot of smack prior to leaving Fort Riley that since he was leaving for Korea that he was going to miss out on the Iraq tour. And now here he is in the Battalion replacing us. How ironic.

6 SEP 04 D + 339 0225 hrs.

Hello again my love. I was delayed for the last few hours, and haven't been asleep yet. Tonight, I had to send off three of my soldiers to ride along with Kuwaiti civilian truck drivers that are driving our equipment down to Camp Arifjan where they'll be cleaned, processed for shipment on the boat, and where we all will eventually fly out of to come home. I absolutely can't stand the thought of breaking the Squad up like this, but it won't get any better until we all get down there. If all of our trucks go out on HET's, then we'll fly down to Kuwait. Either way though, some vehicles will have to convoy down, or that includes our Platoon's Humvee. It's already been decided that one of my Team Leaders will be the gunner on the trip down for that. I already had to let one of my Team Leaders and some soldiers go without me, and I'd not prefer to do it again. I told my guys that I didn't like it and the fact that the Commander was making these decisions without consulting the Squad Leaders, somewhat like picking names out of a hat; and not taking Platoon integrity into consideration. Well, I just plain don't like it. Anyway, I told him that if it came down to it, then I would ask to go along with him instead of flying. I never did like splitting my squad up for any reason, but for the greater good of the entire unit I understand that it's sometimes necessary.

I will close for now because I am very tired my love. I know that we've not spoken for a couple of days now, but things will ease up soon. This is definitely good, and either way it goes, I'll be in Kuwait in a week. I truly can't wait. I love you my darling.

7 SEP 04 D + 340 0930 hrs.

Good morning my love. When I got up this morning, I tried to call you, however, you were at the hospital with Desire at the time, and I couldn't get through on her cell phone either. It was very disheartening to me, and I will have to wait until I get off at 1800 to call you again.

When we spoke last night, you sounded terribly sick, and I wanted to be there with you so badly. I hate the feeling of being so helpless from here, and not being able to do anything for you. One day soon this feeling will end, and there will be no more emptiness like I am feeling now. Yes, even taking you to the hospital in the middle of the night is inviting to me nowadays, anything to be near you honey.

8 SEP 04 D + 341 1830 hrs.

Hello again my love. It's been a very busy 24 hours. The rest of my guys and I were manifested to leave out on a truck convoy last night, but got booted at the last minute. Matt came to Junction City last night on a convoy heading south, and was only there for a few hours. His convoy heading out was our shot, but we were promised that if we didn't get out last night, then we would be heading out to TQ Air Base, and then flown down south to Ali Al Saleem, and then catch a bus over to Camp Arifjan, which is our departure point for coming home.

As I sit here, I'm in the PAX terminal at TQ writing this. We rode out of Camp Junction City on Marine 7-ton trucks. They're a lot bigger than our 5-tons, and have a lot more armor on them. It was a bench style seat, typical of most military vehicles, and it made my ass sorer than any time that I can recall. The last thirty miles or so, I sat on my camelback, which was half full of water. I decided that I'd rather dehydrate than have a sore ass. We just had MRE's for supper, and they'd been sitting in the sun for most of the day, so it saved me the trouble of heating them up. It was more than hot enough for me. I wouldn't have thought just two short hours ago that I'd ever want another hot meal again as hot as it was. Today topped 140. It's only fitting being as it's our last day in Iraq.

It sounds funny even saying that after all this time, but it's getting easier for those same words to roll right off of my tongue. It's 1900 now, and the troops, however tired, are still a little restless. Our flight doesn't take off until 2110 hrs. I told my guys to relax a while, and take advantage of the opportunity to rest. Not just rest in between missions, or rest for lunch, but truly rest without a care in the world.

At least most of DECON is together now, minus those who already convoyed down to Camp Arifjan. Zhou was left to be a gunner for the LT's vehicle for the remaining fifteen vehicles or so that could not be sent out on flatbed trucks. He's not much for it, and I can't say that I am either, but someone had to do it. Poor guy, has to ride in the back of a Humvee and sitting on top of an igloo cooler. I don't think that anyone will be happier to get to Kuwait than him.

I'm going to try and get a nap in before our flight. We're taking a C-130, and I haven't even sat in one so much as once since being at Bragg. Fort Bragg . . . the place of our beginning. In retrospect, I don't think that I love the rodeo, jumping, or even the fire department so much as I don't have as many memories of any of that combined as I do of you and I and Kevin together. Our little phone call down memory lane last night reminded me of that. You are the beginning for me my love, the middle, and the end as well. I love you so much.

9-11 D + 344 2200 hrs.

Hello my love. It's been a busy couple of days here. The day before yesterday, we flew out of TQ, and landed at Ali Asaleem, outside of Kuwait City and next to Camp Doha. The flight went well, and we landed late. Being inside a darkened C-130 sure brought back a lot of memories for me, and Nick and I told Airborne stories almost halfway through the flight. Then we racked out and I didn't even stir once until the wheels hit the ground. This was about 0100, and the DFAC closed at 0200 hrs. We humped our bags all over the place, and eventually made it to chow. We thought we were going to get some shady leftovers, but instead found T-bone steaks and lobster tails. I just could not believe it. I still had the smell of Ramadi in my nose, and plenty of sand in my clothes and in every orifice of my body, and we walked in as we were into what seemed like a five star restaurant.

Some National Guard guy who's pulling a year of 'combat duty' down here in Kuwait looked at us as though he was going to say something about our appearance, but somehow then thought better of it. He looked at the Big Red One patch on our shoulders and it seemed as though it quietly dawned on him that we had just come from Iraq that night, and it probably wasn't wise to do anything but let us get some chow. We must have sat there for 45 minutes or so, eating like kings, and making a big deal about asking someone to pass the steak sauce, or some butter for our lobster tails. It was a great meal.

We spent the night in a bay of about 200 soldiers, and once I found the phone, I got up at 0500 to go and call you. The A T & T phone cards I had didn't last but about ten minutes or so, but it was enough to let you know that I was no longer in Iraq. That was one of the best phone calls I've ever made. I heard your voice lighten up, and I even heard Kevin scream in the background over the news of me being out if Iraq. It was a long one, but a truly great day nonetheless. We were very fortunate to have such a great day, as those leaving behind us didn't have as much good fortune as we did.

We left so that we could do a preemptive strike on our vehicles here at Camp Arifjan, and get them through the wash rack and over staged at the port. Those who left immediately after us were the soldiers from Main Body 1, who are leaving before us, and flying out first. This is primarily because they have no vehicles, have family issues, or something else that's more pressing in the rear. Their flight was to leave the night after ours. This didn't happen.

The night after we left TQ, the base camp was mortared, and the impact of the explosions destroyed portions of the runway, disabling the ability for planes to takeoff and land. One mortar also struck an Ammunition Supply Point (ASP), which from what I'm told kept cooking off live rounds for two whole days in the aftermath. So here we are now, two days later, and those guys are stuck there still in Iraq. It's never truly over until it's really over.

Well, at this point, those guys are still at TQ, we've finished all of our vehicles that have been line hauled, and our guys brought in another 5-ton, our last one tonight. It's 2240 right now, and I was just told that the line is pretty backed up so he won't even get on the wash rack until about 0100 hrs. or so. More's the pity. I don't feel too bad because we've all done our time on the wash rack, and although it sucks it's still one of the last stages before we go home.

Today I sit here in the Middle East on the third anniversary of 9-11 preparing to come home to you. We've all reminisced about the last year, and are overjoyed to be in a place like this. Today is a direct result of what started all this just three short years ago. At the risk of repeating myself, I will never forget your face when I walked through the door that fateful day. You were sobbing uncontrollably as I walked through the door, and we hugged for what seemed like forever. I will never forget that day for as long as I live.

Coming home means so much more to me now, as I've been gone this last year. I just want you o know my love, that it's not just I that have made sacrifices and paid a price, but you and the children as well. I know this, and I'll make sure that our children know it as well.

Tomorrow, Nick and Valencia are packing their bags and moving to the port itself so they can start loading vehicles. Our boat has apparently come in, and they'll start loading our vehicles. Our vehicles don't even have to all be on the boat, just be at the port for us to go anywhere. So the sooner the LT and the last wheeled convoy get here, the sooner we can wash up our last vehicle and actively start looking for a way out of here.

14 SEP 04 D + 347 2030 hrs.

Hello my love. Today was pretty boring, but I did manage to get a three hour nap in. Somehow I still managed to get up at 0500 and make a run to the little donut shop here on camp. I also ate Burger King for lunch and Subway for dinner. Then Zhou wanted to go and eat, but didn't want to go alone so I went with him to the DFAC just a little while ago. It feels like I just can't stop eating lately. I think that we're just saturated with all these amenities of home, and in a way I'm glad for it. I feel like a big fat blob right now, and by the time we actually make it home, I'll be as used to being around things like this as you and the kids are. I guess the days of me starving myself are gone. I almost have to laugh, because I've eaten more actual sit-down meals in the last week than I have in the last month back at Camp J.C. Anyway, enough on my bad diet.

A buddy of mine just came by and told me that he overheard some bad news. Apparently, somehow our flights got messed up, and instead of pushing the majority of the battalion out tomorrow, we now may not be leaving until the 28th of this month. My heart just sank. Even though we're in relative safety here, and the amenities of home are abundant, it's just not even close to being the same. I've already packed and repacked my stuff three times already. Every time I do laundry, I find something else that I really don't need for the trip home, and discard it without a second thought. Even down to the little things; I had enough shampoo and deodorant to last me through this week, but I suppose that I'll have to get some more now.

The guys who flew out on Main Body 1 were in Shannon, Ireland today. Their families have been notified that they'll be home in a day or so, and I'm sure that it does their hearts good to know that.

I know that it's important for everyone to get home, however I am feeling a little selfish lately. It must be nice for those folks that are already on their way, but considering that they're the ones who didn't do as much as the rest of us, then it really is unsettling for the rest of us. I'm not bitching about it, but the rest of the troops don't even know about it yet. I'm not looking forward to putting that out to them. I've been assured that the powers that be are working on it, but a screw up like this, this late in the game is tough to overcome and we may just have to wait it out. We shall see.

16 SEP 04 D + 349 1000 hrs.

Good morning my love. I just got back from breakfast after a PT session with the Squad at the gym. I rode the exercise bike for about twenty minutes, and I have to confess that it almost wore me out. It's funny that actual exercise can wear you out, but jumping into a gun truck for twelve hours or more wearing full battle rattle in 100 degree plus heat is normal. Still, I look forward to hitting the gym with you when I get home. It'll be something else to do together, besides the fact that it's healthy. God only knows that my body and mind are just worn out.

Later on I think I'll pick up my dry cleaning; my good uniform to come home in, and then maybe get a haircut. My hair is growing in so fast nowadays, since we got to Kuwait. I think my follicles loosened up in an environment with less stress. Who knows? And then there's the daily visit to Baskin Robbins. I think I'm getting prematurely spoiled, and I don't want to gain all the weight I lost back in only a week. Seems like I'm trying though.

The Chely Wright concert last night wasn't too bad, but I left after about the second song or so. People started dancing in the aisles, and again I felt en emptiness inside that can only be filled by dancing with you. I can't tell you how much I really miss that.

19 SEP 04 D + 352 0300 hrs.

Hey honey. It seems as though I've been a little reluctant to write the last couple of days. Even though we've had really good talks over the phone and internet lately, I still wonder about my place at home. I' know that I've changed, and although your unwavering support is more than obvious to me, and really appreciated as well, I think the time away from you has done much deeper damage to me that even I was ready for. I've told you before how needy I am for you, and although this may seem a weakness to many, it's a strength in me as I have chosen wisely in my partner, best friend, and wife.

I think I'm beating around the bush. Although I feel bad about missing so much with the kids, I really feel that in my mind I'm putting them on the back burner. I want some time with you, just you, and I hope that doesn't make me seem selfish. I know that the tour has taken a toll on you as well, and in a way I think that you don't so much harbor that against me, but have a certain distance from me due to that. It's not something that I can see or feel from you, just a hunch. It's just something that I think you could be feeling, whether you show it or not.

And then again maybe it's just the fact that it's 0320 hrs right now and I can't sleep because I'm thinking about going home nonstop these days. I think I'll try and get some sleep now, and see how I feel in the morning . . . . well . . . . much later in the morning. I love you my darling.

0930 hrs.

It's Sunday morning, and I only wish right now that I could jump back in time, literally to Saturday night, only back at Riley with you. I miss you terribly my love, and this time here in Kuwait, feels like it's eroding my soul. The time here is very lonely, as there is entirely too much of it. Most of the Battalion is still asleep, after staying up playing cards and watching movies. I, however, cannot sleep. Every soldier has nightmares to some degree, and it's the price I pay for the time spent.

I caution myself to be patient with others, as I have lived with so many for so long. Even in this bay with over a thousand soldiers, I am surrounded yet alone. I long to be home with you and the children, just as everyone around me I would suspect. Still living in close quarters as we are, people get on each other's nerves at the drop of a hat. People do change though. I have seen soldiers, leaders, and even the top ranks change in this little time away from perhaps the worst place on earth. The daily stresses and concerns of combat are now gone from our daily lives, but not faded. Hopefully, as in the past, they will dissipate with time. I am concerned with driving when I arrive home. I have had my own apprehensions realized when I was home on leave, and heard the stories of others in the same situation. I feel naked without my weapon, which, along with a letter for you carried by another, and the constant fear of never returning home have been my constant companions for as long as I can remember now.

In this place, I have had many, many hours to think. Everyone talks about what to do when they get home; however, I have my own thoughts which are, I think, much more realistic than theirs. I have the burden of knowing what they don't know, and would much rather live in their unknowing ignorance than carry the burden of what I know is to come. They do not know that one day they will leave their homes to go to dinner with their family, and run back in the house before leaving because they forgot their weapon. They have no idea of the confusion, fear, and pain that their families must bear because they sit up in a dead sleep, recalling events of their past, speaking in Army lingo over a radio during a battle from the past. Their wives will wake up, and to their astonishment not be recognized as the spouse they are, but another soldier alongside them for the moment. In the mornings to follow these nights, the soldiers will be silent in some sort of private shame over not being able to control their thoughts, their nightmares.

These things and more I pray you will not have to experience my love, however I know better, and I am not even trying to kid myself. I wonder, my love, that even you, in your everlasting love for me will one day look upon me as some sort of pity, as if observing a wounded animal that can't help itself. This is one of my worst fears, more than that of death itself.

2320 hrs.

Hello my love. Well, although things generally look better in the morning, that doesn't seem to fit today. I'm actually feeling a little bit better tonight. I slept a lot today, and I'm heading over to try and get you on the internet. I was thinking about a lot of things today, and although it goes unsaid that everyone is looking forward to going home, it doesn't seem like reality yet. I think that we're past the point of decompression here, and everyone is starting to get on each other's nerves. Even though I think that I have some issues to work out, some apprehensions to deal with, I think that they'll only be resolved by being home for a while. I was just lying here today, and it dawned on me that we'll be home in a week. I should be home by Monday night. When I think of it that way, it suddenly looks a whole lot brighter.

I miss being with you so much today, and the thought of that happening again very soon is almost overwhelming to me. I'm at a cross between the guilt of being away and wanting to be home so much. At the same time hoping that you aren't too scarred emotionally from all this and somehow, even subliminally hold it against me. I'm not saying that you would do something like that my love, but I need you to know and totally believe that there's nothing in the world that I want more than to be with you. It's been difficult on both of us being apart, and we just have to remember that we really couldn't do anything about it. And on that note, I do try to look at the positive aspects of all this. For the rest of our lives, we can be proud that we did more than our part with the War on Terrorism. Our children can be proud of us, and speaking of that, I couldn't be prouder of you my darling. I really don't know how God saw fit to bless my life with you, but it seems that every time I turn around I am more amazed than the last.

And now I get to come home to you my love. That is probably one of the greatest privileges of my life. You already know how big of a deal that coming home from war is to me. And not even just me, it's a national tradition. Since World War II, men in uniform have been coming home to their wives. A more special bond, I don't think, could exist. It's a very special part of great military marriages and is yet another gift from God. It's a part of what's helped build our country, and I'm so proud to be your husband, and that we're a part of that.

20 SEP 04 D + 353 0945 hrs.

Good morning honey. I got up about 0500 this morning and got to talk to you for a few minutes before getting cut off. I was happy to hear your voice, and although the call was short, I was glad to have the first voice I heard this morning be yours.

At this point, I'm sure that this journal is becoming a little redundant, in that all I seem to mention is the trip home, seeing you and the kids, and not being here. Sorry if it's getting a little boring, but the only action we'll see now is a long plane ride through Europe, over the ocean, and a short drive from the hangar to the house. I still can't wait.

When I talked to you last night, Abby wasn't feeling well, and although she was running a small fever, you said she seemed to be clingy and a little snappy due to not feeling well. I wish that I could be there right now to hold you all.

The days are long and boring here. People seem to mind less and less calling their families in the middle of the night back home, as the phone lines seem to be longer and longer by the day. I can understand their enthusiasm though. Being so close to leaving now, it almost feels like we're running uphill on a treadmill. The real enemy here, as it has been for much of the last year, is time. At home it's a precious commodity, however here its abundance makes for long days and nights. I am trying to make the best use of this time as best I can. Although my sleep habits are all screwed up after the last year, I'm trying this week to get on a reverse sleep cycle so that I can be somewhat normal when I get home.

25 SEP 04 D + 358 1115 hrs.

Hello my love. The last few days have been a little more eventful than when we first arrived at Arifjan. Firstly, I have been able to talk to you a lot more frequently than I have in the past, which seems to have weaned me back into my life somewhat. I haven't really noticed it so much over the last year, I think because it was just assumed that opportunities to call and email and such were a luxury and subject to being cut off abruptly.

I ran into my old Platoon Sergeant and good friend from Fort Bragg, Don McRavin. Don is a great guy, and went through the paces with me with my divorce, the birth of the twins, and was a pillar of strength in my weakest hours. We also go way back to Somalia, where he was awarded for heroism for taking a soldier from one of the lost convoys off the back of a truck. The soldier was already dead, as he had an unexploded RPG round imbedded in his chest. It was a gory detail in the movie, however, it always reminds me of my brave friend and how I'm lucky to have been able to have walked with heroes for most of my years. We were there for each other, as I recall gravely the day that he found out that his mother had passed away. He's from a small town in North Carolina, and thankfully was only a short drive from Bragg itself when it happened. I really can't say enough about Don, as he was also the one that sent me off to Airborne school. He was really motivated about it, and mentored me by taking me out to every jump the unit had to get some exposure to it. When I went off to school down at Fort Benning, I didn't feel so awkward due to my exposure to it already. I spent a couple days at work with Don, and we ate lunch together both days.

On the last day of our hanging out at Arifjan, yesterday, he took me to lunch once again and we bade each other a fond farewell. Upon my departure Don also gave me a gift, a really nice ring. I told him that he surely didn't have to do that, but he of course insisted. He told me that when my wife asks me where I got it, I should tell her that my good friend gave it to me.

So here I sit at Camp Doha, Kuwait. We've been searched, gone through customs, and are now sitting in a really nice MWR area. There's free Gatorade, muffins, and other snacks as well. It's really nice, and they pushed it to finish all of our necessary briefings earlier than planned. They know that we're going home now, and that one small courtesy goes a long way . . . especially today.

As for my journal chronicling this, hopefully my last war, I look back on the past year with many feelings. I have felt the short but sweet victory on the field of battle, and the heart wrenching sting of comrades lost. My relationship with God has improved considerably, and only in his eternal grace and wisdom do I return home now. Although separated by the miles, my family and I have explored many different aspects of our relationships that most folks will never touch upon. I long to see my family again, as I suspect everyone on this plane does as well. I will close this out now. Until I get home my love, and we begin the next chapter of our lives. For now this mission is over and perhaps I can finally get some real rest just knowing that I'll be with you again soon. As always, I love you.

Printed in the United States
55103LVS00010B/5